Hermann Bendl

The New Companion to English Literary Texts

Analysis and Interpretation

MANZ VERLAG

Manz Verlag
© Ernst Klett Verlag GmbH, Stuttgart 2005
Alle Rechte vorbehalten
Muttersprachliche Beratung: Mary Ratcliffe, München
Lektorat: Harald Kotlarz, Rottenburg
Herstellung: Karin Schmid, Baldham
Umschlaggestaltung: Werkstatt München: Weiss/Zembsch, München
Illustration: Atelier Georg Lehmacher, Friedberg
Satz: Karin Schmid, Baldham
Druck: Druckhaus Beltz, Hemsbach
Printed in Germany

ISBN 3-7863-2111-6

Preface

This book is meant to act as a "companion" to all aspects of working with English literary texts for study and examination.

Like *Your Companion to English Literary Texts* (in two volumes, Manz, 1981 and 1984), it deals comprehensively and in a thorough-going and systematic manner with all aspects of the analysis and interpretation of poetry, of drama (including film) and of fiction. It also offers helpful language material to be used in your own work. However, it is different from its predecessors in providing

- more text samples
- a far more concentrated presentation of the subject matter
- a greater depth of analysis
- many demonstrations of the step-by-step procedure that leads from assignment to finished answer
- concise overviews of the main points of each section in lucid synopses.

You can use this book for private study, and especially for exam preparation. It can also be a valuable help in course work as **a mine of information** and as **a practical guide** to dealing with all the assignments commonly found in test papers based on literary texts of all types, and it can function as **a work of reference** for student and teacher alike. Consult the index for guidance.

Contents

1 Poetry

1.1 What is poetry?

1.1.1 Poetry and prose

When you look at a poem, you may be struck by the thought that poems are rather strange things. Consider the following example:

The Tide Rises, The Tide Falls

The tide rises, the tide falls,
The twilight darkens, the curlew calls;
Along the sea-sands damp and brown
The traveller hastens toward the town,
    And the tide rises, the tide falls.

Darkness settles on roofs and walls,
But the sea, the sea in the darkness calls;
The little waves, with their soft, white hands,
Efface the footprints in the sands,
    And the tide rises, the tide falls.

The morning breaks; the steeds in their stalls
Stamp and neigh, as the hostler calls;
The day returns, but nevermore
Returns the traveller to the shore,
    And the tide rises, the tide falls.

Henry Wadsworth Longfellow (1807 – 1882)

Notes
curlew: G Brachvogel – *steeds* (poet.): horses – *neigh:* G wiehern – *hostler:* man looking after the horses at an inn

A quick glance at this poem will reveal

- that the words of the poem you see before you have been organised into fixed lines;

- that those lines have further been arranged into regular sections known as stanzas;

- that the lines show a certain rhythmical pattern called metre;

- and that the words at the end of the lines rhyme according to a certain pattern known as a rhyme scheme (aabba aacca aadda).

Yes, there is definitely something artificial about this text – people in ordinary life don't usually speak or write like that. It is important to realise, however, that poetry is precisely *not* like everyday speech or like ordinary writing. The words of a poem have been deliberately arranged so that a new object – made from words – has been created.

The difference between poets and other artists lies in the different ways they present their ideas.

- Poets implement their ideas by arranging them in lines of words, as indicated above, and call those lines "verse".

- Composers arrange sounds, and call the result of their labours "music".

- Visual artists draw, paint, etch or sculpt images, and they call their products "art" – as if there weren't any other art.

Non-poetic writers also work with words, with the materials of language, but they don't arrange their words in lines, and we call this use of language "prose". It is worth our while to explore the difference between "verse" and "prose" a little further.

Generally speaking, verse is writing in which the text is arranged in lines and stanzas and the words used are organised into stressed and unstressed syllables forming a rhythmic pattern. This metrical arrangement may include the use of end-rhyme, perhaps in itself again conforming to a certain pattern, for instance aabb ccdd (pair rhyme) or abab cdcd (cross rhyme), etc. Both the visual and aural effect is quite remarkable – verse is not easy to miss.

Prose on the other hand is much more diffuse and unregulated. Sentences usually vary in length and so do paragraphs. The structure of the sentences employed by the writer is often highly irregular in the sense that a pattern cannot be discovered, and yet prose is not entirely without its own rhythms. A skilful prose writer will be able to use sentence length to good advantage, for instance through the use of parallelism, patterns of repetition, and other rhythmic arrangements, e.g. the order of sentences within a paragraph or the structure of the sentences themselves. They may be structured in such a way, for example, that they establish a *climax* (or *anti-climax*). Or the writer may employ complex sentence structures to establish a measured tone for his text. Or he may opt for a number of short sentences in quick succession and thus create a fast-paced rhythm and a hectic and a breathless tone. And he may naturally have recourse to other stylistic devices, e.g. *accumulation*, *antithesis* and *paradox*, to create certain effects.

In short, prose writing is not necessarily a shapeless and sloppy affair, but the point is that whereas prose more or less submerges its stylistic elements, verse parades them quite openly, drawing attention to them, as it were, especially if end-rhymes and stanzas are used. And there is always a distinctive typographical arrangement of the lines on the page.

As compared with prose, poetry generally tends to be

- more emotionally charged

    - through a heightened use of language;
    - through a more direct appeal to the emotions;
    - through frequent use of imagery and symbolic language.

- more formal in structure

    - through the use of stanzas and refrains;
    - through the recurrence of certain lines;
    - generally through the use of repetition;
    - often through the use of end-rhyme.

- more rhythmical in movement and more metrically balanced

    - through the use of rhythm and often a regular metre;
    - through the tendency to use lines of equal length and equal metrical structure.

- differently delivered (when read aloud or performed for an audience) so that it is set apart from everyday life and language.

- in the case of oral performance, poetry is usually presented in a musical setting, as a song, and with musical accompaniment.

1.1.2 Poetry and verse

Another important terminological distinction must be made here. It has to do with how "verse" is distinguished from "poetry". Put at its simplest, *not all verse is poetry*, and *not all poetry is written in verse*.

Here are some well-known examples of verse:

> As with my hat upon my head
> I walk'd along the Strand
> I there did meet another man
> With his hat in his hand.
>
> *Attributed to Dr. Samuel Johnson (1709 – 1784)*

> Humpty Dumpty sat on a wall.
> Humpty Dumpty had a great fall.
> All the king's horses and all the king's men
> Couldn't put Humpty together again!
>
> *Nursery rhyme*

> Johnny used to drink a lot,
> But now he drinks no more;
> For what he thought was H_2O,
> Was H_2SO_4.
>
> *Anonymous*

Contrast these examples of verse now with two instances of poetry:

The Eagle

> He clasps the crag with crooked hands;
> Close to the sun in lonely lands,
> Ringed with the azure world, he stands.
> The wrinkled sea beneath him crawls;
> He watches from his mountain walls,
> And like a thunderbolt he falls.
>
> *Alfred, Lord Tennyson (1809 – 1892)*

Grass

Pile the bodies high at Austerlitz and Waterloo.
Shovel them under and let me work –
     I am the grass; I cover all.

And pile them high at Gettysburg
And pile them high at Ypres and Verdun.
Shovel them under and let me work.
Two years, ten years, and the passengers ask the
     conductor:

    What place is this?
    Where are we now?

    I am the grass.
    Let me work.

Carl Sandburg (1878 – 1967)

Notes

Austerlitz: a place where in 1805 Napoleon led an outnumbered French army to victory over Austrian and Russian forces.

Waterloo: Napoleon was finally defeated near this town in Belgium in 1815 by a European coalition including Austria, Great Britain, Prussia and Russia.

Gettysburg: a decisive victory by the Union army in the American civil war was won near this Pennsylvania town in July 1863.

Ypres: a town in Belgium at which three battles were fought in World War I (1914, 1915, and 1917) resulting in over 600,000 casualties and stalemate.

Verdun: during most of 1916 the Allied and German armies fought over this French town and castle, the battles ending indecisively with nearly 700,000 casualties.

It is not difficult to work out the difference between verse and poetry from a study of these examples.

The three instances of verse printed above show that verse, i.e. a metrical arrangement of words in lines plus the use of end-rhyme, may be employed when people intend to make a trite remark *(with my hat upon my head)*, when they play with words as children like to do when they first learn to speak (cf. the second example, which is one of the best-known nursery rhymes) or when they try to introduce a light-hearted note into what is really a very serious business – Johnny drank sulphuric acid (H_2SO_4) instead of water (H_2O) and it killed him.

The use of verse is very common.

- Verse has been with us for as long as we can remember. Nursery rhymes gain respect and attention from children from an early age. Alliterating and rhyming words are pleasant, tongue twisters are fun, rhyme books filled with precious. melodious sound are a source of joy for a small child and all children delight in simple but effective word manipulation.

- Wherever people put a few lines together for somebody's birthday or wedding anniversary and the like, they use verse, i.e. they base their text on some underlying metrical arrangement or rhythm and use end-rhyme. The result is generally verse of relatively poor quality, but it is usually quite appropriate for the occasion.

- We are surrounded by verse virtually all the time. It tries to touch our souls in greeting cards, in song lyrics, and in radio and television jingles. Verse combined with music (song lyrics) can have an especially powerful effect on people.

Genuine poetry, by contrast, is not an everyday commodity, but serves an aesthetic purpose, i.e. it tries deliberately to create from the materials of language an artistic object so that it takes on a life of its own, as it were.

Like all true literature, poetry

- has something of importance to communicate;

- deals with aesthetic matters in the widest sense;

- is used as a vehicle for articulating feelings – it can make us laugh, cry, or it may persuade us to do something or it may make us angry;

- provides an emotional experience and talks to our hearts, as it were; it can be intensely personal, especially in love poems;

- may want to stimulate a sensory experience, making us taste, see, hear, touch and smell.

1.1.3 Oral and written poetry

Much of what has been said about poetry and verse is also true of poetry and lyrics (i.e. the words of songs, especially pop songs).

Poetry and lyrics are not synonymous even though both involve the skilful and artistic use of language. The major points of difference are as follows:

Poetry	Lyrics
provides immediate visual contact with the poem on the page.	are primarily absorbed through the ear as the song is played on the radio or from a recording.
allows the reader to go back to the text as often as he likes.	allow the listener only one chance to listen to the song unless it is available as a recording.
may use abstract and even esoteric vocabulary for creating a certain atmosphere.	must not use too obscure or complicated language, but rely on simple sensory images to engage the listener's mind.
is almost unlimited in its format and style – it can be rhymed or unrhymed, it can conform to a standard format (e.g. blank verse) or be written as free verse (i.e. lines of irregular metre defined by thought and rhythm rather than by syllabic count).	are sharply defined by form and metre as they must be combined with the measured rhythm of music and are therefore constrained to follow the count of each measure of melody.
may have any number of rhymes and rhythms – or none at all.	have a distinct rhythm and a definite rhyme scheme which are consistent in parallel sections of the song.
can be of any length.	are limited to what the music allows.

Lyrics are an example of oral literature, which is literature that has been orally composed, is orally transmitted and orally performed.

Today oral poetry can no longer be totally separated from written literature in any absolute sense. In fact, many of the poems widely regarded as "oral" – many ballads and folk songs, for instance – have also appeared at some point in written or printed form. This means that in practice it is impossible to draw up a precise and indisputable definition of "oral", a definition that would make the distinction between "oral" and written poetry a clear-cut matter. A poem may well be orally composed, then later transmitted in writing, or perhaps written down initially, but then performed and circulated by oral means.

If we regard the oral delivery aspect as significant, then it is easy to see that oral poetry in the wider sense is a living art form in the modern world, and one that is even likely to expand and develop as a result of our increasing reliance on the at least partially "oral" media of radio and television. There is in fact a great deal of oral poetry in English in circulation right now, almost exclusively in the form of songs – anything from Negro spirituals to pop songs.

1.1.4 Textual variability

Folk songs are of unknown origin and of anonymous authorship, both with regard to lyrics and tune. Songs were passed on orally from singer to singer, from generation to generation, and from one region to another. Quite a number of songs have thus "travelled" from their area of origin to other regions and virtually throughout the whole English-speaking world so that they can now be found in many regional variations and of course also in individual versions. The old song *A-Roving* is a case in point.

Here is the beginning of a first version:

> In Amsterdam there lived a maid.
> Mark well what I do say.
> In Amsterdam there lived a maid.
> And she was mistress of her trade.
>
> *Chorus*
> *I'll go no more a-roving with you, fair maid*
> *A-roving, a-roving*
> *Since roving's been my ru-i-in*
> *I'll go no more a-roving with you, fair maid.*

The motif of this popular song is very old indeed – a young man is ruined by a girl – and it appears again and again in slightly varying forms. Some place the maid in Amsterdam, as in the version above, whereas others speak of places like Plymouth or Portsmouth.

The song possibly goes back as far as the early seventeenth century. It was certainly extremely popular at the time and was presumably taken on board by sailors and used as a shanty to be sung during their work. Versions of the song have also been found in Dutch, Flemish and French as well as English.

The chorus was very often sung as either "I'll" or "We'll". Other alternative words are "roamin'" for "rovin", "false maid" for "fair maid", and "overt'row" or "downfall" for "ruin".

In some other songs, more than a few words were altered as the song was passed on to others. The whole setting of the song was changed as well so that we now have a number of highly different versions, as in the ballad of *Barbara Allan*.

One version has the following four lines as its first stanza:

> It was in and about the Martinmas time,
> When the green leaves were a-falling,
> That Sir John Græme, in the West Country,
> Fell in love with Barbara Allan.

Another version has this text:

> In Scarlet town where I was born,
> There was a fair maid dwelling,
> Made every youth cry, "Wellaway,"
> And her name was Barbry Allen.

This is how a third version begins:

> In Reading town a lad was born,
> And a fair maid there was dwelling;
> So he picked her out to be his bride,
> And her name was Barbara Allan.

(all quoted from the Internet)

And so on. The only common ground is the girl's name, Barbara Allan (with variations) and the story outline (unrequited love ending in death).

This textual variability is a feature that many, if not most of these songs share with much of oral poetry generally. So there is no single "correct" version; several apparently equally authentic versions of the same song may exist side by side, a fact which can underline the basically oral character of these songs as they circulated (and in many cases still circulate) among singers and their audiences.

In fact, the most distinctive characteristic of oral poetry is precisely its fluidity of text, its textual variability. This can be seen most clearly in long epic songs, where the very length of the song made it almost impossible for the performer to remember every single word and every individual line, so that he was expected to make up some of the lines as he went along. We can also find flexibility in much shorter poems, however, even though here the text tends to become more stable in direct proportion to the number of times that the song is performed by an individual singer. It is important to note that such stability is the result of habit and does not arise from any idea that there is a single unalterable text. Textual variability is thus not something extra-ordinary but something to be expected.

It is only when songs are written down and possibly even appear in print that they come to be seen as unchangeable and the particular version that was printed may then be regarded as the only authentic one.

Synopsis

Poetry
- is not like everyday speech or ordinary writing.
- is often in verse.
- tends to be emotionally charged.
- is usually very formal in structure.
- is rhythmical in movement and metrically balanced.
- is sometimes performed in a musical setting.
- serves an aesthetic and artistic purpose.
- is in some way concerned with aspects of the human condition.
- may deal with serious subject matter, but can also be used for humorous or ironical purposes.

Verse
- is usually arranged in regular lines and stanzas.
- may be highly regulated.
- organises its words into stressed and unstressed syllables forming a pattern.
- is based on a metrical arrangement, often supplemented by the use of end-rhyme and a rhyme scheme.
- is often used in song lyrics and light-hearted entertainment.
- may be whimsical and sometimes nonsensical.
- is not necessarily poetic in quality.

Prose
- is diffuse and unregulated.
- is often highly irregular.
- may include poetic elements.
- tends to submerge its stylistic elements.

Lyrics
- are the words of a song, especially a pop song.
- are primarily absorbed through the ear.
- usually rely on simple sensory images.
- follow a strict rhythm and rhyme scheme.
- are constrained by what the music allows.

> **Oral poetry**
> - may be orally composed.
> - may be orally transmitted.
> - may be orally performed (sung or at least chanted).
> - can no longer be totally separated from written literature.
> - may exist in several different versions.

1.2 The oral tradition

The two traditions of oral and written poetry have largely merged since oral poetry began to find its way into print from the late eighteenth century onwards. And yet, there are without doubt many texts, traditionally meant to be sung, where the oral element can still be felt to be so dominant that these songs clearly warrant the designation of "oral poetry", and this despite the fact that all of the texts in question are now available in print.

The text samples from the oral tradition offered in this section are of course highly selective. To attempt to provide a comprehensive survey of the categories of the oral tradition would be self-defeating.

1.2.1 Negro spirituals

One of the most memorable categories of oral poetry is that of the Negro spiritual, which is closely linked with the history of African Americans and their hard lives as slaves in the South.

Slaves were allowed to meet for Christian church services, and many of them used to stay on for singing and dancing after the regular service had come to an end. Often they also had secret meetings because they needed to share their joys, pains and hopes. The songs the members of this illiterate group sang were closely connected with their lives as slaves. They were used for expressing personal hopes and beliefs and for cheering one another. Work songs dealt with their daily life, expressing discontent with harsh living and working conditions and their many privations. They also served to maintain hope in the face of hardship.

Spirituals were different. They were inspired by the message of Jesus Christ and his Good News, "You can be saved". The lyrics of these simple and direct songs were thus often based on Gospel themes and generally on biblical motifs and characters. They spoke of redemption and of their hope of eventual triumph and freedom. Many express a Christian hope in a better after-life – that they are going to be liberated in the Promised Land. These spirituals were sometimes improvised by a single singer but usually contained recurring lines or refrains so that everybody could join in.

Negro spirituals are now largely seen as an integral part of the American heritage and are frequently performed by amateurs and professionals alike.

Here is a representative text. Spelling and grammar have not been changed:

I's gonna shine

I's gonna shine
Whiter dan snow,
When I gits to heaven
An' dey meets me at de do'.

Oh, shine, I will shine,
How dey shine, glory shine,
When I gits to heaven
An' dey meets me at de do'.

Shine, God a'-mighty shine,
All de sinners shine in de row;
But I'll be de out-shinedest
When dey meets me at de do'.

Oh, shine, de brudders shine,
Dey sisters shine ever mo',
When we all gits to heaven
An' dey meets us at de do'.

Traditional, quoted from the Internet

The singer imagines here what will be happening at the end of his life when he goes to heaven and enters through the pearly gates. He is going to be met and welcomed, probably by angels *(dey at de do')*.

The idea is that after his hard life as a slave he will be rewarded by God in a Christian heaven. The outward expression of this reward will be this *shine*, and this despite the fact that he is a sinner. Indeed, his sins will no longer be important *(all de sinners shine in de row)* – even sinners will go to heaven. He will go there with *de brudders* and *dey sisters* and they will all *shine*.

This insistence on "shining", which is repeated throughout the text (it appears twelve times), is meant to express the singer's and his fellow slaves' idea of what heaven will be like. For all of them it is closely connected with being glorified by God, and the outward sign of this glorification will be that the colour of their dark skin will all be gone (or be insignificant) and they are all going to be as white as snow and truly *shine*. They will be happy ever after (*ever mo'*).

1.2.2 The blues

It was as a direct result of the worsening of the social and economic conditions for blacks in the South after the end of the Civil War that another distinct form of oral poetry and folk music developed – the blues. It arose both as a form of social protest and as a means of expression. And as the blacks moved north in search of jobs, they took the blues with them. This was the beginning of a process that led from urban blues to *rhythm and blues*, which in turn became *rock 'n' roll*.

The blues were born during the era of slavery in the American south. Work songs often relieved the stress of labour and conveyed conspiratorial messages about eventual freedom from oppression. They spoke directly about poverty and the difficulties of making ends meet. The blacks discovered that confronting these fundamental, everyday problems head-on through their songs was better than simply wishing them away. The blues were therapeutic – the songs somehow lifted the pain, and life could go on in all of its complexity. To sing about your troubles was to conquer them.

Blues lyrics are however not only about oppression and hard times. They are often intensely personal and frequently deal with the pain of betrayal, desertion and unrequited love or with situations like being jobless, hungry, broke, away from home, lonely, or downhearted because of an unfaithful lover. The blues abound in songs about lost love and a partner's infidelity.

The structure of blues lyrics usually consists of several three-line verses. The first line is sung and then repeated to roughly the same melodic phrase, whereas the third line is different from the first two, as in the following representative example.

I'm Goin' Down the Road

Goin' down this road and I'm feelin' bad, baby,
Goin' down this road feelin' so miserable and bad,
I ain't gonna be treated this way.

I'm tired of eatin' your corn bread and beans, baby,
Tired of eatin' your corn bread and beans, right now,
I ain't gonna be treated this way.

I'm goin' down this road and I'm feelin' bad, baby,
Goin' down this road feelin' so low and bad,
I ain't gonna be treated this way.

These two dollar shoes is killin' my feet, baby,
Two dollar shoes is killin' my feet right now,
I ain't gonna be treated this way.

Take ten dollar shoes to fit my feet, baby,
Ten dollar shoes to fit my feet right now,
I ain't gonna be treated this way.

I'm goin' down this road and I'm feelin' bad, baby,
Goin' down this road feelin' so miserable and sad,
I ain't gonna be treated this way.

I'm goin' where the weather suits my clothes, baby,
Goin' where the weather suits my clothes tomorrow,
I ain't gonna be treated this way.

I'm goin' where that chilly wind don't blow, baby,
Goin' where the chilly wind don't blow tomorrow,
I ain't gonna be treated this way.

I'm goin' down this road and I'm feelin' bad, baby,
Goin' down this road feelin' so miserable and bad,
I ain't gonna be treated this way.

Traditional, quoted from the Internet

This is an example of a blues song which revolves around the singer's basic unhappiness. He repeats the same lament about his *miserable and bad* situation several times (stanzas 1, 3, 6 and 9 are thus identical) so that it acts like a refrain, hammering in the message of his deep-seated sadness. But he is certain of one thing – he *ain't gonna be treated this way*, with which every stanza ends. In other words, he is fed up with the life he is leading and wants something better for himself.

- He wants better food *(Tired of eatin' your corn bread and beans)*.

- He wants better shoes *(Two dollar shoes is killin' my feet)*.

- He wants a warmer climate *(I'm goin' where the weather suits my clothes* and *I'm … Goin' where the chilly wind don't blow)*.

He is leaving his old home behind *(goin' down this road)*, but he is still *feelin' bad*. It is not quite clear why he is feeling this way. One can only assume that leaving behind everything he is used to has produced a reaction of sadness in him. In fact, the singer finds himself in a somewhat paradoxical situation; he doesn't like the life he is leading, but the idea of leaving it behind and striking out for something new doesn't make him happy either. This attitude of an all-pervading and deep-seated sadness is typical of the blues.

1.2.3 Songs of various occupational groups

Another important category of oral poetry is to be found in the songs of various occupational groups, like those of the railworkers, the miners, the cowboys and the migrant workers. The tramps, the soldiers, the lumbermen in the forests, the prison inmates and members of many other groups all had their songs. They kept them going and helped them to mark out and consolidate their separate identity. What all these songs have in common is that they were brought forth by members of what might be called "marginal groups" of society, in other words by groups of people who lived, and often still live, a life separate from the mainstream.

Small wonder then that the songs they produced should never really have become part of the book culture of the establishment. It is true that by now many of the most famous songs have found their way onto records and CDs and made it into collections of such songs published in book form. But despite this development, these songs have remained very much a performed art rather than a written one.

One famous performer of such songs was Woody Guthrie (1912 – 1967), who became something of a spokesman for many groups because he made their songs known to a much wider audience in live performances and in broadcasts of his concerts on the radio and later also on television. One of the songs he recorded about the hard life of a disadvantaged group – here that of the migrant workers – is *Pastures of plenty*.

Pastures of plenty

It's a mighty hard row that my poor hands have hoed,
My poor feet have travelled a hot dusty road,
Out of your dust bowl and westward we roll,
Through deserts so hot and your mountains so cold.

I've wandered all over your green growing land,
Wherever your crops are I've lent you my hand,
On the edge of your cities you'll see me and then,
I come with the dust and I'm gone with the wind.

California, Arizona, I've worked on your crops,
Then north up to Oregon to gather your hops,
Dig beets from your ground, I cut grapes from your vines,
To set on your tables that light sparklin' wine.

Green pastures of plenty from dry desert ground,
From the Grand Coulee Dam* where the water runs down,
Ev'ry state of this Union us migrants have been,
We come with the dust and we're gone with the wind.

It's always we ramble that river and I,
All along your green valleys I'll work till I die,
I'll travel this road until death sets me free,
'Cause my Pastures of plenty must always be free.

It's a mighty hard row that my poor hands have hoed,
My poor feet have travelled this poor dusty road,
On the edge of your cities you'll see me and then,
I come with the dust and I'm gone with the wind.

Traditional, quoted from the Internet

* **Grand Coulee Dam:** the largest concrete structure in the U.S., forming the centrepiece of the Columbia Basin Project in the state of Washington.

The song covers a number of activities usually undertaken by migrant workers. They

- work in the fields;
- labour in vineyards;
- harvest crops – anything from beets to hops.

And they are constantly on the move, travelling through all the States of the continental U.S.; they even expect to die during their travels, a death which "sets them free" at long last, as the text says.

It is a hard life, exposing the migrants to the elements, especially to dust, heat and cold, but in contrast to what the blues singers have to say, who always seem to lament their situation and to express their deep-seated sadness, the singer of *Pastures of plenty* appears to be happy enough – despite the hardships on the road.

1.2.4 Folk ballads

The folk ballad is a short narrative poem usually relating a single, dramatic event. It was composed to be sung and goes back as a literary form at least to the thirteenth century and may well be older. These anonymous ballads were passed along orally from singer to singer and from generation to generation. In this process, a particular ballad would be slightly changed again and again so that a number of versions now exist side by side.

The singers drew their material from community life, from local and national history, and from legends and folklore. Their stories are usually of adventure, love, betrayal, war, violence and death, and the supernatural. The story usually begins abruptly and moves rapidly. It is told mainly through dialogue and action. The theme is often tragic and the events tend to be sensational or melodramatic. A folk ballad typically presents a single episode, with minimal imagery and little attempt to develop character, as in the following example.

Lord Randal

"O where ha' you been, Lord Randal, my son?
And where ha' you been, my handsome young man?"
"I ha' been at the greenwood; mother, mak my bed soon,
For I'm wearied wi' huntin', and fain wad lie down."

"And wha met ye there, Lord Randal, my son?
And wha met you there, my handsome young man?"
"O I met wi' my true-love; mother, mak my bed soon,
For I'm wearied wi' huntin', and fain wad lie down."

"And what did she give you, Lord Randal, my son?
And what did she give you, my handsome young man?"
"Eels fried in a pan; mother, mak my bed soon,
For I'm wearied wi' huntin', and fain wad lie down."

"And wha gat your leavin's, Lord Randal, my son?
And wha gat your leavin's, my handsome young man?"
"My hawks and my hounds; mother, mak my bed soon,
For I'm wearied wi' huntin', and fain wad lie down."

"And what becam of them, Lord Randal, my son?
And what becam of them, my handsome young man?"
"They stretched their legs out an died; mother, mak my bed
   soon,
For I'm wearied wi' huntin, and fain wad lie down."

"O I fear you are poisoned, Lord Randal, my son!
I fear you are poisoned, my handsome young man."
"O yes, I am poisoned; mother, mak my bed soon,
For I'm sick at the heart, and I fain wad lie down."

"What d' ye leave to your mother, Lord Randal, my son?
What d' ye leave to your mother, my handsome young man?"
"Four and twenty milk kye; mother, mak my bed soon,
For I'm sick at the heart, and I fain wad lie down."

"What d' ye leave to your sister, Lord Randal, my son?
What d' ye leave to your sister, my handsome young man?"
"My gold and my silver; mother, mak my bed soon,
For I'm sick at the heart, and I fain wad lie down."

"What d' ye leave to your brother, Lord Randal, my son?
What d' ye leave to your brother, my handsome young man?"
"My houses and my lands; mother, mak my bed soon,
For I'm sick at the heart, and I fain wad lie down."

"What d' ye leave to your true-love, Lord Randal my son?
What d' ye leave to your true-love, my handsome young
   man?"
"I leave her hell and fire; mother, mak my bed soon,
For I'm sick at the heart, and I fain wad lie down."

Anonymous

Notes

fain wad: gladly would – *wha:* who – *leavin's:* leftovers – *kye:* cows

At the heart of the ballad is a case of poisoning – Lord Randal has apparently been poisoned by his "true-love" and is on the point of dying when the conversation with his mother takes place.

The ballad is instructive for us because it utilises many of the typical ballad devices.

- It employs *dialogue*, with each question and answer providing more and more information on what has happened:

  - Where have you been? (at the greenwood)
  - Who did you meet? (my true-love)
  - What did she give you? (eels fried in a pan)
  - And so on.

  The realisation that the young man has been poisoned leads to more questions and answers: What are you going to leave to your mother? Your sister? Your brother? Your true-love? (my milk cows, my gold and silver, my houses and my lands, hell and fire).

- It makes use of a *refrain*, i.e. lines and phrases repeated at regular intervals, here:

  - "Lord Randal, my son"
  - "my handsome young man"
  - "mother, mak my bed soon, / for I'm wearied wi' huntin', and fain wad lie down"

- It relies on *incremental repetition* to carry the story forward, i.e. a few words are changed from stanza to stanza so that additional information is provided, here:

  - I have been at the greenwood
  - O I met with my true-love
  - Eels fried in a pan
  - And so on.

- It uses a *strong rhythm* because ballads were of course meant to be heard:

  - The brief stanzas are arranged according to an identical rhyme scheme (abcb; in other ballads frequently abab)

–   The text is presented in lines of four stresses (tetrameter [te'træmɪtə]):

O whére have you béen, Lord Rándal, my són?

More often, however, we find a mixture of tetrameter and trimeter ['trɪmɪtə], i.e. alternating lines of four and three stresses, as in the following excerpt from *Bonny Barbara Allen*:

"O móther, móther, máke my béd
O máke it sóft and nárrow
My lóve has díed for mé todáy
I'll díe for hím tomórrow."

- The text is based on a *simple vocabulary*, usually of words of one or two syllables.

- There is *no additional refinement* such as descriptive detail or the portrayal of the characters' feelings.

Some people have associated the ballad with a real-life case of the poisoning of a young nobleman, but we have no means of knowing if such speculations have any basis in fact. It is certainly not unlikely that the rumours surrounding a suspicious death may have given rise to the ballad.

1.2.5 Songs of protest and oppression

Songs of protest and oppression can be found wherever groups of people find themselves in situations that seem hopeless or at the very least depressing. Unsurprisingly, such songs were created by oppressed groups such as the blacks in America, by social outcasts and even by prison inmates. Some of these songs are particularly striking because one would not always expect a down-trodden group of people to respond to their situation with such humanity and also artistry. To be able to release some of their tensions and anxieties through song – and of course also to protest against their situation – must have been a great help to many of these people.

In the song selected here, a song from Ireland for a change, the singer remembers the terrible plight of the Irish potato *(praties)* famine of the 1840s during which a million people starved to death and another million people were forced to emigrate overseas.

Famine song

O the praties are so small
　　Over here, over here,
O the praties are so small
That we dig them in the Fall,
And we eat them skin and all,
　　Full of fear, full of fear.

O I wish we all were geese*
　　Night and morn, night and morn,
O I wish we all were geese,
For they live and die in peace,
Till the day of their decease,
　　Eatin' corn, eatin' corn.

O we're down into the dust,
　　Over here, over here,
But the Lord in whom we trust
Will yet give us crumb for crust
　　Over here, over here.

Quoted from Ruth Finnegan, The Penguin Book of Oral Poetry, 1978

* refers to the geese that were fattened up for the landlords to eat. The landlords were living in England, where there was no famine; the general feeling was that they did not care for the fate of their Irish tenants.

The song needs little explication; it speaks for itself. The people were forced to eat the small potatoes even with their skins because there was next to nothing to eat and they were starving. The idea that the geese are far better off than they even though they are being fattened for slaughtering is deeply ironic – at least the geese will die peacefully, and with a full stomach *(Eatin' corn, eatin' corn)*. Only the Lord can help them now and divine intervention is their only hope under the circumstances – God will provide when everything seems to be lost.

This protest of the *Famine song* against starvation – and against the passivity of the English who are held responsible for it – must be seen as a largely impotent form of protest.

Not all protest was quite as impotent, however. The singer in the following song is not satisfied with protesting peacefully against a situation he finds unjust ("No Irish need apply"), but proceeds to take the law into his own hands.

No Irish Need Apply

I'm a decent boy just landed
From the town of Ballyfad;
I want a situation, yes,
And want it very bad.
I have seen employment advertised,
"It's just the thing," says I,
"But the dirty spalpeen ended with
'No Irish Need Apply.'"

"Whoa," says I, "that's an insult,
But to get the place I'll try,"
So I went to see the blackguard
With his "No Irish Need Apply."
Some do count it a misfortune
To be christened Pat or Dan,
But to me it is an honor
To be born an Irishman.

I started out to find the house,
I got it mighty soon;
There I found the old chap seated,
He was reading the *Tribune*.
I told him what I came for,
When he in a rage did fly,
"No!" he says, "You are a Paddy,
And no Irish need apply."

Then I gets my dander rising
And I'd like to black his eye
To tell an Irish gentleman
"No Irish Need Apply."
Some do count it a misfortune
To be christened Pat or Dan,
But to me it is an honor
To be born an Irishman.

I couldn't stand it longer
So a hold of him I took,
And gave him such a welting

As he'd get at Donnybrook.
He hollered, "Milia murther,"
And to get away did try,
And swore he'd never write again
"No Irish Need Apply."

Well, he made a big apology,
I told him then goodbye,
Saying, "When next you want a beating,
Write 'No Irish Need Apply.'"
Some do count it a misfortune
To be christened Pat or Dan,
But to me it is an honor
To be born an Irishman.

Traditional; quoted from the Internet

Notes
Ballyfad: place name (Ballyfad is in central Ireland) – *spalpeen:* an Irish term for a good-for-nothing fellow; here: the revolting advert – *blackguard:* a scoundrel – *I gets my dander rising:* I became extremely annoyed – *welting:* a severe thrashing – *Donnybrook:* Donnybrook Fair (near Dublin), held annually, is notorious for its brawls – *Milia murther:* a Gaelic phrase that means "a thousand murders"

It is not surprising that this song, which reflects the discrimination against Irish immigrant workers in nineteenth century America, became immediately popular among the Irish immigrant population and was spread far and wide. The idea that all you had to do was to beat up the oppressors and discriminators is of course incredibly naïve. The serio-comic picture of the wronged but still proud and aggressive Irishman appears however to have struck a chord in many people's hearts, even though they must have been well aware that the procedure of our Irish hero was highly irregular and even counter-productive. What is really important in the song is of course the refrain-like ending of each other stanza:

Some do count it a misfortune
To be christened Pat or Dan,
But to me it is an honor
To be born an Irishman.

This appeal to people's sense of national pride and the confirmation of this pride by our hero's action (which coincided with many people's wishful thinking) endeared the song to many at the time and has since made the song something of a classic.

1.2.6 Songs of courtship and married life

Courtship songs and love laments make up the great bulk of the folk songs, but there are also many humorous songs about married couples and their difficulties with each other. Whereas in the love songs marriage is seen as the desired goal, love is rarely mentioned in the songs about married people. Frequently we see a situation described in the love songs in which one of the two lovers deplores the other's betrayal of their love or is pining for the love of a person that is beyond their reach.

It is customary in the folk songs concerned with courtship and love to include a little twist in the courtship stories that they tell – there is usually something that isn't quite right. In the following song a proper courtship does not even develop.

Where are you going, my pretty maid

"Where are you going, my pretty maid"?
"I'm going a-milking, sir," she said.

"May I go with you, my pretty maid?"
"You're kindly welcome, sir," she said.

"What is your father, my pretty maid?"
"My father's a farmer, sir," she said.

"What is your fortune, my pretty maid?"
"My face is my fortune, sir," she said.

"Then I can't marry you, my pretty maid."
"Nobody asked you, sir," she said."

Anonymous

The reasons for the failure of this courtship scenario are obvious. The young man was attracted by the girl's beauty *(my pretty maid)*, but when he learns that he cannot hope for a large dowry if he marries her *(my face is my fortune)*, he is no longer interested.

The young woman's reaction is interesting. She invariably replies calmly and politely, and in the end she shows herself to be fully in control of the situation – it is the young man who does not come off too well here.

The next song, *I wish I was single again*, is a typical example of the songs about married people. It exists in versions for both sexes and pokes fun at people's desire to have it both ways – to enjoy married life and also to have their freedom.

I wish I was single again

Once I was single, then O then
Once I was single, O then
Once I was single, my pockets did jingle
An' I wish I were single again

I got me a wife, then, O then, O then
I got me a wife, O then
I got me a wife, she's the plague of my life
An' I wish I were single again

My wife got th' fever, O then, O then
My wife got th' fever, O then
My wife got th' fever, an' I wish it never leave 'er
So I could be single again

My wife she died, O then, O then
My wife she died, O then
My wife she died, an' I laughed till I cried
So glad t' be single again

I got me another, a lot worse than the other
An' I wish I were single again

This is how the female version begins:

Once I was single and lived at my ease,
But now I am married with a husband to please,
Four young children to maintain;
Oh how I wish I were single again!

Anonymous

The singer sketches the situation with supreme irony. All the time he (or she) wishes to be single again and yet when the partner dies and he (or she) is in fact free, the first thing he / she does is to get married again. And immediately the wish to be single again comes back to him / her. People always want what they can't have – they try to have their cake and eat it, which is of course impossible.

The oral character of these songs is underlined through the use of

- repetitions and recurring lines and phrases;
- simple language and words of only one or two syllables;
- colloquialisms *(I got me a wife)* and contracted forms;
- clear rhythmic arrangements;
- the use of dialogue (in the first song).

All these factors mark them out as belonging to the oral tradition.

Synopsis

The oral tradition
- cannot be strictly separated from written poetry any more.
- has largely merged with the written tradition.
- is still going strong in some areas.

Negro spirituals
- are inspired by Gospel themes.
- are based on biblical motifs.
- express a Christian hope for a better after-life.
- speak of redemption and the hope of eventual triumph and freedom.
- maintain hope in the face of hardship.
- help to cheer the singer and his audience.

Blues songs
- came into being after slavery had been abolished.
- are often about the hard life of disadvantaged groups.
- are concerned with situations like being jobless, hungry, broke, away from home, etc.
- frequently deal with the pain of betrayal, desertion and unrequited love.
- often revolve around the singer's basic unhappiness.
- show an attitude of all-pervading and deep-rooted sadness.
- paved the way for "rhythm and blues" and eventually for rock 'n' roll.

Songs of various occupational groups
- were brought forth by "marginal groups".
- kept the workers going.
- helped members of particular groups to mark out and consolidate their separate identity.

Folk ballads
- are short narrative poems relating a single, dramatic event.
- may exist in a number of versions side by side.
- are usually based on tragic themes and sensational events.
- tell of adventure, war, love, death, violence, betrayal, and the supernatural.
- take their material from community life, from local and national history, and from legends and folklore.
- often begin abruptly and move rapidly.
- are told as impersonal narratives, mainly through dialogue.
- employ incremental repetition as a structural principle.
- make little attempt to develop character.
- are based on a simple vocabulary and a strong rhythm.
- offer minimal background information.
- show no additional refinement.

Songs of protest and oppression
- were created by members of oppressed groups.
- are intended as a protest against an intolerable situation.
- can provide a release of tension and anxiety.
- can help the oppressed to bear their lot.

Songs of courtship and married life
- tend to be humorous.
- often deplore the unfaithfulness of the beloved.
- often show one of the two lovers as heartbroken.
- see marriage as the goal for unmarried people.
- tend to make fun of married life.

1.3 The main elements of poetry

1.3.1 The language of poetry

The language of poetry tends to be richer, more suggestive, and more powerful than the language of prose. This may seem a little strange at first, because in a sense both poetry and prose make use of exactly the same language. The difference is that in poetry aspects of language like sound devices, rhythm, figurative language and the like are made to count for more; they carry more meaning. It is for this reason that we speak of the "language of poetry" as if it were separate from the language of prose.

All language is made of speech sounds and these speech sounds are organised into words. When people communicate, they make sentences from these words and use certain words in certain contexts so that meaning is established. In a poem the words are organised in lines and stanzas, which are not just convenient ways of printing a poem so that it looks good on the page but the very mode of existence of a poem. A particular poem consists of these particular words arranged in these particular lines, and each word has been selected for a particular reason, often for its various connotations and implications.

Many words can refer to more than one thing and may suggest or call to mind a number of objects or ideas. The little word "red", for instance, refers first of all to a familiar colour (this is its denotation), but it can also suggest things like love, blood, passion, revolution, danger, anger, and so forth. All these implied meanings are its connotations.

Poets love to use words that have acquired clusters of association and suggestion. They tend to pay close attention to the connotations of their words for they are often interested in conveying not only broad meaning but nuances of meaning. Some of the manuscripts of poems that have survived show poets experimenting with words so as to get what they want to say just right, which means finding a word that carries the desired connotation better than another word.

In one of the stanzas of *The Eve of St. Agnes* by John Keats (1795 – 1821), for instance, which describes Porphyro preparing a feast of rich, exotic food, Keats changed several words to improve their connotations. In the lines

> … he from forth the closet brought a heap
> Of candied apple, fruits, and plum, and gourd;

he crossed out the word *fruits* and replaced it with *sweets*, and when he was still not happy with the result, he put *quince*, and these are the lines as we have them now:

> … he from forth the closet brought a heap
> Of candied apple, quince, and plum, and gourd;

The connotations of *quince* (G Quitte) contribute to the rich sensuous effect of the line; *quince* is much more in keeping with the other fruits listed in that line than either of the two previous words. Sound plays a part here, too. Indeed, sounds of words and phrases often have an evocative quality that appeals to people's emotions.

What puzzles us, catches our interest, or gives us pleasure in a poem is usually something to do with the way words work. Poets use words in an intriguing, suggestive and enriching way. The reader is invited to let them impress him and to think about them, working out their connotations and implications. This is what poetry does with words – it enriches and deepens their meaning.

A common way for poets to attract the reader's attention and point him to words that carry a special significance is to make use of repetitions. When a poet uses a word more than once within a short space, it is often because it is particularly important for the building up of the poem's meaning. Here is a good example from William Blake's poem *London*:

> I wander through each chartered street,
> Near where the chartered Thames does flow,
> And mark in every face I meet
> Marks of weakness, marks of woe.

William Blake (1757 – 1827)

Why are the words *chartered* and *mark* repeated? It looks as if the speaker is angry at the way in which each of the streets in London is given over to trade (a *charter* is a licence to sell), and not even the river is exempt from it. This, he feels, has marked the people, and also marked him, for although he uses the word as a verb in line 3, it sounds harsh, as if he, too, is aware of the *marks of woe* in him. The whole poem shows that life in London marks people like a disease, and this is what the poem is about – the outer and inner corruption that London generates in people.

Words can also be striking in combination. Their suggestiveness can be enhanced when they appear as part of a figure of speech, such as a simile or metaphor. Both these figures of speech can make important contributions to a poem because both speak of one thing in terms of another and can thus help to bring out a particular shade of meaning, deepen an impression or enrich an experience.

In a simile the words *like* or *as* are employed to make the relation clear between the two things that are compared, whereas in the case of a metaphor those two things become one. Here is an example:

simile: the fog descended *like* a blanket
metaphor: a blanket of fog descended

Or in lines from an actual poem:

simile: … a grin
               Like the slash of a knife on his face

metaphor: His pale face was the lantern
           By which they read in life's dark book …

both examples from R.S. Thomas "On the Farm"

Metaphors come in different varieties. In metonymy [mɪ'tɒnɪmɪ], the poet replaces the name of the thing with the name of something closely associated with that thing. A famous example is the following:

The *pen* is mightier than the *sword*.

Edward Bulwer-Lytton (1803 – 1873); the quote is from his play Richelieu

The meaning is that human history is influenced more by the written word (= the *pen*) than by warfare (= the *sword*).

In synecdoche [sɪ'nekdəkɪ], people take a part of the thing and use it to stand for the whole thing. In *The Love Song of J. Alfred Prufrock*, for instance, the poet T.S. Eliot has his speaker say

I should have been *a pair of ragged claws*
Scuttling across the floors of silent seas.

He doesn't mean, of course, that he should be just claws, but instead some lowly, crablike animal, an excellent metaphor for Prufrock's dissatisfaction with himself.

Another commonly used figure of speech is personification, a kind of metaphor in which non-human things (animals, inanimate objects, abstract ideas) are given human qualities. It is one of the most frequently used resources of poetry. Here is a particularly charming example:

The fog comes
on little cat feet.

Carl Sandburg, Fog

What personification can do particularly well is to suggest that in the poet's mind the whole world can come alive and inanimate things can appear to "live".

The language of poetry is not only suggestive; it is also vivid. Regardless of whether the poem tells a story, discusses ideas, attitudes and feelings, or seeks to evoke a sense of physical experience, the poet usually relies on words that appeal to our senses. They appeal to us not in a physical sense; they appeal to our "senses of the mind". We can see and hear something in the mind, and much the same is true, though perhaps to a lesser degree, of the other senses of smell, touch and taste. To these five senses should be added the sense of heat (or cold) and the sense of motion. We refer to these senses as follows:

- sight   –   the visual sense
- hearing   –   the aural sense
- smell   –   the olfactory sense
- taste   –   the gustatory sense
- touch   –   the tactile sense
- heat   –   the thermal sense
- motion   –   the kinetic sense

When a poet uses words that appeal to our senses, that appeal takes the form of a mental representation, of an "image" in our mind. All of the images suggested by a poem are known as its imagery. People react differently to imagery – some are more, others are less sensitive to them, but this sensitivity to imagery can be improved with a little practice.

Let's take a close look at a passage from the Keats poem already mentioned, *The Eve of St. Agnes*, in which the poet appeals to the reader's thermal sense and paints images of "cold".

St. Agnes Eve – ah, bitter chill it was!
The owl, for all his feathers, was a-cold;
The hare limp'd trembling through the frozen grass,
And silent was the flock in woolly fold;
Numb were the Beadsman's fingers, while he told
His rosary, and while his frosted breath,
Like pious incense from a censer old,
Seem'd taking flight to heaven, without a death,
Past the sweet Virgin's picture, while his prayer he saith.

Notes
St. Agnes: a saint of the Roman Catholic Church, a martyr of the fourth century A.D.; her feast day is January 21, so "St. Agnes' Eve" would be January 20, usually a fairly cold time. St. Agnes is the patron saint of virgins. If a virgin performed the correct rituals on St. Agnes' Eve, she would dream of the man she would marry – *fold:* enclosure for sheep – *Beadsman:* a person who is paid to pray for someone else's soul – *tell one's rosary:* G den Rosenkranz beten – *incense:* G Weihrauch – *censer:* an implement from which incense is dispensed

Isn't it fascinating to see how the poet here manages to convey a sense of the extreme cold of the evening by creating appropriate imagery?

The poem is also interesting in the sense that it can demonstrate how helpful it can be for the poet when he can enrich his text with a number of appropriate cross-references and allusions. In the quoted passage they can assist him to set the stage for a superbly strange poem. A bland reference to "wintertime" as the time of the action would not have been half as attractive as referring to *St. Agnes' Eve*. The mystical environment can be brought to intense life by the reference to a popular saint, to incense and rosaries, and finally to the Virgin Mary herself. The problem is that the ordinary reader often lacks the background knowledge that would enable him to see and enjoy the extra richness that a poet has tried to achieve for his poem.

Poets allude, i.e. make references, to things outside the poem. In his epic *Paradise Lost*, for instance, John Milton wanted his readers to feel the gentle sweetness of Adam's words to Eve. So he lets Adam speak

with voice

    Mild, as when *Zephyrus* on *Flora* breathes

but unless the reader knows that *Zephyrus* is the Western wind that blows in spring and brings nature back to life again and that *Flora* is the goddess of the world of flowers and plants (and often stands for flowers in general), the allusion is lost on him. The poem thus has a male god breathing on a female god, and Adam breathes sweetly on Eve, who comes to life as a result – a wonderful moment.

Allusions can be shorthand for larger stories and contexts the poet expects his readers to be familiar with. Such allusions help him to set the material of the poem on a larger stage and they help the reader to understand the characters and their feelings more closely.

Another challenge the reader faces when he studies poetry is that poets like to work with symbols. This is not surprising since symbols are central to the way our world works. Words themselves are symbols, of course; they *stand for* the thing they refer to. We simply couldn't function without symbols.

Symbols unite a concrete thing with an idea or concept greater than that thing. A wedding ring, for instance, is in reality just a piece of gold given this particular shape. But the gold stands for marriage, and marriage means lifelong commitment and never-ending love, all of which is symbolised by that never-ending line of the wedding ring.

Literature often contains common symbols such as flowers, storms, sunrises, etc. which come ready-made with their own meanings. Storms, for example, usually symbolise trouble, whereas sunrises often symbolise hope. Other symbols need a little more effort to be fully understood.

What symbolic meaning can you detect in the following poem by William Blake, *The Sick Rose*:

O rose, thou art sick.
The invisible worm
That flies in the night
In the howling storm

Has found out thy bed
Of crimson joy,
And his dark secret love
Does thy life destroy.

William Blake (1757 – 1827)

We can understand this poem literally, of course – a worm is destroying a flower – but we can appreciate the poem more and understand it more deeply if we can figure out what the symbols mean.

In this case, both rose and worm are well-established symbols:

- Roses often signify love and beauty,
- and the worm usually stands for death and decay.

We therefore see a symbol of death destroying a symbol of beauty. Although literally all you read about is a worm destroying a flower, you feel that there is some extra significance, making you think of other kinds of destruction, perhaps, and of how other beautiful objects lose their beauty or their lives. This feeling is reinforced when you take a closer look at what else the poem says. You probably sense that the words *howling storm*, *night* and the *invisible* flying *worm* that destroys the rose with its *dark secret love* are all scary notions. These words invest everything that happens with a heightened significance, giving it a melodramatic or frightening character. The worm is *invisible* and his love *secret*, implying furtiveness and stealth, as though something malevolent was causing the rose's death.

Another useful observation here is that the speaker addresses the rose as *thou* – certainly an unusual way to talk to a plant. Blake is using *personification* here, endowing something non-human with human attributes. The rose had a prior life of *crimson joy* that it is now losing, and the reader may feel sympathy for the rose. Human characteristics seem to be placed on the worm as well – it is said to feel *dark secret love* for the rose and to show a destructive will. The rose, on the other hand, appears innocent and vulnerable; but it doesn't stand much of a chance in that *howling storm* carrying death-bringing worms. The rose's *bed /*

Of crimson joy can be understood as a symbol of sexual love, which gives the worm a sexual significance, too, representing a man deflowering a woman, possibly against her will, i.e. raping her and destroying her innocence. The *howling storm* can be seen in this reading as symbolising the use of violence and force, and the *dark secret love* as standing for the man's lust and desire. (Other interpretations of the poem's symbols can of course also be attempted.)

In *The Sick Rose* Blake shows us a world in which the interplay of love, joy, violence, sickness and death and especially the use of rich and suggestive symbols make a deep impression on the sensitive reader.

In general, whenever an image seems to evoke meanings that go far beyond literal understanding, we are probably dealing with a symbol. Trying to make out what the symbols in a poem are meant to stand for makes the experience of studying it richer and more rewarding.

1.3.2 Rhythm and metre

Rhythm in poetry is created by the repetition of sounds and ideas so that a regular pattern is established. Study the following stanzas from Coleridge's *The Rime of the Ancient Mariner* and notice the rhythm:

[An old sailor (= the ancient mariner of the title) stops a wedding-guest at the door to tell him about a strange experience he had at sea.]

> The sun came up upon the left,
> Out of the sea came he!
> And he shone bright, and on the right
> Went down into the sea.
>
> Higher and higher every day,
> Till over the mast at noon –
> The Wedding-Guest here beat his breast,
> For he heard the loud bassoon.
>
> The bride hath paced into the hall,
> Red as a rose is she;
> Nodding their heads before her goes
> The merry minstrelsy.
>
> The Wedding-Guest he beat his breast,
> Yet he cannot choose but hear;
> And thus spake on that ancient man,
> The bright-eyed Mariner.

Samuel Taylor Coleridge (1772 – 1834)

Notes

The sun ... he: the sun is considered masculine in English – *bassoon:* G Fagott – *minstrelsy:* musicians – *spake:* old form of "spoke" – *mariner:* sailor, seafaring man

The patterns of sound have an enchanting effect here. The accent (i.e. where the stress is placed) and the final sound of the second line in the third stanza, "Red as a rose is she," echoes the second line of the first stanza, "Out of the sea came he!" This focus on "ee" sounds, and the repetition of the words *Wedding-Guest – breast* contribute in equal measure to the flowing sound of the poem and the chanting effect of internal rhyme (*Guest – breast*).

We can see from this that rhythm is created out of the patterned use of words, sounds and stress (accent), which establishes in the mind a collection of associations of sound and meaning. *The Rime of the Ancient Mariner* is divided up into seven parts and throughout the poem the rhythm seems to be gathering momentum. Readers have always shown a strong emotional response to its rhythm, because they are almost literally swept up in the even, chant-like flow of its lines and stanzas.

Rhythmical pattern is established in two ways:

- in the repetition of lines showing the same number of syllables,
- and in the regular use of word stress (accent) in the same way.

We call this arrangement of lines according to a regular pattern of a certain number of syllables, some of which are accented (receive stress) and some of which are not (receive no stress), the metre.

When we want to indicate that a particular syllable should be accented, we mark it with an accent, a slanted dash (/). A syllable that does not carry any stress is not marked:

>   /   /   /   /
> The sun came up upon the left,
> /   /   /
> Out of the sea came he!

Sometimes a simple accent is preferred:

> The sún came úp upón the léft,
> Óut of the séa came hé!

When lines of poetry are marked in this manner, we speak of *scanning* the lines. A frequently used alternative to scanning lines by putting accents or slanted dashes directly above the accented syllables is by using accented and unaccented x's below the line, like this:

> The sun came up upon the left,
> x x́ x x́ x x́ x x́
> Out of the sea came he!
> x́ x x x́ x x́
> And he shone bright, and on the right
> x x́ x x́ x x́ x x́
> Went down into the sea.
> x x́ x́ x x x́
>
> Higher and higher every day,
> x́ x x x́ x x́ (x)x x́
> Till over the mast at noon –
> x x́x x x́ x x́
> The Wedding-Guest here beat his breast,
> x x́ x x́ x x́ x x́
> For he heard the loud bassoon.
> x x x́ x x́ x x́

Have you noticed how Coleridge has avoided giving his lines a sterile and monotonous rhythm by varying the accent ever so slightly here and there:

- In the second line of the first stanza the first syllable *(Óut)* needs to be stressed, and not the second syllable *(of)*.

- Similarly, the first line of the second stanza does not put the stress on the second syllable *(Highér)*, but on the first *(Hígher)*.

- In the second line of that stanza, the first accented syllable *(óver)* is followed by two unaccented ones *(óver the)*.

- The last line of the quoted passage opens with two unaccented syllables *(For he héard)* and does not stress the *he*, as one might expect.

- Finally, the last line of the first stanza ought to be scanned *Went dówn ínto the séa* so that two accented syllable follow one another here. *Went dówn intó the séa* is not in keeping with the natural speech rhythm.

The point is that a regular rhythmical pattern is established despite these deliberate irregularities. In fact, it is precisely the small breaks in the rhythm that set up a tension at certain points between what we expect and what we get, a tension that is interesting and pleasurable. Do not be distracted by such seeming irregularities and rather expect to find them in good poetry. The poet does not feel obliged to force his words into a metrical strait jacket, nor should we read them with barrel-organ regularity. Monotony is the deadly enemy of good rhythm.

You will have noticed as you studied the stanzas of the Coleridge poem that not all of the lines have an equal number of stressed syllables. Lines 1 and 3 of each stanza have four accented syllables, whereas lines 2 and 4 have only three, but the basic rhythm is the same – first an unstressed syllable and then a stressed one. This unit of rhythm is known as a metric foot; each line of poetry therefore has a number of metric feet. And as the pattern of one foot is repeated (or sometimes varied), a pattern for the entire line and then for the whole poem is established, the metre.

Metric feet are based on different numbers of syllables, stressed and unstressed. They are known by different names.

The iambic foot, for instance, is composed of an unstressed syllable followed by a stressed one (x ́x), as in *The Rime of the Ancient Mariner*:

> The sun came up upon the left,
> x   ́x   x   ́x x ́x   x   ́x

The iambic metre is in fact by far the most common metre in English because it closely resembles the natural speech rhythm. Other common types of metric feet are trochee, dactyl, anapaest and spondee. This is a tabulated overview of the most common metric feet:

Arrangement of stresses	Name (noun)	Adjectival form	Example
x ́x	iamb [ˈaɪæm]	iambic [aɪˈæmbɪk]	today (x ́x)
́x x	trochee [ˈtrəʊkiː]	trochaic [trəʊˈkeɪɪk]	father (́x x)
́x x x	dactyl [ˈdæktɪl]	dactylic [dækˈtɪlɪk]	beautiful (́x x x)
x x ́x	anapaest [ˈænəpest]	anapaestic [ænəˈpestɪk]	overturn (x x ́x)
́x ́x	spondee [ˈspɒndiː]	spondaic [spɒnˈdeɪɪk]	sidewalk (́x ́x)

One or two subtle variations must be mentioned here. For example, many lines end with an extra, or additional, unaccented syllable. These "soft" endings are called feminine endings. If, on the other hand, the line ends on a "hard", accented syllable that completes the metrical foot, is has a masculine ending. Most rhymes are masculine in English because the language is so rich in monosyllabic words. Masculine rhyme can sound settled and determined, whereas feminine rhyme tends to be fluid and musical. Throughout the dramatic poem *Is My Team Ploughing?* by Thomas Hardy (1840 – 1928) for instance, the text alternates between feminine and masculine endings. Here is the first stanza:

> /
> "Is my team ploughing,
>
> /
> That I was used to drive
>
> /
> And hear the harness jingle
>
> /
> When I was man alive?"

The metre is iambic here, but every other line does not end in a full foot. There is instead an extra unaccented syllable at the end of the line. The alternating rhythm between feminine and masculine line endings that results from this is often felt to be a pleasing variation of the metre and we can find it in quite a number of poems.

A further distinction must be mentioned. There are lines of poetry which pause naturally at the end because the syntactical unit comes to an end at this point; we call them end-stopped lines. There are other lines however which run on past the end of the line into the next one before pausing naturally because the end of the sentence has been reached. Such lines are known as run-on lines or as instances of enjambment [ɪn'dʒæmmənt].

A second step in determining the metre of a line (and often of the whole poem) is to count the number of feet in the line. The appropriate technical terms are as follows:

	1 foot		monometer [mɒ'nɒmɪtə]
	2 feet		dimeter ['dɪmɪtə]
	3 feet	is	trimeter ['trɪmɪtə]
A line of	4 feet	known	tetrameter [te'træmɪtə]
	5 feet	as	pentameter [pen'tæmɪtə]
	6 feet		hexameter [he'ksæmɪtə]
	7 feet		heptameter [hep'tæmɪtə]
	8 feet		octometer [ɒk'təʊmɪtə]

Iambic tetrameter is quite a common metre, but far more important is iambic pentameter, especially in an unrhymed form known as blank verse. Blank verse is the metre of English dramatic and epic poetry. All of Shakespeare's plays and Milton's *Paradise Lost* were written in blank verse, for instance. (There are a few prose passages here and there in Shakespeare plays, but we are not concerned with them here.) Since no rhyme is used, the units of thought form the stanzaic divisions, and through the use of techniques like run-on-lines, end-stopped lines, etc., the poet is able to write verse units without rhyme. The form became the standard mode of expression for dignified verse forms such as poetic drama and the epic, although it has been used for every kind of poetry since then.

Lines of more than five feet and lines of only one foot are relatively rare in English. Iambic pentameter is the most common metre. Anapaestic metres are rare, but individual anapaests occur as a variation in basically iambic poems. Trochaic metres are less common than iambic ones, and dactylic metres are very rare.

At this point we need to look at another device of *prosody* (= the study of versification, covering rhythm, metre, rhyme, and verse-forms), the caesura [sɪˈzjʊərə]. The caesura is related as closely to meaning as to verse technique. It signifies a break in the flow of sound within a line and it is caused by a break in meaning – the end of one sentence and the beginning of another, for instance. That break in meaning occasions a rhetorical pause in the reading, often at about the middle of the line. The use of caesura adds variety to the music of the line and the entire poem. Here is an example from Alfred Tennyson's (1809 – 1892) *The Lotus-Eaters*.

> Let us alone. ‖ Time driveth onward fast.
> And in a little while our lips are dumb.
> Let us alone. ‖ What is it that will last?

The poet's choice of a particular metre for expressing his thoughts and feelings is usually significant. There are no hard and fast rules governing the character of metres, of course, but rhythm is always in some measure bound up with meaning and so there are certain aspects of metres that make them particularly suitable for certain subjects.

Iambic metres tend to be thoughtful and full of recollections, moving as they do from the uncertainty of an unaccented syllable to the certainly of an accented one. Look at this passage from Wordsworth's *Tintern Abbey*, for instance, in which the poet explains how his mind works:

With many recognitions dim and faint,

x   x́ x x́ x x́ x   x́   x   x́

And somewhat of a sad perplexity,

x   x́   x   x́ x x́   x   x́ x x́

The picture of the mind revives again …

x   x́ x   x́ x   x́   x x́   x x́

William Wordsworth (1770 – 1850)

The iambic rhythm of the last line perfectly mimics the revival of recollected experiences which it speaks of, the stresses on *the picture* (x x́), *the mind* (x x́), *revives* (x x́) and *again* (x x́) create the increasing certainty that comes with the mind's revival. This is particularly so in the case of the last two words (*revíves* and *agáin*) where the verse follows the natural iambic speech rhythm.

Trochaic metres, by contrast, because they begin with a stressed syllable, are likely to sound assertive. Consider the opening lines of Blake's *The Tyger*, for example:

Tyger, Tyger! Burning bright

x́ x   x́ x   x́ x   x́

In the forests of the night …

x́ x   x́ x x́   x   x́

The *Tyger* bursts upon the scene in assertive trochees here. You cannot expect all trochee metres to be quite as powerful as that, but more often than not a trochaic rhythm tends to hammer out the meaning of the lines.

Dactylic metres tend to be tinged with sadness. The two unstressed syllables which follow the stressed syllable create a feeling of decline, of a falling away from certainty. It is not surprising, therefore, that a poem of regret, Robert Browning's *The Lost Leader* should be written in sad, heavy dactyls:

We that had loved him so, followed him, honoured him,

x́ x x   x́   x   x   x́ x   x   x́ x   x

Lived in his mild and magnificent eye …

x́   x x   x́ x   x   x́ x x   x́

Robert Browning (1812 – 1889)

The sad regret of *loved him so* (x́ x x) is created by the two unstressed syllables that follow *loved*. It is as if the dactyl enacts the way love for the lost leader fades away.

Anapaestic metres, on the other hand, build up emotional tension by taking the reader from two unstressed syllables to the stressed one. Byron's "The Destruction of Sennacherib" is a famous example:

The Assyrian came down like the wolf on the fold,

x   x x x́ x   x   x́   x x x́ x x x́

And his cohorts were gleaming in purple and gold.

x   x   x́ x   x   x́ x   x x́ x x x́

George Gordon Byron (1788 – 1824)

The unstressed syllables create an anticipatory [æn'tɪsɪpətərɪ] tension which is released in the powerful syllables of *down* (x́), *wolf* (x́), and *fold* (x́).

Spondees on their own cannot sustain whole poems, but they are sometimes used to slow the rhythm of a line, making it "heavier" for a particular effect, as when Ted Hughes (1930 –) in *View of a Pig* says that it weighed *as much as three men* (x x́ x x́ x́) and that *Such weight and thick pink bulk* (x x́ x x́ x́ x́) / *Set in death seemed not just dead.* Look at the way the words *as three men* (x x́ x́) and *thick pink bulk* (x́ x́ x́) can create an impression of the dead pig's weight through the equal stress of the spondees.

A word must also be said here about **free verse**. Like traditional verse, free verse (sometimes referred to by the French term *vers libre*) is poetry printed as individual lines and not as continuous text as in ordinary prose. It differs from traditional verse in that its rhythmic pattern is not organised into a regular metrical form. Most free verse has lines of irregular length and is either totally without rhyme or uses it only sporadically. *Blank verse* is different from free verse in the sense that it is metrically regular; it is written in iambic pentameter.

It was probably the famous American poet Walt Whitman (1819 – 1892) who did more than anyone else to develop free verse and establish it as a major form. He startled the literary world in 1855 with his poem collection *Leaves of Grass,* in which he employed verse lines of varying length, lines that depended for rhythmic effect not on regular metric feet, but on the careful arrangement of stressed and unstressed syllables. (Such an arrangement, along the lines of natural speech rhythm, is known as a *cadence* ['keɪdəns].) He also made use of repetitions, balanced and varied his words, his phrases, and whole lines. He also experimented with sound effects to good advantage.

Here is a typical example of Whitman's work:

Sparkles from the Wheel

Where the city's ceaseless crowd moves on the livelong day,
Withdrawn I join a group of children watching, I pause aside with
  them.

By the curb toward the edge of the flagging,
A knife-grinder works at his wheel sharpening a great knife,
Bending over he carefully holds it to the stone, by foot and knee,
With measur'd tread he turns rapidly, as he presses with light but
  firm hand,
Forth issue then in copious golden jets,
Sparkles from the wheel.

The scene and all its belongings, how they seize and affect me,
The sad sharp-chinn'd old man with worn clothes and broad
  shoulder-band of leather,
Myself effusing and fluid, a phantom curiously floating, now here
  absorb'd and arrested,
The group, (an unminded point set in a vast surrounding,)
The attentive, quiet children, the loud, proud, restive base of the
  streets,
The low hoarse purr of the whirling stone, the light-press'd blade,
Diffusing, dropping, sideways-darting, in tiny showers of gold,
Sparkles from the wheel.

Walt Whitman (1819 – 1892)

Notes
Sparkles: poetic word for "sparks" – *flagging* (here): area covered with
flagstones (i.e. the pavement) – *effusing and fluid* (here): feeling unreal –
unminded: nobody pays any attention – *restive:* constantly on the move

The speaker describes a scene in the street where he is watching a *knife-
grinder* at work *at his wheel*. He is concerned with the strong
impression this scene makes on him, with how *the scene and all its
belongings ... seize and affect* him. He says very little about most of the
objects involved in the scene he is describing. He merely mentions a few
things, but when he talks about the grindstone *(the wheel)*, there is a
marked change. He is not content with simply listing the grindstone as
one more object among a few others, and suddenly achieves poetic
heights in his description of what the knife-grinder is doing. The
whirling stone is said to give off a *low hoarse purr* (as if it were an

animal), and when the man *presses with light but firm hand*, sparks fly from the wheel *in copious golden jets* and in *tiny showers of gold, diffusing, dropping, sideways-darting*.

Have you noticed how the poet

- uses repetition (*Sparkles from the wheel*, at the end of each of the sections / stanzas) to good effect; it helps him to emphasise what the poem is about.

- relies a great deal on sound effects to bind his text together:
  - alliteration (e.g. <u>c</u>ity's / <u>c</u>easeless; live<u>l</u>ong; <u>w</u>ithdrawn / <u>w</u>atching; <u>w</u>orks / <u>w</u>heels, etc.)
  - assonance (e.g. withdr<u>aw</u>n / p<u>au</u>se; <u>o</u>ver / h<u>o</u>lds / st<u>o</u>ne; m<u>ea</u>sur'd / tr<u>ea</u>d / pr<u>e</u>sses, etc.)
  - consonance (e.g. <u>c</u>ity'<u>s</u> <u>c</u>ea<u>s</u>eless; measur'<u>d</u> / trea<u>d</u>; sa<u>d</u> o<u>ld</u> man / broa<u>d</u> / shoul<u>d</u>er-ban<u>d</u>, etc.)

These special sound effects (for details on alliteration, assonance and consonance see below), and especially their great number, help to distinguish this text as verse, as different from ordinary prose.

Many modern poets have tried out diverse rhythmic possibilities. In their poems, the verse is released from the constraints of a regular line and of a recurrent rhythm. Instead, conspicuous visual clues are often used to control pace, pause, and emphasis in the reading. In this way a tension is achieved between suspense and release, depending on how the line endings coincide with or work against the pull towards bringing the syntactical unit to an end. (The poems of the American poet e.e. cummings [1894 – 1962] are typical of such efforts.)

1.3.3 Sound and rhyme

In everyday situations people are hardly aware of the sounds that words make, but in poetry sounds play an important role in the impact of a poem. Depending on what impact the poet wants to achieve, poems can sound

- majestic and powerful,
- soft and lyrical,
- grave and sonorous,
- fluid and agile.

Every word is both a sound (or a series of sounds) and a meaning. When a poet manages his words sensitively, sounds can express or supplement meaning. As Alexander Pope (1688 – 1744) said in *An Essay on Criticism* (1711): *The sound must seem an echo to the sense*.

This is self-revealing in the case of onomatopoeia [ˌɒnəmætəˈpɪːə], the imitation in sound of the thing described. It is perhaps the most obvious of all phonic devices. Words whose sound resembles the thing or action denoted by the word include *buzz, jangle, rustling, bubbling, crackle,* and so on. Listen for instance to the way Wilfred Owen (1893 – 1918) manages to imitate the harsh, mechanical sounds of guns and rifles in his *Anthem for Doomed Youth* (1917), a poem about the First World War:

> Only the monstrous anger of the guns,
> Only the stuttering rifles' rapid rattle …

The sounds of *monstrous anger* hint at the explosive power of big guns, and *stuttering rifles' rapid rattle* is remarkably close to the repetitive sound of infantrymen's rapid firing.

More subtle sound effects are achieved through manipulation of vowels and consonants. The repetition of consonant sounds at the beginning of words or of stressed syllables is known as alliteration (also sometimes known as *head-rhyme* or *initial rhyme*), which is a very old device in English verse (older than end-rhyme). It is common in verse generally and is used occasionally in prose, e.g. in the formulation of newspaper headlines. Alliterative verse became increasingly rare after the end of the fifteenth century however and now tends to be reserved for the achievement of special stylistic effects:

- to reinforce the meaning,
- to link related words,
- and to create the tone of the poem.

All of these can be felt in the vigorous opening of Percy Bysshe Shelley's (1792 – 1822) *Ode to the West Wind*:

> O Wild West Wind, thou breath of Autumn's being

The alliterated words powerfully enact the awe the poet feels in the presence of such a mighty force. You can hear it in the expansive sounds of *Wild West Wind* and feel its power again in *breath* and the skilfully delayed echo of the b-sound in *being*.

Two further sound effects can be mentioned in passing – assonance and consonance. Assonance is the repetition of internal vowels (e.g. *bird – thirst*), whereas consonance means the reverse of assonance – the consonant sounds are the same, but there are different vowel sounds (e.g. *wood – weed*). These two phonic devices are often employed when the poet is working with imperfect rhymes (see below).

When sounds are repeated, the effect is pleasurable, and the most important repetition of sounds in poetry is of course end-rhyme. It delights the ear as music does, especially when it is used in popular songs and ballads, but the effect is also similar in serious poetry. It functions as a mnemonic device – it assists the memory. In a poem using a regular pattern of end-rhyme, the reader is constantly curious as to what word will appear to complete the rhyme; he anticipates the need for a word of matching sound, and when it appears he recognises it as fitting, or he is surprised when the rhyme is imperfect.

The patterning of end-rhymes is also part of the architecture of a poem. The rhyme seems to bind together the unit in which it is used and it can intensify the logical connections and the unity of meaning. In the hands of a skilful poet, it is a device that seems not to be imposed from without, but dictated from within. A group of rhyming lines thus appears bound together in an almost magical way that can enhance both the meaning and the music of the lines.

A succession of rhymes can assist the progression of thought and differentiate one unit from another. A strong contrast in the rhyme sounds can contribute to the contrasting of ideas. Cross-rhyme, on the other hand, can assist in an interlocking of ideas. Here is an example of perfect interlocking rhyme:

> That time of year thou mayst in me beh*old*
> When yellow leaves, or none, or few, do h*ang*
> Upon those boughs which shake against the c*old*,
> Bare ruined choirs, where late the sweet birds *sang*.

This is the beginning of Shakespeare's *Sonnet 73*. The lines demonstrate perfect end-rhyme, i.e. the rhyming words repeat exactly the stressed vowel and all of the speech sounds following that vowel: beh<u>old</u> – c<u>old</u>; h<u>ang</u> – s<u>ang</u>.

When we want to describe the pattern of rhyme in a poem, we label the first rhyme-sound "a," the next "b," then "c," "d," etc. When the sound reappears, we use the same letter originally used to label that sound. Here is the full text of *Sonnet 73*, with the rhymes labelled as described:

That time of year thou mayst in me behold	a
When yellow leaves, or none, or few, do hang	b
Upon those boughs which shake against the cold,	a
Bare ruin'd choirs, where late the sweet birds sang.	b

In me thou seest the twilight of such day	c
As after sunset fadeth in the west,	d
Which by and by black night doth take away,	c
Death's second self, that seals up all in rest.	d
In me thou see'st the glowing of such fire	e
That on the ashes of his youth doth lie,	f
As the death-bed whereon it must expire	e
Consumed with that which it was nourish'd by.	f
This thou perceivest, which makes thy love more strong,	g
To love that well which thou must leave ere long.	g

When the entire stanza is labelled in this way, the rhyme of the stanza can be summarised by saying that the pattern of rhyme is abab cdcd, etc. Even if the words don't rhyme (unrhymed lines), they should still be given a letter. This is known as the stanza's rhyme scheme. An ability to classify the rhyme scheme is however only half the battle. What really matters is whether we can show how the form of the poem, as created by the rhyme scheme, can assist in enacting its meaning. In other words, you ought to be aware of the particular effects certain verse forms make possible (for details see below).

Until recently almost all English writers of serious poems have limited themselves to perfect rhymes, except for an occasional poetic licence such as eye-rhymes – words in which the endings are spelled alike (so that they look alike: eye-rhyme), and in most instances were once pronounced alike, but have in the course of time acquired a different pronunciation. Examples include *love – move*; *come – home*; *daughter – laughter*.

Many modern poets, however, deliberately employ approximate rhyme (also known as *imperfect rhyme*, *partial rhyme*, *half-rhyme*, *slant rhyme*, or *pararhyme*; see also *assonance* and *consonance* above). These poets like playing with rhyme and systematically exploit partial rhymes. Strictly speaking, imperfect rhyme is not rhyme at all, because words either rhyme or do not rhyme. Nevertheless, it depends on rhyme for its effectiveness because the ear wants, and naturally expects, the full harmony of perfect rhyme, but in a sense this expectation is disappointed, and poets exploit this disappointment for their own purposes. Look at how Wilfred Owen uses the incompleteness of imperfect rhyme in the following poem to echo the break-up of order and harmony that occurs in war. Here is the first stanza of his poem *Insensibility* in which he talks of those who have become insensible to the horrors of the war surrounding them:

Happy are the men who yet before they are killed
Can let their veins run cold.
Whom no companion fleers
Or makes their feet
Sore on the alleys cobbled with their brothers.
The front line withers,
But they are troops who fade, not flowers,
For poet's tearful fooling:
Men gaps for filling:
Losses, who might have fought
Longer; but no one bothers.

Notes

fleers: mocks – *cobbled with their brothers:* paved with the skulls of their dead fellow soldiers – *Men gaps for filling:* the men are thought of merely as "gaps for filling" – *no one bothers:* nobody is interested in their fate

The text is full of imperfect rhymes (of instances of consonance): *killed – cold, fleers – flowers, feet – fought, brothers – bothers*, and *fooling – filling*. These half-rhymes enact the disarray of the war situation by hinting at thymes that do not come. There is discord also in ideas – people should be concerned for their *brothers*, the soldiers, but in war *no one bothers* about them. The sounds of the half-rhymes thus echo and reinforce the poem's meaning.

Rhyme may occur elsewhere than at the ends of lines. It is frequently used in a pattern of internal rhyme (inner rhyme) that usually comes in the middle and at the end of a long line. A good example of internal rhyme is found in Edgar Allan Poe's (1809 – 1849) *The Raven*, which employs a regular pattern of internal and end rhyme.

Open here I flung the *shutter*, when, with many a flirt and *flutter*,
In there stepped a stately Raven of the saintly days of yore;
Not the least obeisance *made he*; not a minute stopped or *stayed he*;
But with mien of lord or *lady*, perched above my chamber door –
Perched upon a bust of Pallas just above my chamber door –
Perched and sat, and nothing more.

Notes

yore: long ago – *obeisance* (here): a bow of respect – *perched* (of a bird): sat – *Pallas:* in classical mythology name given to Athena

Blocks of lines separated from other such blocks of lines in a poem are known as stanzas. A stanza is therefore a division separated by spacing from other similar units. Most lyric poems are made up of a group of stanzas of the same length, but this is not always so. Often a poet may prefer to use stanzas of irregular length, corresponding to paragraphs in prose, the lines being grouped solely according to the logic of their content. Regular stanza forms, however, may continue the thought from one stanza to another. A fresh thought may be started in mid-stanza if desired. On the other hand, one stanza may constitute a complete poem.

The stanza may be defined according to the number of lines it contains. Some of the more common stanza forms follow.

A stanza of two lines is called a couplet – one line coupled to another. The heroic couplet, found frequently in English poetry, is a stanza composed of two rhyming lines of iambic pentameter. The couplet as a separate stanza form is not common, but the couplet as part of connected verse is. Shakespeare, for instance, uses it frequently to round off his sonnets; his *Sonnet 73* (quoted above) is a case in point.

The couplet tends to be affirmative. What is said in the first line is developed in the second and then completed by the rhyme to make a strong, self-contained statement. The second line and the rhyme develop and complete what the first line began. It is a form that is particularly suited to argument and to bringing a poem to a firm conclusion.

A stanza of three lines' length (called *triplet* or *tercet*) is rare in English, but quatrains, four lines of verse, are the most popular stanza form in lyric poetry. They tend to be neat and economical, as in the following excerpt from Robert Herrick's (1591 – 1674) *To The Virgins, To Make Much of Time*:

> Gather ye rosebuds while ye may,
> Old time is still a-flying:
> And this same flower that smiles to-day
> To-morrow will be dying.

The argument is neatly arranged – its four stages are given a line each. And there is a pleasing contrast between the masculine rhymes that deal with what might be done and the flowing feminine rhymes that express the quick passing of time. Like all successful quatrains, this one creates the feeling that it needs just four lines to say all that needs to be said.

There are stanza forms of five, six, seven, eight, and nine lines in length. Some of the best English poetry has been written in stanzas of seven lines (known as *rhyme royal*), e.g. Geoffrey Chaucer's (c. 1343 – 1400) *Troilus and Criseyde*, or even in nine-line stanzas, Edmund Spenser's (c. 1552 – 1599) *Faerie Queene*, for instance, but the fact remains that these long stanzas are not common.

The sonnet, consisting of a single stanza of fourteen lines, has been very popular. The Italian sonnet is divided into an *octave* (the first eight lines) and a *sestet* (the last six lines). The English sonnet, by contrast, may present three arguments concerned with its theme in three *quatrains* and draw a conclusion in the final *couplet*. A more detailed discussion of the sonnet will be attempted later (see 1.4.4 Lyric poetry).

1.3.4 Speaker and persona

In the Shakespeare sonnet quoted above, *Sonnet 73*, the poet seems to be speaking in his own voice, preparing his young friend, not perhaps for the approaching literal death of his body, but for the metaphorical "death" of his youth and passion. The speaker of the poem and the poet are presumably identical here, but this is by no means always the case, though it probably happens more often in poetry than in narrative literature that speaker / narrator and poet / writer are one and the same person. This is because poetry, and especially lyric poetry, invites the poet to lay open his innermost feelings and to write about his own emotions, whereas autobiographical outpourings are relatively rare in fiction, which is usually concerned with the conflicts of some characters the writer has invented.

An element of doubt remains even with the Shakespeare sonnet; are the first-person speaker and the poet really identical? If we assume that the sonnets are at least partly autobiographical, i.e. that Shakespeare was writing about himself and his own feelings, it becomes relevant that he was still a young man when *Sonnet 73* was composed. It is generally accepted that all of his 154 sonnets were written before 1600, so the poet would have been hardly over 30 at the time, not a ripe old age even by Renaissance standards. So the speaker of this sonnet may be a slightly different persona than the poet himself, created by him for artistic purposes, namely for representing a much older man than the poet himself was at the time.

This persona-concept is important for understanding poetry. "Persona" was the Latin word for the mask worn by the actors in the classical theatre. (The term for the list of characters having a role in a play, *dramatis personae* [ˌdrɑːmətɪs pɜːˈsəʊnaɪ], derives from this; and ultimately so does the English word "person", a particular individual.) Within the context of literary discussion, "persona" is usually applied to the first-person speaker whose "voice" we hear in a lyric poem.

Such a "persona" is always, to some degree, adapted to the requirements and the artistic aims of a particular work. Consider for instance the opening of *Ulysses* (1842) by Alfred Tennyson's (1809 – 1892):

> It little profits that an idle king,
> By this still hearth, among these barren crags,
> Matched with an aged wife, I mete and dole
> Unequal laws unto a savage race,
> That hoard, and sleep, and feed, and know not me.

Notes
crags: pieces of rock – *mete and dole:* give out – *hoard:* collect stuff to keep in a safe, often secret place

It is self-evident here that the Ulysses that speaks in the first person *(I mete and dole / Unequal laws …)* is not the poet Tennyson; he is a distinctive persona created by the poet for the purpose of this poem – Ulysses is here not the vigorous war hero of the battles about Troy (see the *Iliad*) or of the adventures on his way home to his island of Ithaca (see the *Odyssee*), but an old man, tired and discontented, who is obliged only to look back on his glorious past and appears to have nothing to look forward to. This is the character that interests the poet, and so he creates for this man the persona that comes across from the lines above. The man is in despair, he is exhausted and dispirited so that the reader may well wonder whether such a man could ever change again. Yet in the very next line, the attitude of the persona does in fact change:

> I cannot rest from travel: I will drink
> Life to the lees …

It becomes obvious that Ulysses is trying to stir himself and find a new start. The caesura after *travel* marks the beginning of a deliberate effort to force himself into action. In the end he summons his companions from the past to accompany him on one final journey:

> Come, my friends,
> 'Tis not too late to seek a newer world.
> Push off, and sitting well in order smite
> The sounding furrows; for my purpose holds
> To sail beyond the sunset, and the baths
> Of all the western stars, until I die.

Ulysses, the aged voyager who once felt such a great longing for his island of Ithaca after the fall of Troy and simply wanted to get home, is depicted here as having grown weary of a life of idle comfort. He wants, and in fact needs, to be up and about again and will have no rest until his death.

The few lines quoted above thus reveal Ulysses as the man he is. There are a number of forceful imperatives here (*Come … Push off … smite* [= hit]), but we can also detect a weariness – the persona Tennyson has created contemplates not success but his own death (*until I die*). A tired old man still longs for action, even though death is close at hand.

The upshot of all this is that the "I" that gives a poem unity is rarely the "I" of the poet. The voice *within* the poem should not be confused with the voice of the poet *outside* the poem. The "I" of the first-person speaker can safely be assumed to have been specially created for that particular poem. In Robert Browning's dramatic monologues (see 1.4.3 below for details), for instance, the personae range from a famous painter ("Fra Lippo Lippi") to a young man who strangles his girl friend with her own long and beautiful hair ("Porphyria's Lover"). Nobody should identify the poet with either. It is however always worth asking why a poet was interested in the persona he or she has created, and why he created this particular persona and not another one.

1.3.5 Form and content

The previous sections of this chapter have looked at the various elements of poetry individually and separately, but the point is, of course, that all these elements are nothing in themselves; they receive their significance exclusively from their contribution to the poem as a whole. All the individual elements are fused together, so to speak, and produce out of this fusion a new whole – the poem. The interplay of all the separate aspects of poetry can thus not only create a specific *tone* for the poem (anything from "sad" to "joyful and amusing"), but also *enact its overall meaning*.

It is possible to say something separately about the form elements (such as metaphors, rhythm, rhyme, choice of words, etc.) and about the content elements (i.e. the "experience" which the poem crystallizes and distils), but we should be clear about the fact that form and content must not, and indeed cannot, be separated. You can't have the one without the other; they form an organic whole in the poem and *together* enact its meaning. A look at an example, *Dover Beach* by Matthew Arnold's (1822 – 1888) can perhaps help to make this clear. The poem is about the poet's thoughts and feelings while he is listening to the waves breaking on the shore. At one point he writes about the sounds and rhythms they make:

> Listen! you hear the grating roar
> Of pebbles which the waves draw back, and fling,
> At their return, up the high strand,
> Begin, and cease, and then again begin,
> With tremulous cadence slow, and bring
> The eternal note of sadness in.

The sounds and rhythms of those words enact two things – the ebbing and flowing of the waves, which begin, and cease, and then begin again, and the overwhelming sadness those sounds stir in the poet. We can hear the waves crashing onto the shore and then relapsing before its inevitable return, and then the whole movement seems to slow down, as if we were experiencing it in slow motion, as we hear about the *tremulous cadence slow*. The waves bring *The eternal note of sadness in*. The word *eternal* is well chosen here because it suggests the never ending movement of the sea.

The point about the words used in this passage is that they are not just decorating the idea of the sea's movement and sadness, but actually enact the movement of the waves and the poet's feelings of sadness. Form and content cannot be separated.

Synopsis

The language of poetry
- uses words in an intriguing and enriching way.
- tends to be suggestive and to make the reader curious.
- is full of words that carry many associations.
- is also vivid and often relies on words that appeal to the senses.
- is rich in similes, metaphors, symbols and other figures of speech.
- frequently relies on the use of imagery.
- often contains cross references and allusions.

Rhythm
- is created by the repetition of sounds and ideas so that a regular.
- pattern is established.
- is created out of the patterned use of words, sounds and stress.
- can have an enchanting effect.
- can have a strong emotional impact on the reader.
- establishes associations of sound and meaning in the mind.

Metre
- is based on a rhythmical pattern of stressed and unstressed syllables.
- consists of a regular number of metric feet.
- can be iambic, trochaic, dactylic, anapaestic, or spondaic.
- can tolerate slight irregularities in the rhythmical pattern.

Lines
- may end in a hard, accented syllable.
- may end in a soft, unaccented syllable.
- may have a masculine or feminine ending.
- may alternate between masculine and feminine endings.
- may be end-stopped.
- may run on past the end of the line into the next.
- may show instances of enjambment.

The caesura
- signifies a break in the flow of sound within a line.
- is caused by a break in meaning.
- occasions a rhetorical pause in the reading.
- adds variety to the music of the lines.

The various metres are traditionally associated with certain moods.

Iambic metre
- tends to express certainty.
- conveys seriousness and solemnity.

Trochaic metre
- is likely to sound assertive.
- can exhibit a tripping movement.

Dactylic metre
- tends to move slowly.
- is often tinged with sadness.

Anapaestic metre
- is likely to be galloping and joyful.
- tends to create emotional tension.

Spondees are sometimes used to slow down the rhythm of a line.

Free verse
- is not organised into a regular metrical form.
- tends to have lines of irregular length.
- is either totally without rhyme or uses it only sporadically.
- often experiments with sound effects.
- releases the verse from the constraints of a regular line and a recurrent rhythm.
- depends for rhythmic effect on cadences of stressed and unstressed syllables.

Sounds
- play an important role in the impact of a poem.
- can express or supplement meaning.
- may be onomatopoeic in character.

Alliteration
- is based on the repetition of consonant sounds at the beginning of words or stressed syllables.
- can reinforce meaning.
- can link related words.
- can help to create the tone of the poem.

Assonance
- is the repetition of internal vowels, but with different consonants.
- is often found in imperfect rhyme.

Consonance
- means the repetition of consonant sounds, but with different vowel sounds.
- is sometimes used in free verse.

End-rhyme
- repeats at the end of a line a stressed vowel and all of the speech sounds following that vowel.
- is a technique that is basic to versification.
- is an important feature of verse.
- delights the ear and creates soothing, pleasurable effects.
- functions as a mnemonic device, assisting the memory.
- is part of the architecture of a poem, tying individual lines into the larger pattern of a stanza.
- binds together the unit within which it is used.
- can intensify the logical connections.
- can establish unity of meaning.
- can contribute to the contrasting of ideas when there is contrast in the rhyme sounds.
- can assist in the interlocking of ideas, especially if cross rhyme is used.
- can highlight certain words.
- can be used to achieve a comic effect.

Imperfect rhyme
- is also known as approximate rhyme, partial rhyme, half-rhyme, slant rhyme, or pararhyme.
- is usually based on assonance or consonance.
- can be exploited for particular purposes.
- can reinforce a poem's meaning.

Internal rhyme usually comes in the middle and at the end of long lines.

Stanzas
- are groups of lines in a poem.
- are recognisable units in a poem.
- are often of the same length, but sometimes of irregular length.
- are divisions in a poem separated by spacing from other similar units.

The couplet
- may be a stanza of two lines.
- is usually two lines of iambic pentameter.
- is particularly suited to argument.
- is often used to conclude a poem.
- often appears as a heroic couplet, two rhyming lines of iambic pentameter.

The quatrain
- is the most popular stanza form in lyric poetry.
- tends to be neat and economical.

Iambic pentameter
- is the preferred line in dramatic and epic poetry.
- usually appears in the form of blank verse.
- closely resembles the natural speech rhythm.

The speaker
- of a poem must not be confused with the poet's own voice.
- is a *persona* created by the poet for artistic reasons.
- is a *persona* created for a particular poem.

Form and content
- are inseparable in a poem.
- form an organic whole in the poem.
- together enact the poem's meaning.

1.4 Genres of poetry

Poetry can be divided into a number of broad classifications:

- narrative poetry,
- dramatic poetry,
- lyric poetry
- and light verse.

1.4.1 Narrative poetry

The principal categories of the second group, narrative poetry, are

- epic,
- verse romance
- and ballad.

What they all have in common, however, is that they tell a story, but they do so in different ways.

The most dignified and elaborate form of narrative poetry is the epic, which is a composition on a grand scale – a narrative in verse celebrating warlike adventures, the mysteries of religion or personal romance. Epics probably date back to prehistoric times. The earliest of them were performed by singers who accompanied themselves on a stringed instrument and made up their lines as they went along. In doing this they followed the outline of a well-known myth or traditional story revolving around the exploits and adventures of a hero.

In Western literature, epic poetry begins with the *Iliad* and the *Odyssey*. Both epics are generally attributed to Homer, a blind Greek poet living around 700 B.C. He based his texts on the cycle of tales surrounding the half-historical, half-mythical Trojan War. His two epics became so famous that they served as models for later poets who all tried to write epic poetry in the Homeric manner:

- invoking the Muse for divine inspiration at the beginning;
- starting *in medias res* (in the middle of things),
- and presenting their material in a dignified style.

These rules or conventions were largely forgotten during the Middle Ages and poets produced epics in a more natural style. Important medieval epics include the Old English epic *Beowulf*, which probably dates from the eighth century A.D. but was not written down until the end of the tenth century. The action it unfolds is set in southern Scandinavia. The epic is still essentially pagan in character and

Beowulf's fights with monsters and dragons are related in terms of the Germanic heroic age with its intense code of loyalty to the feudal lord. The action is however interpreted and commented on from a decidedly Christian viewpoint.

The poetic method used in *Beowulf* is based on the use of head-rhyme, not end-rhyme. This is to say the verse is *alliterative*, repeating the word-initial consonant sounds in the same lines. Here is a short extract from *Beowulf* in a modern English translation that can show what is meant:

Soon he saw	– that shepherd of sorrows –
that he'd never met	in all middle-earth,
all ways of the world,	a warrior who wielded
a grip this grievous,	so strong he groaned
in frenzy, fear,	no breaking free.
He hurt to be home,	flee to his hideout,
lair of devils –	but no such doings
as he'd done before	in olden days!

From Part I, XI

Notice how in the first line words beginning with s-sounds *(soon, saw, sorrow)* are employed, then, in the second line, we find words beginning with the m-sound *(met, middle-earth)*; there are four words beginning with w in the third line *(ways, world, warrior, wielded)*, and so forth.

During the Renaissance, which came late to the British Isles, the classical models of epic writing were rediscovered and so the English poet John Milton (1608 – 1674) imitated them when he composed his *Paradise Lost* (1667). Milton struck out on his own however when he decided against the idea of writing on a romantic or historical theme and instead sought inspiration in the myths of the Biblical tradition, which also gave him an opportunity to put forward his own theological views. Thus he turned to the creation of the universe and especially to the myths of a war among the heavenly powers. As a result of his insubordination (and his defeat in battle), Satan is cast out from Heaven and eventually makes his way to Paradise where he induces Adam and Eve to eat from the fruit of the Tree of Knowledge, a deed which brings sin and death into the world and leads to their expulsion from Paradise.

Milton opens his poem in a traditional and conventional manner:

Of Man's first disobedience, and the fruit
Of that forbidden tree, whose mortal taste
Brought death into the world, and all our woe,
With loss of Eden, till one greater Man
Restore us, and regain the blissful seat,
Sing Heavenly Muse, [...]
                                        I thence
Invoke thy aid to my adventurous song,
That with no middle flight intends to soar
Above th' Aonian mount, while it pursues
Things unattempted yet in prose or rhyme.
And chiefly Thou O Spirit, that dost prefer
Before all Temples th' upright heart and pure,
Instruct me, for Thou know'st; [...]

Notes
one greater Man: the Messiah – *Aonian Mount:* Mt. Helicon, in Aonia, sacred
to the classical muses

It is interesting to note that Milton not only invokes the help of the
Heavenly Muse in the traditional manner (probably Urania, the muse
of astronomy), but *chiefly* the aid of the *Spirit* (the Holy Spirit) who is
to instruct the poet because He "knows" *(Thou know'st)*. The classical
epic tradition and Milton's Christian outlook are combined here and
seem to march hand in hand.

Paradise Lost is conceived on the grand scale of Milton's classical
models and thus features invocations, digressions, legend, folklore,
magic, history, the supernatural, eloquent speeches, dangerous
journeys, battles and scenes in the underworld. The range of *Paradise
Lost* is truly colossal, its sweep majestic, and Milton is fully aware of
the magnitude of the task before him – he attempts to pursue *Things
unattempted yet in prose or rhyme* – and critics are all agreed that he
succeeds brilliantly.

Many see *Paradise Lost* as the last poem that can unreservedly be called
an epic. Maybe so, but it is also true that since Milton's day a number
of narrative poems have been produced which can be said to have
continued the epic tradition by virtue of their scale, their heroic themes
and their elevated style. The rise of realistic prose fiction, especially
novels, has certainly led to a decline of epic poetry. The novel, the
cinema and to some extent also the theatre appear to have become the
preferred vehicles for narratives on an epic scale. Famous instances of
such novels are Leo Tolstoy's *War and Peace* (1865 – 1872) or John

Steinbeck's *The Grapes of Wrath* (1939) or his *East of Eden* (1952). All these novels and others like them offer such a large-scale picture of society and the various problems besetting a whole generation during a difficult historical period that they can truly be said to be modern epics – not in verse however, but in prose.

Another narrative verse form which was gradually superseded and replaced by prose writing is the verse romance. It flourished from the Middle Ages until far into the nineteenth century and even later. The verse romance is different from the epic in the sense that the stories it offers are presented on a much reduced scale. We do not find the majestic sweep of the epic or the grand style in the presentation of the story, but the metrical romance also features

- heroic adventures,
- love stories,
- tales of knightly chivalry,
- often an element of mystery,
- possibly a touch of the supernatural,
- and generally exciting action.

Quite a number of nineteenth century poets felt moved to try their hand at verse romances and some produced very fine poems. Examples include *The Lady of Shalott* (1832; revised 1842) by Alfred Lord Tennyson (1809 – 1892).

The Lady of Shalott tells of a mysterious lady of Shalott who lives on the island of Shalott in the river which flows down to *many-towered Camelot*. The lady sings and weaves, sitting in front of a magic mirror which reflects what is happening in the world. She appears to be under a curse and never looks directly at the real world until she tires of this way of life one day when she sees Sir Lancelot riding to Camelot. She leaves her weaving behind and looks directly down on Camelot. At this moment the curse takes effect, her magic *mirror crack[s] from side to side* and she knows that she is doomed. She writes her name on a boat, lies down in it and sings her death song as she floats down to Camelot.

These are the two final stanzas:

> Under tower and balcony,
> By garden-wall and gallery,
> A gleaming shape she floated by,
> Dead-pale between the houses high,
> Silent into Camelot.
> Out upon the wharfs they came,
> Knight and Burgher, Lord and Dame,

And around the prow they read her name,
The Lady of Shalott.

Who is this? And what is here?
And in the lighted palace near
Died the sound of royal cheer;
And they crossed themselves for fear,
All the Knights at Camelot;
But Lancelot mused a little space
He said, "She has a lovely face;
God in his mercy lend her grace,
The Lady of Shalott."

The legends surrounding King Arthur and his Knights of the Round Table provided the background to the poem (even though the inspiration originally came from an Italian story) and Tennyson used the mystery surrounding Camelot, the seat of King Arthur's court, to good advantage here, transferring it to his own poem and creating a romance of wonderful and mysterious charm.

Tennyson was not the only nineteenth-century poet to be interested in narrative poetry. The Romantic poets in particular had their interest captured by the possibilities of verse narrative, especially by the ballad. They deliberately chose the sort of themes found in folk ballads and adapted them to their own purposes. The ballad form was felt to be particularly attractive because it gave them an opportunity of combining the traditional with the exotic and to endow their poems with connotations of simple folkloristic authenticity.

The resulting literary ballad, unlike the folk ballad and the broadside ballad, is a sophisticated rather than a popular form and it is not an anonymous composition but is the work of a single known poet. It differs from the folk ballad in several respects.

Folk ballads	Literary ballads
• are meant to be sung. • use simple language. • present a single event. • are subject to variations and continual change.	• are meant to be read. • use sophisticated literary devices. • deal with complex ideas. • have a firmly established, unalterable text.

As a rule the literary ballad is far more elaborate and complex, even though the poet may have retained some of the devices and conventions of the folk ballad. Examples of the form include John Keats' *La Belle Dame sans merci* (The Beautiful Lady Without Mercy / Pity) and Samuel Taylor Coleridge's *The Rime of the Ancient Mariner*, which is possibly the best-known literary ballad. Oscar Wilde's *The Ballad of Reading Gaol* is also a famous literary ballad.

Here is the text of *La Belle Dame sans merci*:

La Belle Dame Sans Merci, 1819

Oh what can ail thee, knight-at-arms,
Alone and palely loitering?
The sedge has withered from the lake,
And no birds sing.

Oh what can ail thee, knight-at-arms,
So haggard and so woe-begone?
The squirrel's granary is full,
And the harvest's done.

I see a lily on thy brow,
With anguish moist and fever-dew,
And on thy cheeks a fading rose
Fast withereth too.

I met a lady in the meads,
Full beautiful – a faery's child,
Her hair was long, her foot was light,
And her eyes were wild.

I made a garland for her head,
And bracelets too, and fragrant zone;
She looked at me as she did love,
And made sweet moan.

I set her on my pacing steed,
And nothing else saw all day long,
For sidelong would she bend, and sing
A faery's song.

She found me roots of relish sweet,
And honey wild, and manna-dew,
And sure in language strange she said –
'I love thee true'.

She took me to her elfin grot,
And there she wept and sighed full sore,
And there I shut her wild wild eyes
With kisses four.

And there she lullèd me asleep
And there I dreamed – Ah! woe betide! –
The latest dream I ever dreamt
On the cold hill side.

I saw pale kings and princes too,
Pale warriors, death-pale were they all;
They cried – 'La Belle Dame sans Merci
Hath thee in thrall!'

I saw their starved lips in the gloam,
With horrid warning gapèd wide,
And I awoke and found me here,
On the cold hill's side.

And this is why I sojourn here
Alone and palely loitering,
Though the sedge is withered from the lake,
And no birds sing.

John Keats (1795 – 1821)

Notes

sedge: marsh grass – ***woe-begone:*** sorrowful, miserable – ***meads:*** meadows –
zone: belt – ***manna dew:*** heavenly food – ***grot:*** grotto – ***full sore:*** very heavily
– ***woe betide:*** alas – ***latest*** (here): last – ***in thrall:*** enslaved – ***gloam:*** twilight

An anonymous speaker asks a knight what is wrong with him (stanzas
I–III). The knight replies that he met a beautiful, wild-looking lady in a
meadow, made flowers garlands for her and became convinced that she
loved him. He sat her on his horse and walked beside her. He saw
nothing but her, because she leaned over to him and sang a faery's song
to him. She gave him wonderful food to eat and made it clear to him in
a strange language that she loved him. He kissed her to sleep and when

he also fell asleep, he dreamt of a number of kings, princes and warriors who were all deadly pale. They were the woman's slaves and warned him about her, about *La Belle Dame sans Merci*. And now he was her slave, too. When he woke up, the woman was gone and he found himself on the cold hillside.

It is easy to see that Keats was imitating the conventions of the folk ballad by

- using mostly simple language,

- establishing a dialogue situation,

- focussing on a single event,

- not making any judgments,

- and relying on the ballad meter – with one exception: the last line of each stanza is shorter than usual, carrying only two stresses. This makes it special and calls attention to the line.

The poem is vastly different from folk ballads in the sense that the knight's physical and mental state and his dream are very important and that at the end we are back at the beginning – the poem describes a circular movement, an observation which is reinforced by the use of almost the same words. A folk ballad, by contrast, has a definite ending and concentrates on action.

The unusual character of this ballad is further underlined by the use of realistic and familiar details and of unearthly and strange elements side by side. The result is the creation of a sense of mystery which has intrigued and also puzzled many readers. Whereas a folk ballad must be understood on a literal level only, this ballad is not so easy to interpret – what does it all mean?

- What is the character of the strange lady?

- Was the knight deceived by the strange lady *(a faery's child)* or is he himself deluded?

- What is the meaning of his experience and especially of his dream?

- Why has the knight become sick with anguish by his experience, and was the experience real or only a dream vision? The telltale signs of a serious illness are quite prominent – he is described as *pale*, *haggard* and *woe-begone*, has a *lily* on his *brow with anguish moist and fever dew* and there is a *fading rose* in his cheeks, i.e. we see the flush and pallor and the sick sweat indicative of a deadly illness.

These and similar questions can be asked of the poem. In fact, a case can be made for a number of plausible and even compelling readings of this ballad. This multi-valence of serious literature, i.e. the possibility of interpreting it in a number of ways, is also a feature that distinguishes it from simple folk literature, which is usually to be understood in the literal sense only.

Useful language material

The epic
- This section / extract presents a battle scene.
- It describes the meeting / fight of / between X and Y.
- It shows how X is captured / taken prisoner.
- It depicts a wedding ceremony.
- It centres on X's speech / his escape / his triumph.
- It sets the scene for the next episode.
- The poet fills in some background information here.

The verse romance
- The first stanza sets the scene / sets … before us / describes the wild landscape / introduces the topic.
- The … stanza shows us / introduces the hero / the protagonist.
- It prepares the reader for the meeting between X and Y.
- It paints a romantic scene.
- This section is concerned with creating atmosphere.
- It deepens the mystery.
- The effect of this section depends largely on the poet's use of metaphorical language.
- The final stanza solves the riddle / sees X and Y reunited / ends on a peaceful note.

The literary ballad
- This poem is a literary ballad.
- The story focuses on a single event, namely …
- The poet creates a sense of mystery, when …
- He shows us an enchanted landscape / introduces unearthly and strange elements.
- The first few lines establish a dialogue situation.
- The poem has the typical four-line stanzas of the folk ballad.
- It imitates the conventions of the folk ballad.
- It can be interpreted in a number of ways / shows a certain multi-valence.

1.4.2 Dramatic poetry

As the name indicates, dramatic poetry is intricately bound up with drama, which was always written in poetry in classical times. Within the English tradition, it was Shakespeare who introduced prose passages into his plays, especially for the lowly characters, and used blank verse for the others. It was not until comparatively modern times however that the drama began to be written entirely in prose.

Dramatic poetry within the context of a play focuses chiefly on the revelation of character. The characters created by the dramatic poet for his play are placed by him in situations which involve some conflict and it is precisely the development of this conflict that moves the play action along. It is a dramatic convention for the audience to accept without question the idea that in critical moments a character, alone on the stage, may utter his thoughts aloud. This device, which is known as a soliloquy [səˈlɪləkwi], enables the audience to get to know more about the character's motives, thoughts and feelings, and generally his state of mind.

The following text is one of Shakespeare's best-known soliloquies from one of his masterpieces, *Macbeth*. The context is that Macbeth, the title hero, has just been told that his wife has died.

> She should have died hereafter;
> There would have been a time for such a word.
> To-morrow, and to-morrow, and to-morrow,
> Creeps in this petty pace from day to day
> To the last syllable of recorded time,
> And all our yesterdays have lighted fools
> The way to dusty death. Out, out, brief candle!
> Life's but a walking shadow, a poor player
> That struts and frets his hour upon the stage
> And then is heard no more: it is a tale
> Told by an idiot, full of sound and fury,
> Signifying nothing.

Macbeth, V.v.17–28

Notes

She … hereafter: This line has caused much debate. Four possible meanings are (1) she should have died after the battle when there would be time to mourn properly; (2) she should have waited for me, seeing that my death is so near; (3) she would have died at sometime, either now or later; (4) she should have died after the battle for now, with her gone, I know I shall not win. – *such a word:* namely "death" – *petty pace:* at this meaningless pace – *syllable* (here): final trace – *recorded time:* as opposed to eternity – *frets:* worries

Macbeth's terrible acts throughout the play have led him to this last, horrible conclusion about life – it is utterly meaningless. People's life on this earth serves no other purpose than to push them towards *dusty death*. It is a seemingly endless and depressing succession of bleak days creeping along at a *petty pace*. Life is so insubstantial that it can only be compared to a *shadow*; so unreal that it is like a temporary *stage* on which a poor actor gives a pitiful performance, and when it is over, his character disappears into nothingness; he is quickly forgotten and leaves nothing of any significance behind.

In short, this soliloquy is an important step in the revelation of Macbeth's character at this point in the play. It can show what sort of person he has become – he comes across as a completely disillusioned man who has lost all hope and can see no meaning in life whatsoever. All he has tried so very hard to accomplish throughout the action of the play is totally and absolutely worthless.

A soliloquy in a play – such as we have just seen – must not be confused with a dramatic monologue, which is something quite different. It does not denote a component in a play, but is a type of lyric poem. The dramatic monologue is a species of lyric poem that reveals a "soul in action" through the speech of a character in this poem who addresses one or more silent listeners. The circumstances surrounding the speaker's monologue are made clear by implication, i.e. they can be inferred from what the speaker says. A dramatic monologue is thus like a speech out of a play or a film and the speaker may well unintentionally reveal certain aspects of his or her character.

The poetry of Robert Browning (1812 – 1889) is famous for its dramatic monologues – see for instance his *Soliloquy of the Spanish Cloister* (1842), in which the speaker, a monk in a Spanish monastery, feels a savage, obsessive hatred of Brother Lawrence, a fellow monk at this monastery. What the speaker says shows him up as an unfair and hate-obsessed, vengeful character.

Dramatic monologue makes new demands of the reader, who must work out what the dramatic situation is the poet wants the reader to imagine. He has to piece together scraps of information to complete a picture of the speaker, and even, sometimes, to figure out what is going on. The reader must become engaged in the game of imagination which the poet asks him to play before he can attain a detached, critical view of the text.

The following sample poem can show what is meant. The poem was published in 1902 and refers to the Boer War in South Africa (1899 – 1902), in which the British government, in a military action noted for its brutality, struggled to put down a rebellion by the "Boers", Dutch-speaking peasants whose ancestors had settled there many generations before. Note that the "he" of the title points to the same person as the "I" in the poem.

The Man He Killed

"Had he and I but met
By some old ancient inn,
We should have sat us down to wet
Right many a nipperkin!

"But ranged as infantry,
And staring face to face,
I shot at him as he at me,
And killed him in his place.

"I shot him dead because –
Because he was my foe,
Just so: my foe of course he was;
That's clear enough; although

"He thought he'd 'list, perhaps,
Off-hand like – just as I –
Was out of work – had sold his traps –
No other reason why.

"Yes; quaint and curious war is!
You shoot a fellow down
You'd treat, if met where any bar is,
Or help to half-a-crown."

Thomas Hardy (1840 – 1928)

Notes
nipperkin: a half-pint glass or a smaller one, or small amount of beer, wine, or spirits – *'list:* enlist – *traps:* belongings – *half-a-crown:* British coin worth 12,5 pence, which was a lot of money then.

The speaker here ("I") is of course not identical with the poet; he is an unnamed young British soldier and it is that soldier who is speaking. The circumstances in which he communicates the text to his listener, also unnamed and silent, can only be guessed at, but the speaker's musing and reflective tone in the last three stanzas suggests that we must be in some place where the two people involved are relaxed. They are possibly sharing a drink or two in a tavern where they happen to find themselves standing next to each other at the bar, strike up a conversation, get to talking about the speaker's stint in the military, and then this stretch of reminiscence comes out. The speaker is in fact saying that the person he killed could just as well have been the person he's talking to, sharing a beer with him, a person from pretty much the same social circumstances as his own.

The poem turns on a separation between two situations: the war situation the speaker narrates and the one in which the speaker is doing the narration, and reflecting upon it, in the presence of the silent companion. The paradox of the first situation is conveyed in the first 2 stanzas. Beginning with the third stanza, the urgencies of the present situation come to the fore. The speaker attempts to explain, to his companion, how the event just described in stanza 2 could have happened. But this doesn't come off: the speaker gets stuck explaining, because, he discovers, he doesn't *have* an explanation himself.

> I shot him dead because –
> Because he was my foe,
> Just so: my foe of course he was,
> That's clear enough; although,

The first line ends in a pause, as he gropes for a reason. The second – back-stepping to re-undertake the task (repeating the word *because*) – supplies the reason that comes, eventually, to mind: *he was my foe*. In the third, he repeats this explanation twice, and still a third time in the first part of the fourth line. We see a man trying to convince himself – which is to say, a man who is working to overcome a vague feeling that the explanation he has come up with is somehow insufficient and won't do. The stanza comes to an end that is not an end – the second-thought *although* spills over into the fourth stanza, where he finishes by drawing a generalization – war is strange – and then to illustrate it with a condensed version of the paradox already laid out in the first and second stanzas (though this time with the facts deployed in reverse order).

The generalization coming at the end of a meditation on a narrative constitutes a familiar pattern – the moral of the tale. But as the sum of wisdom afforded by the whole process, as the sense that was sought, the answer doesn't work. If we look carefully at the content of the generalization in the light of the specific circumstances of the problem, and the question that it raised – why did I shoot a person who wasn't any different from me than you are, a person whom, given the circumstances of my own life history, I spontaneously identify with? – we notice that the proposition "war is strange" doesn't qualify as an answer. In effect, rather than laying the question to rest, it provides an excuse to change the subject by pretending that an understanding has been reached. As an answer it begs the question; it rephrases the curiosity we began with and serves it up as if it were the answer. Instead of an insight into the speaker's history, we get a profound-sounding mystification of it – a pseudo-answer. The declaration, then, has the form of an answer, but on inspection, it's a kind of substitution for an answer, a deflection from it. The reader is left to work out his own response to the problem posed in the poem.

Most critics have seen it as an anti-war statement, and the whole poem as a condemnation of the stupidity of war. Hardy uses a fine imaginative device here when he lets the returned soldier say every word and, paradoxically, it is his inarticulate, awkward, stumbling prose which so clearly conveys to the reader the puzzled thoughts going through his mind. Why do men who might easily be good friends kill each other in wartime? The man's hesitation, the repetitions, the awkward, interrupted rhythm of his speech, all tell us that this returned soldier, naïve though he may be, is questioning the usefulness of all this fighting. When will they ever learn, Hardy seems to be implying.

Hardy's poem can demonstrate very clearly how the reader must be alive to what the poet is doing when he presents a dramatic monologue, and how he must work out a number of answers to tacit questions raised by the speaker of the poem and draw inferences from what is said – and left unsaid.

Generally speaking, dramatic monologues differ greatly in subject-matter and in presentation, but they all share a number of characteristic features:

- The reader needs to achieve a measure of imaginative sympathy with the speaker and the situation he or she presents, for instance by taking the part of the listener. Indeed, the listener may by absent, dead, out of earshot, or simply inattentive.

- The speaker uses some kind of case-making, argumentative tone.

- And the form requires the reader to complete the dramatic scene from within, by means of inference and imagination.

Useful language material

▬ **Dramatic poetry**
- This poem is a ballad based on a dramatic dialogue.
- The story is presented in dramatic form / as question and answer dialogue.
- The two characters are having a dramatic exchange.

▬ **The soliloquy**
- This soliloquy informs us about X's state of mind at this point in the play.
- These lines form a soliloquy in which X lets the audience know about his innermost feelings.
- They show us his doubts concerning … / his expectations of what the future holds.
- They let us see into his heart / make clear how he tries to come to terms with his experiences / reveal his immediate plans.

▬ **The dramatic monologue**
- This poem is a dramatic monologue.
- These lines reveal a "soul in action" / reveal X for what he really is, namely …
- The speaker appears to address a silent listener.
- He reveals his views of … / opinion of … / doubts concerning … / hopes of …
- The speaker talks about … and his words make clear that he hates him / despises him.
- His monologue unintentionally reveals certain aspects of his character, namely …
- It shows a man trying to convince himself of …
- The speaker wants to share with his silent companion an experience that has been on his mind.

1.4.3 Lyric poetry

This category is the most common type of poetry and has proved particularly fertile. There are literally thousands, if not tens of thousands of lyric poems for every occasion in life. A lyric is usually a short poem that expresses a speaker's personal feelings or thoughts – not necessarily those of the poet. It may consist of solitary contemplation, or be addressed to someone, ranging from short expressions of a speaker's mind to longer forms.

As we have seen, narrative poetry concentrates on telling a story and dramatic poetry on revealing character in an appropriate dramatic situation. Lyric poetry, by contrast, cannot be narrowed down like that. It is the most inclusive (and elusive) category of poetry and the least easy to pin down, encompassing not only expressions of love, but also statements of personal values, observations and meditations. The lyric mode can accommodate almost any subject or mood, private or public. It includes many specific forms such as sonnet, ode, elegy and dramatic lyric; they can all be considered types of lyric poems. They are particularly well-known possibilities of lyric expression and we are going to look at examples of each of these four types in turn.

The term sonnet derives from the Italian *sonetto* ("little sound" or "song") and as a form developed in Italy probably in the thirteenth century. Petrarch, in the fourteenth century, raised the sonnet to its greatest Italian perfection and so gave it his own name – the *Petrarchan sonnet*, also known as the *Italian sonnet*. The sonnet was introduced into England in the early sixteenth century by Thomas Wyatt, who translated Petrarchan sonnets into English and left over thirty sonnets of his own. Gradually the Italian sonnet pattern was changed and an English form created, the *English sonnet*, also known as the *Shakespearean sonnet* after its greatest practitioner.

The sonnet is a fourteen-line lyric poem in iambic pentameter with a carefully patterned rhyme scheme. The Petrarchan sonnet falls into two main parts: an octave (eight lines) rhyming abbaabba followed by a sestet (six lines) rhyming cdecde or some variant, such as cdccdc. It usually projects and develops its subject – the hopes and pains of a male lover – in the octave, then executes a turn at the beginning of the sestet, which means that the sestet must in some way release the tension built up in the octave. In other words, the first eight lines contain the argument of the poem, while the final six lines suggest how the argument might be solved.

The following text by Thomas Wyatt can demonstrate the Italian form of the sonnet.

Farewell love and all thy laws forever

Farewell love and all thy laws forever;
Thy baited hooks shall tangle me no more.
Senec and Plato call me from thy lore
To perfect wealth, my wit for to endeavour.
In blind error when I did persever,
Thy sharp repulse, that pricketh aye so sore,
Hath taught me to set in trifles no store
And scape forth, since liberty is lever.
Therefore farewell; go trouble younger hearts
And in me claim no more authority.
With idle youth go use thy property
And thereon spend thy many brittle darts,
For hitherto though I have lost all my time,
Me lusteth no lenger rotten boughs to climb.

Sir Thomas Wyatt (1503 – 1542)

Notes

Senec: Lucius Annaeus Seneca: Roman stoic philosopher, rhetorician, and tragedian – *wealth:* well-being in mind (not in money) – *pricketh aye so sore:* Love is traditionally blind and shoots arrows at or "pricketh" its victims (cf. 12) – *lever:* dearer, more loved – *use thy property:* "be yourself"; exhibit your distinguishing quality – *Me lusteth:* I want – *lenger:* Middle English comparative of "long" – *rotten boughs to climb:* follow a worthless pursuit

The first thing to notice about this poem (apart from its old-fashioned language) is that it follows the theory of the Petrarchan sonnet very closely. The rhyme scheme is abbaabba cddcee, which is typical, and the structure of the poem is also as one would expect in an Italian sonnet. The octave states the speaker's decision to turn away from the unprofitable pursuit of love and its *baited hooks*, to turn to philosophy instead and to enjoy a new-found freedom. The *Therefore* at the beginning of the sestet indicates the "turn" in the poem. The speaker has come to the conclusion that love is a futile pursuit that only befits an *idle youth*, but not an older and more experienced person. The concluding couplet clinches the argument – love is an unprofitable use of a wise man's time, like the climbing of *rotten boughs* that break just when a man seems to be making progress.

What makes this poem quite fascinating is that the surface text obviously has a lot of subtext. Recent rejection has made the speaker fearful of returning to love's pursuit and embittered towards its pains.

But his renunciation of love seems to be subtly ironic. Even as he proclaims that *liberty is lever*, one can sense that in reality he is deeply sorry to have lost his love. Although he claims that love's *sharp repulse* has taught him to place no value in *trifles*, it seems that he is merely trying to convince himself that he has chosen the more valuable goal, despite his heart's testimony to the contrary. Just as long goodbyes often indicate a reluctance to leave, the speaker's extended farewell in Wyatt's poem may indicate his reluctance to leave love behind. The repetition of *farewell* at the turn may reflect this, leaving the reader to wonder why one *farewell* to love was not enough. It is most likely that the speaker still desires to return to love's attractions despite his fear of its *hooks*.

The Shakespearean sonnet consists of three quatrains (four lines) and a rhyming couplet – that is, it rhymes abab cdcd efef gg – and has a wider range of possibilities. Generally speaking, it introduces an idea in the first quatrain, complicates it in the second, complicates it even more in the third quatrain, and resolves everything in the final epigrammatic couplet, which either clinches the argument or reverses the whole trend of the previous twelve lines.

Sonnet 138

When my love swears that she is made of truth
I do believe her, though I know she lies,
That she might think me some untutor'd youth,
Unlearned in the world's false subtleties.
Thus vainly thinking that she thinks me young,
Although she knows my days are past the best,
Simply I credit her false speaking tongue:
On both sides thus is simple truth suppress'd.
But wherefore says she not she is unjust?
And wherefore say not I that I am old?
O, love's best habit is in seeming trust,
And age in love loves not to have years told:
Therefore I lie with her and she with me,
And in our faults by lies we flatter'd be.

William Shakespeare (1564 – 1616)

Notes

made of truth: faithful in love, unable to lie (also a pun on "maid of truth") – ***untutor'd:*** inexperienced – ***unlearned:*** with no knowledge of, not having studied (the final -ed syllable is pronounced) – ***the world's false subtleties:*** the ways of the world; the cynical tactics used by older people to advance themselves – *vainly:* ineffectually – *my days are past the best:* the days of my youth are past – *simply:* absolutely, like a simpleton – *credit:* believe – *wherefore:* for what reason, why – *love's best habit:* the best practice for lovers to adopt – *seeming trust:* the appearance of trusting one another – *age in love:* older lovers – *I lie with her and she with me:* I deceive her and she deceives me; we sleep together and make love – *in our faults:* with all our faults – *we flattered be:* we console ourselves (by pretending to be young, truthful and desirable)

The structure of this Shakespearean sonnet follows the established pattern:

First quatrain: The poet pretends to believe his lover's protestations of faithfulness even though he is convinced that she deceives him. He is even willing to be taken for an inexperienced simpleton rather than acknowledge the situation as it really is.

Second quatrain: She on the other hand pretends to think that he is younger that he actually is, even though she must know that his best years are behind him. So neither of them wants to face up to the truth.

Third quatrain: So why don't they simply admit that there is pretence on both sides? Well, they feel more comfortable when they don't look truth in the eye.

Concluding couplet: That is why they lie to each other – their respective lies make the situation easier to bear.

In this sonnet the poet candidly reveals both the nature of his relationship with his lover (the "dark lady", who is in the centre of many of his sonnets) and the insecurities he feels about growing older. The whole text hinges on the contradiction of what his heart tells him to believe (that she is his alone) and of what his critical faculties tell him (she is unfaithful to him). He thus insists on believing something he knows to be untrue.

The opening line sets the scene by suggesting that there is a need to patch up the love relationship between the speaker and his lover; the woman swears that she is true, which implies that doubt has arisen, and the poet has to pretend that he is younger than he is for fear of losing her. The basis for love is therefore flawed, but they seem to have achieved a level of relative contentment with their situation.

Although the two types of sonnet, the Italian and the English types, may seem quite different, in actual practice they are not always easy to tell apart because the rhyme schemes do not always strictly follow either the one or the other form. And the presentation of the argument is not always confined to the octet, etc.

The sonnet is in many respects the most challenging of literary forms. Its fourteen lines are just long enough to make possible the fairly complex development of a single theme, and short enough to provide a challenge to the poet's talent for concentrated expression. Further restrictions are placed upon him by a demanding rhyme scheme and a conventional metrical form (iambic pentameter).

The uncompromising technical discipline of the sonnet ensures that only the greatest poets have excelled at it, but the logical and emotional intensity available in this form has preserved its fascination for many poets right down to the present day. It is significant that the sonnet has not remained confined to its traditional subjects, the joys and pains of love, but has been used for a wide range of other topics. John Donne (1590 – 1640), for instance, made the sonnet a vehicle for passionate and paradoxical argument, whereas others expressed in their sonnets sentimental and even trivial ideas or presented reflections on topical events. Contemporary poets have experimented with unrhymed sonnets on a variety of subjects.

Unlike the sonnet, which tends to focus on personal matters (such as being in love), the ode is usually concerned with celebrating notable public occasions or presenting lofty universal themes such as liberty, justice, the nature of art and truth, and the question of immortality. It generally deals with one main idea and can be written as a song of praise or to celebrate an experience or a person.

The ode originated in ancient Greece and the first odes seem to have been composed to be chanted to music by a dancing chorus. The demands of music and dance resulted in highly elaborate metrical structures patterned on sets of three movements – moving in a dance rhythm to one side *(strophe)*, then to the other *(antistrophe)*, then, standing still *(epode)*.

The odes created in imitation of the classical models by English poets are therefore lyric poems that are serious in subject and treatment and are written in an elevated style. They also often have elaborate stanza forms.

The best odes in English date from the eighteenth and nineteenth centuries, culminating in some of the exalted poems of the great Romantic poets. Since the Romantic era the ode has gone into a decline however – it appears that as a vehicle of high seriousness the ode could not prosper in the cynical climate of the modern age.

Our next category of lyric poetry is the elegy. In classical literature an elegy was a poem composed of elegiac distichs, i.e. alternating hexameter and pentameter lines. There was usually a mourning strain in elegies, especially in epitaphs and commemorative verses. The term "elegy" has now come to mean a poem of mourning for an individual or a lament for some tragic event, usually ending in consolation. It has also acquired the meaning of "poetry natural to a reflective mind" (Coleridge), or, in more general terms, a serious meditative poem.

The language of funeral elegies gave poets an opportunity for plaintive, melancholy generalisations on death or on the state of the world. Thomas Gray's *Elegy Written in a Country Churchyard* (1750) is usually regarded as the archetypal general meditation on the passing of life, unconnected with any specific death.

The following sample poem is in fact connected with a particular death – that of President Abraham Lincoln, who was assassinated on 14 April, 1865.

O Captain! My Captain!

O Captain! my Captain! our fearful trip is done;
The ship has weather'd every rack, the prize we sought is won;
The port is near, the bells I hear, the people all exulting,
While follow eyes the steady keel, the vessel grim and daring:
But O heart! heart! heart!
O the bleeding drops of red,
Where on the deck my Captain lies,
Fallen cold and dead.

O Captain! my Captain! rise up and hear the bells;
Rise up – for you the flag is flung – for you the bugle trills;
For you bouquets and ribbon'd wreaths – for you the shores
    a-crowding;
For you they call, the swaying mass, their eager faces turning;
Here Captain! dear father!
This arm beneath your head;
It is some dream that on the deck,
You've fallen cold and dead.

My Captain does not answer, his lips are pale and still;
My father does not feel my arm, he has no pulse nor will;
The ship is anchor'd safe and sound, its voyage closed and
    done;

From fearful trip, the victor ship, comes in with object won;
Exult, O shores, and ring, O bells!
But I, with mournful tread,
Walk the deck my Captain lies,
Fallen cold and dead.

Walt Whitman (1819 – 1892)

O Captain! My Captain! is probably Walt Whitman's most popular poem. He wrote it as an elegy to Abraham Lincoln, the immensely popular American president who was assassinated by a Southern fanatic at the end of the Civil War, in which the North triumphed. The poem depicts Lincoln as the captain of a ship that has suffered the wild storms of the sea – a metaphor appropriate to the leader of the union following the ravages of the Civil War. Although the ship has weathered the storms and has entered the harbour safe and victorious, the captain – like the recently assassinated Lincoln – is dead.

The ship imagery makes clear that the speaker is a sailor who is mourning his fallen Captain. Every stanza opens with an appeal to the Captain, and every stanza also ends with a reference to the fact of his death *(Fallen cold and dead)*. The speaker seems to feel very acutely dismay and horror at realizing that his Captain has died, he mentions the *bleeding drops of red*, which may as much refer to the Captain's wounds as to his own wounded heart *(O heart! heart! heart!)*. It seems that at first he is having trouble admitting to himself that his Captain is indeed dead and asks him to *rise up and hear the bells*, or he tries to find consolation in the hope that it may all be only a bad dream *(It is some dream that on the deck …)*. It takes him until the third stanza to understand that his Captain is indeed irrevocably dead and *has no pulse nor will* any more. This realisation causes him to walk *with a mournful tread* to where his *Captain lies, / Fallen cold and dead.*

In this last stanza the speaker expands the Captain metaphor beyond the more limited range of a military leader into that of a father figure *(My father)*, one whose wisdom and skill has guided his children on their way through life and who has become like a father to an entire nation. The speaker's grief, which is central to the poem, is therefore shared by the rest of the country, who are also at one with him in feeling both joy at the victory and dismay and grief at the loss of their leader.

The speaker's state of mind is only one aspect of the poem. It also owes much of its impact to the ambiguous character of a number of elements, which all contribute to bringing out the strange feeling of simultaneous joy and grief-stricken horror. There are first of all the *bells*; they can be rung in celebration of military victory, or they might symbolise funeral bells. Similarly, the flying of the *flag* can be seen either as a symbol of victory and rejoicing, or it can refer to a flag flown at half-mast in mourning. Again, *bouquets and wreaths* can stand for both celebratory receptions and funerals. It is precisely this tension between joy and grief that gives this poem its poignancy and appeal.

The poem thus captures the emotional upheaval felt in America at the time by both the triumph and the grief of the end of the war and is an elegy remembering a beloved president.

There is one more type of poem that can be found among the possibilities of "lyric poetry" – the dramatic lyric. In a poem of this type, the speaker addresses one or more silent auditors (recognized only indirectly by the reader) within the context of a particular dramatic situation. Emphasis is placed not so much on the speaker's character, as is the case in a dramatic monologue, but rather upon the poem's subject. John Donne's *The Flea* (1633) is an example of the type. In this poem the speaker addresses a lady in the dramatic moment of trying to seduce her; the main interest of the poem is his ingenious (perhaps over-ingenious) argument of comparing a fleabite with the act of love:

The Flea

Mark but this flea, and mark in this,
How little that which thou deniest me is;
Me it sucked first, and now sucks thee,
And in this flea our two bloods mingled be.
Thou know'st that this cannot be said
A sin, or shame, or loss of maidenhead;
Yet this enjoys before it woo,
And pamper'd swells with one blood made of two;
And this, alas, is more than we would do.

O stay, three lives in one flea spare,
Where we almost, yea, more than married are.
This flea is you and I, and this
Our marriage bed, and marriage temple is.
Though parents grudge, and you, we're met,
And cloister'd in these living walls of jet.
Though use make you apt to kill me,
Let not to that self-murder added be,
And sacrilege, three sins in killing three.

Cruel and sudden, hast thou since
Purpled thy nail in blood of innocence?
Wherein could this flea guilty be,
Except in that drop which it suck'd from thee?
Yet thou triumph'st, and say'st that thou
Find'st not thyself nor me the weaker now.
'Tis true; then learn how false fears be;
Just so much honour, when thou yield'st to me,
Will waste, as this flea's death took life from thee.

John Donne (1590 – 1640)

Notes
mark (here): regard – *this:* i.e. this flea – *maidenhead:* virginity – *pamper'd:*
looked after too kindly – *stay* (here): don't kill the flea – *jet:* black

The "I" of the poem is lying in bed with a lady and is trying to make
her give up her virginity to him. While lying there, he notices a flea,
which has evidently bitten them both. Since the idea at the time
(seventeenth century) was of sex as a "mingling of the blood", he
argues that by mixing their bloods together in its body, the flea has
done what she hasn't dared to do. So, he goes on to argue, since the flea
has done it, why shouldn't they? To reinforce his argument, he refers to
the marriage ceremony, in which it is stated that the man and the
woman "shall be one flesh". Since they have mingled their bloods, he
argues, they are therefore "one blood" – virtually "one flesh" – and
therefore as good as married.

When the woman prepares to kill the flea, the speaker is moved to
argue that by spilling his blood and hers by crushing the flea on her
finger nail, she is practically committing a double murder, and not only
that – by breaking the holy bond of marriage in this way, she is
committing a sacrilege – in fact, three sins in a single action.

However, the flea is killed, and the speaker is obliged to change tactics.
Killing the innocent flea, he says, has left them none the weaker; so
giving up her resistance and yielding to him will be just as easy and
painless.

The poem breaks off at this point, leaving the reader to wonder if the
speaker's line of argument will finally achieve its purpose. The speaker's
character is not in question here – he is a man bent on seducing a lady.
It is the quality and indeed the ingeniousness of his argumentation that
the poet appears to be interested in – the "conceit" he is making use of,
i.e. the comparisons and the religious imagery, from *Confess it* to
sacrilege and *blood of innocence*, etc. The lady's objections are never

noted, by the way, just reacted to, but she makes the most powerful statement in the poem, a non-verbal one, by crushing the flea.

Useful language material

■ **The sonnet**
- This poem is a sonnet / a Petrarchan / Italian / a Shakespearean / English sonnet.
- This sonnet follows the Petrarchan / Shakespearean model very closely.
- The poet has developed his argument in the first eight lines / in the octave / in the three quatrains.
- He executes a turn at the beginning of the sestet / releases the tension in the sestet / resolves the situation in the sestet.
- The concluding couplet resolves the situation / clinches the argument / introduces a surprising turn / reverses the trend of the preceding lines.

■ **The ode**
- This poem is an ode / can be classified as an ode.
- The poet uses elevated diction and establishes a sense of stately argument.
- He employs a steady rhythm and a regular rhyme scheme.
- The writer presents well-balanced sentences and an orderly progression of ideas.

■ **The elegy**
- This poem is an elegy / is an elegy to …
- The speaker mourns the death of … / laments a tragic event, namely …
- The poem shows the speaker's grief and dismay / reveals his grief-stricken horror at what has happened.
- The stanzas capture the emotional upheaval felt when …
- The poet has included general meditations on the passing of life.

■ **The dramatic lyric**
- This poem can be described as a dramatic lyric.
- It presents an argument in dramatic form / lets the speaker present an ingenious argument.
- The lines focus on the speaker's line of argumentation / on his rhetorical skills.

1.4.4 Light verse

"Light verse" is poetry that is playful and humorous. Often serious at bottom, light verse aims to amuse the reader, to make him smile and even laugh. In short, it takes the comic view of life as opposed to the tragic, as in the following few lines:

Résumé

Razors pain you;
Rivers are damp;
Acids stain you;
And drugs cause cramp.
Guns aren't lawful;
Nooses give;
Gas smells awful;
You might as well live.

Dorothy Parker (1893 – 1967)

From the Portable Dorothy Parker (© 1956, Viking Penguin, a division of Penguin Putnam Inc., and Gerald Duckworth & Co. Ltd.)

The reader notices very quickly what this is a "résumé" of. The poem does not mention it directly, but it is not hard to see that the poet is talking about the various methods of committing suicide. The whole tone of the lines is however not tortured or full of fear, as one might expect for such a topic. Instead, the speaker rejects each option for trivial reasons, the implication being that suicide isn't worth it unless it can be achieved easily, painlessly and neatly. The attitude that comes across suggests that both living and suicide are trivial pursuits, which is highly ironic.

There is a great variety of poems that treat their subjects playfully or wittily, or with good-natured satire. The subjects of light verse need not in themselves be trivial or inconsequential, as we have seen above with Dorothy Parker's *Résumé*. It is the tone of voice used and the speaker's attitude towards the subject that make all the difference. *The War Song of Dinas Vawr* begins thus:

The mountain sheep are sweeter,
But the valley sheep are fatter;
We therefore deemed it meeter
To carry off the latter.

And this is how the poem ends:

> We brought away from battle,
> And much their land bemoaned them,
> Two thousand head of cattle,
> And the head of him who owned them:
> Ednyfed, king of Dyfed,
> His head was borne before us;
> His wine and beasts supplied our feasts,
> And his overthrow, our chorus.

Thomas Love Peacock (1785 – 1866)

Notes
meeter (unusual comparative): more befitting, more appropriate – *Ednyfed,*
Dyfed: Welsh names

The speaker's dispassionate attitude towards what he narrates and the pat rhymes all contribute to the creation of wonderfully light verse in a situation which could be seen as serious, if not tragic, namely the killing of beasts and people.

A number of categories of light verse can be distinguished. The most popular are:

- verse satire (vers de société),
- clerihew.
- limerick,
- and nonsense verse.

Verse satire (also known as vers de société, literally "society verse") is verse dealing with the superficial problems and events of a shallow and effete society, as in the following extract (the first three stanzas) from a representative modern example:

In Westminster Abbey

> Let me take this other glove off
> As the *vox humana* swells,
> And the beauteous fields of Eden
> Bask beneath the Abbey bells.
> Here, where England's statesmen lie,
> Listen to a lady's cry.

Gracious Lord, oh bomb the Germans.
Spare their women for Thy Sake,
And if that is not too easy
We will pardon Thy Mistake.
But gracious Lord, whate'er shall be,
Don't let anyone bomb me.

Keep our Empire undismembered,
Guide our Forces by Thy Hand,
Gallant blacks from far Jamaica,
Honduras and Togoland;
Protect them Lord in all their fights,
And, even more, protect the whites.

Think of what our Nation stands for,
Books from Boots' and country lanes,
Free speech, free passes, class distinction,
Democracy and proper drains.
Lord, put beneath Thy special care
One-eighty-nine Cadogan Square.

John Betjeman (1906 – 1984;
written in 1940, shortly after the outbreak of the Second World War)

Notes

vox humana: an organ register – ***the beauteous fields of Eden:*** words from a hymn *(Daily, daily sing the praises / Of the city God hath made. / In he beauteous fields of Eden / Its foundation stones are laid.)* – ***bask*** (here): lie happily – ***where England's statesmen lie:*** they are traditionally laid to rest in the Abbey – ***drains:*** the system of pipes used to carry away waste matter and water – ***Boots':*** a chain store

The speaker is a British lady *(Listen to a lady's cry)* who appears to be attending a service in Westminster Abbey during the Second World War *(oh bomb the Germans)*, but she doesn't follow the liturgy and lets her mind wander to a number of things that worry her. As she does so, her thoughts turn into the parody of a prayer, in which she shows herself to be full of prejudice and to be principally concerned for her own welfare: *Don't let anyone bomb me* and *Lord, put beneath Thy special care / One-eighty-nine Cadogan Square.* This is clearly her own address.

The humorous effect of these lines is heightened by the use of a word like *undismembered* (with reference to the Empire, which was beginning to be dismembered in the forties) and the grouping together of completely incongruous elements like *Democracy and proper drains*. The effect is humorous and satirical because it shows up people's self-centredness in a funny way. The humour has survived the years, perhaps because readers may recognise just a little of themselves in this lady's approach to God – "looking out for number one" (i.e. thinking only of oneself) is still a very widespread attitude.

Generally speaking, we can say that verse satire *(vers de société)* deals with the relationships, concerns and doings of polite society. It almost goes without saying that it is often satirical, with the stress on humour rather than sarcasm, and the tone it employs is usually urbane, the style polished and elegant, and the sentiments expressed are witty and often presented with a touch of irony.

The clerihew is a form of comic verse invented by Edmund C. (for Clerihew) Bentley (1875 – 1956). It consists of two couplets of unequal length often with complex or somewhat ridiculous rhymes and usually concentrates on presenting a famous person or historical character in a witty, deft and epigrammatic way:

> George the Third
> Ought never to have occurred,
> One can only wonder
> At so grotesque a blunder.

Note
George III was King of England from 1760 to 1820. His bouts of madness together with the stubborn way he handled the American Revolution eroded his support and the power of the Crown. His reign is thus generally seen as disastrous.

The humour of the clerihew relies on the presentation of the trivial, the fantastic or the ridiculous and presenting it with deadpan seriousness as the characteristic, the significant, or the essential. This is what Bentley has to say about a famous scientist, Sir Humphrey Davy (1778 – 1829), who during his prestigious career discovered a number of chemical elements, including sodium and potassium, investigated chlorine and its oxides and invented the Davy Lamp for use in the coal mines.

> Sir Humphrey Davy
> Abominated gravy.
> He lived in the odium
> Of having discovered sodium.

Many people have composed good clerihews and making them up has become a parlour game. Bentley himself stated and illustrated the nature of his work thus:

The Art of Biography
Is different from Geography.
Geography is about Maps,
But Biography is about Chaps.

It is clear that this art from, which bears a certain resemblance to the Limerick (see below), relies for effect on a very British sense of humour, but it has nevertheless attracted many practitioners in other English-speaking countries, notably in America.

The limerick has become one of the most beloved of all forms of light verse. Its origins are obscure and possibly go back to a parlour game popular at the beginning of the nineteenth century. Edward Lear (1812 – 1888) did much to popularise the form. Here is one of his limericks, still much liked by children:

There was an old man with a beard
Who said, "It is just as I feared –
Two owls and a hen,
Four larks and a wren
Have all built their nests in my beard!"

Lear always ended his limericks by repeating the rhyme word of the first line in the last. This is hardly ever done in modern limericks, e.g.

There was a young man from Bengal
Who went to a fancy dress ball.
He went, just for fun,
Dressed up as a bun,
And a dog ate him up in the hall.

The limerick is unique in that it is the only stanza form used exclusively for light verse. It is a single unit with a fixed rhyme scheme (aabba) and metrical pattern (predominantly anapaestic, with three stresses in lines 1, 2 and 5, and two in lines 3 and 4). The final line, at least in modern limericks, usually provides a surprise or witty reversal. Limericks have been composed on a great variety of subjects from philosophic doctrines to jokes of extreme obscenity. Most of them are anonymous.

Nonsense verse is a form of light verse, normally composed for humorous effect, which is paradoxical, silly, witty, whimsical or just plain strange. In a world that makes no sense to many people it may well be that nonsense verse can function as a form of escape. Nonsensical verse has certainly always been popular, in nursery rhymes such as the following sample and in other verse (see the examples quoted above in 1.1.2):

Hey diddle diddle,
The cat and the fiddle,
The cow jumped over the moon;
The little dog laughed
To see such sport,
And the dish ran away with the spoon.

The nonsense poem that has fascinated readers more than any other since it first appeared in *Through the Looking-Glass* (1871) by Lewis Carroll is *Jabberwocky*.

Twas brillig, and the slithy toves
Did gyre and gimble in the wabe;
All mimsy were the borogoves,
And the mome raths outgrabe.

Beware the Jabberwock, my son!
The jaws that bite, the claws that catch!
Beware the Jubjub bird, and shun
The frumious Bandersnatch!

He took his vorpal sword in hand:
Long time the manxome foe he sought
So rested he by the Tumtum tree,
And stood awhile in thought.

And as in uffish thought he stood,
The Jabberwock, with eyes of flame,
Came whiffling through the tulgey wood,
And burbled as it came!

One, two! One, two! And through and through
The vorpal blade went snicker-snack!
He left it dead, and with its head
He went galumphing back.

And hast thou slain the Jabberwock?
Come to my arms, my beamish boy!
O frabjous day! Callooh! Callay!
He chortled in his joy.

Twas brillig, and the slithy toves
Did gyre and gimble in the wabe;
All mimsy were the borogoves,
And the mome raths outgrabe.

Notes (on pronunciation)
slithy toves ['slaɪðɪ 'təʊvz] – *gyre* [gaɪə] – *gimble* [gɪmbl] – *borogoves* ['bɒrəgəʊvz]
– *raths* [rɑːθs]

Since its first publication, this text has become famous around the world, with translations into many languages, including German, French, Latin, Italian, and Esperanto. The translators' achievement is all the more remarkable because many of the principal words of the poem were simply made up by Carroll; they did not exist before and there was no semantic content attached to them. A few of these words, namely *chortle* (a portmanteau word derived from "chuckle" and "snort"), *burble* (a combination of "bubble", "murmur" and "warble"?) and *galumph* have entered the language as generally accepted items. The title word itself, *jabberwocky*, is also sometimes used in a general sense, referring to nonsense language. The meaning of many of the new words can only be guessed at, but the general drift of the poem seems reasonably clear.

Jabberwocky continues to fascinate people because, although it contains many nonsense words, its structure is perfectly consistent with classic English poetry:

- There are seven regularly built stanzas of four lines each (the first quatrain is mirrored in the seventh, providing a frame for the poem).

- The sentence structure is accurate.

- End rhyme (cross rhyme) is used throughout, and only a few lines have no corresponding rhyme.

- The rhythm is a fairly regular iambic tetrameter (four stresses to each line).

- Something like a story line can be discerned in the flow of events;

- and even the general tone of the poem appears to be in keeping with the subject-matter and to be perfectly appropriate for it.

Little wonder then that the result of mixing all this with the many nonsense words should have led some critics to speculate as to whether Carroll's poem is not really intended as a satire on poetry that is impeccable in a formal sense, but inferior in content. Whether or not the text was ever meant as a satire on mediocre and indifferent verse will never be known, but few would dispute that *Jabberwocky* is the greatest of all nonsense poems in English. There is little doubt that it is one of literature's most fanciful texts, yet the made-up words still sound purposeful somehow. The text manages to fascinate the reader no mean achievement in a poem of any sort. *Jabberwocky* beautifully skates the thin edge of being understood and being nonsense. But such glorious nonsense! As Alice put it in *Through the Looking-Glass*, "It seems very pretty, but it's rather hard to understand!"

Useful language material

Light verse
- These lines are playful and humorous / highly ironic.
- They try to amuse the reader / attempt to make him smile.
- The poem shows the comic side of … / treats the subject playfully and wittily.
- The poet has contrived to create a wonderfully light-hearted poem / managed to achieve a playful approach to his subject.

Verse satire
- This poem is a verse satire / can be regarded as an instance of *vers de société*.
- The poet satirises certain assumptions of members of polite society, namely …
- He highlights some common prejudices in an ironical manner.
- He makes fun of some of the attitudes and foibles of mankind.
- The elegant language used by the poet stands in sharp contrast to people's inelegant behaviour as described in the poem.

The clerihew
- These four lines constitute a clerihew.
- This clerihew draws its humour from the juxtapositioning of … and …
- It relies for comic effect on the contrast between the elegant and the banal.
- It exploits to good effect the contrast between … and …

■ **The limerick**
- These five lines are clearly a limerick.
- The rhyme scheme and metrical pattern of these five lines show that the poem is a limerick.
- This limerick focuses on the discrepancy between … and …
- The train of thought presented in the first four lines finds a sharp / witty reversal in the final line, when …
- The final line comes as a surprise / provides an unexpected twist / turn.

■ **Nonsense verse**
- These lines constitute nonsense verse / are an instance of nonsense verse.
- They rely for effect on many neologisms / words invented for the occasion / made-up words.
- The writer has managed to combine the most disparate objects to produce a comic effect.
- These lines show the poet's brilliant flight of fancy.

Synopsis

Ritual poetry
- consists mainly of incantations or charms and ritual songs.
- relies on verse rather than poetry.

Narrative poetry
- basically tells a story.
- focuses on a series of events.

The epic
- is a dignified and elaborate form of narrative poetry.
- relies on heroic themes.
- is a composition on a grand scale presented in a dignified style.

The verse romance
- often has a melodramatic story to tell.
- relies principally on native traditions.
- is not on quite such a grand scale as the epic.

The literary ballad
- is not anonymous, but the work of a single known poet.
- is a sophisticated rather than a popular form.
- deals with complex ideas.
- sometimes imitates the conventions of the folk ballad.

Dramatic poetry
- may take the form of a soliloquy.
- is not only found in the drama.
- is often based on question and answer dialogue in ballads.
- may occur as dramatic monologue.

The soliloquy
- shows a dramatic character uttering his thoughts aloud.
- focuses on the revelation of character.
- lets the audience know more about a character's motives.

Dramatic monologue
- is a type of lyric poem.
- is a dramatic poem in which a speaker addresses a silent listener.
- makes great demands on the reader, who has to work what is going on.

Lyric poetry
- expresses a speaker's personal feelings or thoughts.
- can accommodate almost any subject or mood.
- includes many specific forms.

The sonnet
- is a fourteen-line lyric poem in iambic pentameter with a carefully patterned rhyme scheme.
- divides into an octave and a sestet, or into three quatrains and a concluding couplet.
- exists in an Italian and an English form.

The ode
- celebrates notable public occasions.
- presents lofty universal themes.
- is serious in subject and treatment.
- is written in an elevated style.

The elegy
- can be a poem of mourning for an individual.
- may be a lament for some tragic event.
- is a serious meditative poem.

The dramatic lyric
- is a variation of the dramatic monologue.
- is not so much concerned with the revelation of character as with the presentation of an argument.

Light verse
- is poetry that is playful and humorous.
- aims to amuse the reader.
- takes the comic view of life.
- treats its subjects playfully, wittily, or with good-natured satire.

Vers de société
- deals with the relationships, concerns and affairs of polite society.
- is characterised by wit, elegance and a conversational tone.
- is often satirical.

The clerihew
- consists of two couplets of unequal length.
- concentrates on presenting a famous person in a witty, deft and epigrammatic way.

The limerick
- is a single unit of five lines with a fixed rhyme scheme and metrical pattern.
- often provides a surprise or witty reversal in the final line.

Nonsense verse
- is composed for humorous effect.
- can function as a form of escape from the pressures of life.

1.5 The interpretation of poetry

When you have to give an interpretation of a poem, what you are being asked to do is this:

- You must elucidate the meaning of the poem,

- and you are expected to do it by showing how the form of the poem enacts its meaning. In a good poem the form the poet has given it and the ideas he or she wants to express through it, its content, are interdependent.

The following procedure can lead you to good results:

- Read the poem through several times, trying first of all to get a good general idea of the poem, but then concentrating on the details of what the poem has to say.

- Mark the poem as shown on the next page. This will help you take note of significant elements of the poem.

- Ask a number of questions of the poem; the answers to these questions can guide you in your interpretation.

Composed Upon Westminster Bridge

September 3, 1802

Earth has not anything to show more fair:
Dull would he be of soul who could pass by
A sight so touching in its majesty:
This City now, doth, like a garment, wear
The beauty of the morning: silent, bare,
Ships, towers, domes, theatres, and temples lie
Open unto the fields, and to the sky;
All bright and glittering in the smokeless air.
Never did sun more beautifully steep
In his first splendour valley, rock, or hill;
Ne'er saw I, never felt, a calm so deep!
The river glideth at his own sweet will:
Dear God! The very houses seem asleep;
And all that mighty heart is lying still.

William Wordsworth (1770 – 1850)

The first thing to do, obviously, is to look up in your dictionary any unknown words and phrases you are not quite sure of. This will hardly be necessary here, but perhaps these notes are still useful:

Notes
garment: dress – *steep something in splendour:* make it bright and glittering

Not all poems come with line numbers already provided. So it will be useful to write the line numbers down on the left as you mark the text of the poem, possibly like this:

Composed Upon Westminster Bridge

trochaic opening	1	Earth has not anything to show more fair:	a	*wonder and admiration*
	2	Dull would he be of soul who could pass by	b	
	3	A sight so touching in its majesty:	b	
octave	4	This City now, doth, like a garment, wear	a	*simile*
	5	The beauty of the morning: silent, bare,	a	
	6	Ships, towers, domes, theatres, and temples lie	b	*enumeration*
	7	Open unto the fields, and to the sky;	b	
	8	All bright and glittering in the smokeless air.	a	
	9	Never did sun more beautifully steep	c	*repetition*
sestet	10	In his first splendour valley, rock, or hill;	d	
	11	Ne'er saw I, never felt, a calm so deep!	c	
	12	The river glideth at his own sweet will:	d	*personification*
	13	Dear God! The very houses seem asleep;	c	
	14	And all that mighty heart is lying still.	d	*metaphor*

description of the city

poet's reflections

After going through the text several times and marking it, a first impression can be jotted down. With reference to our poem this could be:

William Wordsworth's "Composed Upon Westminster Bridge" is a poem that describes the magnificence and the tranquillity of the City of London at daybreak.

Such a preliminary statement can have a positive influence on the rest of your analysis of the poem because it can serve as a point of reference and as a guideline.

Every poem is of course unique and the observations made about one particular poem can hardly ever be transferred to another poem. What can and should be done however is to ask a number of standard questions of the poem under discussion.

1. **Questions concerned with a general understanding of the poem**

- What sort of poem / what **genre** of poetry is it?
  - narrative? dramatic? lyric?
  - light verse?

  ➜ a lyric poem (largely descriptive), a sonnet (Italian type)

- Who is the **speaker** of the poem?
  - the poet in his own voice?
  - a persona specially created for the artistic purposes of the poem / adapted to its requirements?
  - what sort of listener or reader is being addressed?

  ➜ the speaker seems to be the poet himself as the poem is obviously autobiographical; no particular audience – the poet could be speaking to himself.

- What is the **central idea** of the poem? What is its **theme**? What is it concerned with?
  - love? beauty? a description? a declaration of love?
  - the presentation of a narrative or dramatic scene?
  - the poet's reflections?

  ➜ the beauty of London shortly after sunrise

- What seems to be the **poet's intention**?
  - to speak of his love?
  - to appeal to the reader's / listener's emotions?
  - to present an argument?
  - to describe an object / scene (of great beauty)?
  - to tell a fascinating / melodramatic / mystical story?
  - to reveal his thoughts / reflections of … / on …?

  ➜ he wants to bring to mind again a wonderful moment when he was struck by the beauty and tranquillity of the City of London one early morning

- What is the prevailing **tone** of the poem?
  - solemn and grave?
  - light-hearted and humorous?
  - enthusiastic and full of praise?
  - tranquil and peaceful?
  - critical, even sarcastic?
  - sad and melancholic?

  ➜ enthusiastic and full of praise for the beauty of the city

Useful language material

▰▰ General understanding of the poem
– The poem is an instance of narrative / dramatic / lyric poetry / of light verse.
– It is largely descriptive / it describes a scene of great beauty / …
– It narrates a complex story about … / an important event in the life of … / an unusual occurrence / a significant moment …
– It presents a dramatic scene / moment.
– It offers the poet's reflections on … / is concerned with the presentation of …
– It describes / deals with / treats of / is concerned with …

▰▰ The speaker of the poem
– is / seems to be the poet himself / a persona invented / specially created by the poet.
– seems to be addressing a friend / his beloved / the general reader / nobody in particular.

▰▰ The central idea / the theme / what the poem is concerned with
– is the conflict of human and material values.
– is death and immortality.
– is the nature of truth.

▰▰ The poet's intention seems to be
– to speak of his love.
– to describe an object / scene of great beauty.
– to present an argument / to argue for / against …
– to tell a fascinating / melodramatic / mystical story.
– to reveal his thoughts about … / his reflections on …
– to appeal to reader's emotions / sense of beauty / …
– to stir / arouse the reader's feelings / sympathy for / disgust / …

▰▰ The prevailing tone of the poem is
– solemn and grave.
– tranquil and peaceful.
– sad and melancholic.
– enthusiastic and full of praise.
– critical, even sarcastic.
– light-hearted and humorous.
– ironical / satirical.
– detached / matter-of-fact.

2. Questions for a detailed analysis

What is important here is that you must not only name the elements you have found, but you must also say what their function is in the particular instance and what effect is intended.

- What **sounds** and what **sound effects** has the poet used?
  - Are there more light or more dark vowels?

  → there are generally more light vowels *(fair – City – wear ...)* – to indicate the bright light of the early morning

  - Are sounds repeated anywhere (alliteration)?

  → an instance of alliteration occurs in line 6 *(towers – temples)* – of no particular significance here

  - Can onomatopoeic elements be found?

  → no onomatopoeic elements in this poem

- What sort of **vocabulary** does the poem contain?
  - Which speech level is predominant (colloquial, neutral, formal, poetic)?

  → mainly neutral style, a few formal elements *(garment, steep in splendour)* – to underline both the general significance of the experience and its extraordinary nature

  - What word classes do the words mainly come from (nouns, verbs, adjectives)?

  → many descriptive adjectives *(fair – dull – touching – silent ...)*, also many nouns *(City – ships – towers – domes – theatres ...)*, but a conspicuous scarcity of verbs *(show – pass by – wear ...)* – to emphasise the static nature of the poet's impression; the scene he is viewing is not of moving objects; everything, *even the very houses seem asleep.*

  - Are the words taken from a particular area or field (nature and countryside, city life, warfare, religion, etc.)?

  → vocabulary taken from the field of city architecture (esp. line 6), but also from the field of nature and countryside (esp. line 10) – underlines the fact that the poet sees the City virtually as part of the landscape; also a few items from the field of religion *(soul, temples, God)* – appears significant in view of the fact that the poet is so enthusiastic about his experience that what he describes appears to strike him almost with the force of a religious revelation and the London he describes thus takes on features of the Heavenly Jerusalem

– Which words stand out / are particularly striking and rich in connotations? Has the poet used allusions?

➜ a number of words and phrases are striking, esp. *a sight so touching in its majesty, garment, splendour, at his own sweet will, that mighty heart* – all of them can contribute to conjure up the scene for the reader and set up associations in that reader's mind, helping to deepen that sense of wonder that pervades the whole poem.

There are only some indirect allusions to elements of the Heavenly Jerusalem and these allusions are relatively obscure. For those who recognise the allusion the scene described can take on an additional significance.

– Can we find repetitions and which words are repeated?

➜ We can find two repetitions of *never* (the word occurs for the first time in line 9 and is twice repeated in line 11) – the triple negation emphasises the uniqueness of the experience.

– Do certain words form a contrast to each other?

➜ There is contrast in the poem, but it is only implied:

– *heart* will be pulsating with life again;

– there is the contrast between city and countryside;

– finally there is the contrast between *fair* and *dull* in lines 1 and 2 – the speaker appears to be convinced that hardly anybody would be left untouched by *A sight so touching in its majesty*.

– Is there a discrepancy between content and vocabulary (e.g. to create ironic distance)?

➜ There is no discrepancy between content and vocabulary unless we see a discrepancy in the combination of *touching* and *majesty,* which is certainly unusual. The imagery of the city wearing *The beauty of the morning "like a garment"* can perhaps also be seen as somewhat unusual – it is certainly not an idea that would spring readily to mind, but this is what makes it so effective, of course.

Useful language material

▬▬ Sound and sound effects
- The poem contains many light / dark vowels.
- There are some instances of alliteration / a number of onomatopoeic elements.
- A special sound effect is achieved through the use of alliteration / assonance / consonance / internal rhyme.
- The repetition of the sound xxx helps to suggest / evoke the din of a workshop / the swish of wings / the gallop of horses …
- The repetition of the word … emphasises / stresses the poet's deep concern with … / his preoccupation with … / the significance of that particular word.
- The repetitions of … give this word extra significance / reveal something particularly important for building up the poem's meaning / help to give unity to the poem.

▬▬ Vocabulary
- The vocabulary of the poem is mainly / predominantly neutral / formal / poetic in style.
- The words are simple / are difficult / are learned and elevated.
- They refer to concrete objects / to abstract things.
- Many words have been taken from / belong to the field of religion / the world of law / refer to nature / …
- The poet has used / employed many descriptive adjectives.
- He favours a style based on a preponderance of nouns / verbs.
- The poet contrasts *fair* and *dull*.
- The words *fair* and *dull* form a contrast / are contrasted.
- The word *fair* is contrasted with *dull*.
- There is a marked contrast between X and Y.
- There is an ironic contrast between the formal vocabulary and the ridiculous content.
- The ironic contrast between X and Y provides humour.
- The poet has used a number of words that are particularly striking / rich in connotations, namely …
- Some of his words are full of implied meaning / are highly suggestive.
- The connotations of … contribute to the rich sensuous effect of the lines.
- The word … catches the reader's interest / is used in an intriguing way / arouses the reader's curiosity / enriches and deepens the meaning of the line / stanza / poem.

- How do syntax and the structure of the lines contribute to the overall effect of the poem?

  - Has the poet used mainly short or long sentences?

  → Most of the syntactical units are relatively short – in keeping with the brief sense impressions the speaker receives as he surveys the scene before him. In a technical sense, however, the octave, the first eight lines of the poem, is no more than one long sentence – it covers the whole sweep of the speaker's vision, so to speak. The sestet, on the other hand, is divided up into two sentences (9 – 11 and 12 – 14).

  - Does the word order conform to the ordinary rules of syntactical construction?

  → There is a highly unusual inverted word order in line 2 *(Dull would he be of soul who …)* – it helps to emphasise the word *dull* at the beginning of the line, which forms a sharp contrast to the word *fair* in line 1.

  - Are some of the sentences elliptical / incomplete?

  → no elliptical or incomplete sentences, unless we count line 8 as elliptical; technically speaking, the verb is missing, but it can easily be supplemented if we assume that this line is governed by *lie* at the end of line 6 *(All [lie] glittering …)* – no particular significance here.

  - How are the sentences connected? What connectives are used, if any?

  → no connectives; the syntactical units are generally separated by semi-colons – this can underline both the accumulation of the individual elements of the speaker's experience and their interconnectedness.

  - Are the lines always end-stopped or can we find some run-on lines / instances of enjambment?

  → Some of the lines are end-stopped, but by no means all of them. There are quite a number of run-on lines – emphasising the fact that we move from one impression to the next, and often these impression shade into one another.

- How is the metrical form of the poem significant?

  – What metre has been used? Is it regular?

  → The metre is pentameter, mainly iambic, but with some important variations. Lines 1, 2, 6, 7, 9, (10), and 11 all begin with a stressed syllable, a trochaic foot, giving these words a special significance and additional emphasis (and avoiding monotony, of course). This includes the repetition of *Never / Ne'er* (ll. 9 and 11), which helps to underline the uniqueness of the poet's experience.

  – Is there a rhyme scheme and, if so, what is it?

  → the rhyme scheme is abbaabba cdccdc, which makes the poem a sonnet of the Italian type and indicates the division of the 14 lines into octave (abbaabba) and sestet (cdcdcd). The impure rhyme in lines 2 and 3 *(by – majesty)* makes the word *majesty* stand out – as clearly intended by the poet.

  – What stanza form has been employed (e.g. quatrains)?

  → no separate stanzas here; the 14 lines of the poem form a sonnet and the sonnet form seems just the right vehicle for encompassing both the beautiful view and the poet's wonder at it.

- What can be said about the composition of the poem? Which compositional principle is at work?

  – a chronological presentation in which event follows event?
  – a survey of things perceived in space, based on a narrowing or widening of focus?
  – a dialectical arrangement of ideas as thesis – antithesis – synthesis?
  – an argumentative structure that lists a number of points and draws a conclusion?
  – a loosely associative composition in which one idea leads to the next?
  – Do external composition (arrangement of the stanzas) and internal composition (progression of ideas) correspond?

  → The poet moves from the presentation of a general impression of the beauty of the morning to details of the London skyline *(Ships, towers …)* and from there to elements of nature *(valley, rock, or hill)*, then mentions the river and comes back to London as the "heart" of the country – the whole text is thus based on a shifting of focus, as is typical of impressionistic descriptions.

- What imagery does the poet rely on? Which stylistic devices has he employed?

  - What visual, auditory, olfactory, tactile, gustatory, abstract and kinetic imagery can be found?

  → The poem contains visual and auditory images – the poet appeals to sight (e.g. *a sight so touching in its majesty*) and to hearing (e.g. *silent* …).

  - How is the imagery conveyed (e.g. as metaphor or simile)?

  → The poet uses simile *(like a garment)*, metaphor *(the mighty heart)* and personification *(City, sun, river,* and *houses)* to create mental images in the reader's mind.

  - What associations are produced by these devices?

  → The reader associates images of glittering beauty and absolute calm with the speaker's words.

Useful language material

▣ **Syntax and structure of the lines**
- The short sentences speed up / quicken the pace.
- The long sentences slow the poem's pace / have a retarding effect.
- The unusual word order in line … draws attention to / stresses / emphasises / underlines the importance of …
- The poet employs inversion / changes the usual word order here / makes use of elliptical statements / incomplete sentences.
- The lines are mostly end-stopped.
- There are some run-on lines / instances of enjambment.
- The poet relies again and again on the use of enjambment / caesuras / unusual word arrangements to achieve a particular effect, namely …

▣ **Rhythm and metre**
- The rhythm of the poem / its metrical form is significant.
- This poem relies on / is based on a regular rhythmical pattern (with some slight / important variations).
- The rhythm has an enchanting effect here.
- The rhythm is basically iambic / trochaic / dactylic / anapaestic.

- The poem consists mainly of / is made up of iambic / trochaic / dactylic / anapaestic feet.
- The basically iambic metre gives the poem a serious tone.
- The trochaic metre sounds assertive.
- The dactylic rhythm accounts for the note of sadness in the poem.
- The anapaestic metre creates a galloping rhythm that is perfectly in keeping with ...
- The spondees the poet introduces here and there slow down the movement of the poem / add some extra weight to the description of ...
- The poet has tried to avoid monotony by varying the rhythm occasionally / by introducing spondees to break the iambic / trochaic pattern.
- From time to time the poet departs from the established rhythm.
- The metre is (iambic) tetrameter / pentameter / ...
- The poem is written in blank verse.

■■■ **Rhyme and rhyme scheme**
- The poem is based on a regular rhyme scheme, namely ...
- All the lines have a masculine ending, which lends emphasis to what the poet wants to say.
- The masculine rhymes sound settled and determined.
- The feminine rhymes give the poem a fluid and musical quality.
- Masculine and feminine endings alternate so that a pleasing rhythm is established.
- The poem consists of / is made up of rhyming couplets / heroic couplets / is based on cross rhyme.
- This poem is not based on a traditional rhyme scheme / is an example of free verse / unrhymed verse.
- The poet deliberately disregards the traditional rules of rhythm and rhyme here and writes free verse.
- He has used internal rhyme to good effect – its use tends to quicken the pace of the lines.
- In this poem a number of lines do not rhyme.
- The poet relies on imperfect rhyme in lines ...

■■■ **The composition of the poem**
- The poem is based on four-line stanzas / on quatrains.
- It is divided into four stanzas of ... lines each.
- The stanzas are based on a traditional rhythmical pattern and rhyme scheme.
- The poet has devoted a stanza each to the presentation of the various steps of his argument.
- The composition of the poem follows the chronological presentation of the events.

- It is based on a narrowing and widening of focus / on a dialectical arrangement of ideas / on a loosely associative chain of impressions / …
- The poem is a sonnet of the Italian / English type.

Imagery and stylistic devices
- The poet has relied to a large extent on imagery.
- The imagery of the poem helps to conjure up / evoke / suggest the beauty / calmness / majesty of …
- The poem produces visual / auditory / olfactory / tactile / gustatory images in the reader's mind.
- The poem's imagery is conveyed as simile and metaphor.
- The poet has used an appropriate / original / highly suggestive metaphor here.
- A metaphor is employed here to intensify the message of the poem / to make it more vivid and richer in connotations.
- He connects / associates the term "majesty" with the beauty of the city.
- The word "heart" is full of implied meaning / rich in connotations.
- The poet refers to / presents / describes … as if it were alive / as if it had a life of its own.
- He personifies it / endows it with human qualities.
- The poem is full of symbolic significance.
- X is meant to represent / stands for / symbolises Y.

After going through all these questions, we must decide

- which of them are particularly significant,
- how these dominant elements enact the poet's intention,
- and what correspondence there is between form and content.

We must also check whether the preliminary interpretation is still valid. It can now be amended a little to read

William Wordsworth's "Composed Upon Westminster Bridge" is a sonnet that describes the poet's impression of the magnificence and tranquillity of the City of London at daybreak and his reaction to it.

The particularly significant and dominant elements:

- The poem is largely descriptive (impressionistic description).
- The poet's intention is to bring to mind again a wonderful moment of great beauty and quasi-religious significance.
- The metre is mainly iambic, but the trochaic feet at the beginning of certain lines and some spondees later on emphasise particularly important words and reinforce the calm the poet feels.

- Images of magnificent beauty are produced in the reader's mind through the use of unusual language (vocabulary, simile, syntax).
- The sonnet is clearly divided into octave (mainly descriptive) and sestet (mainly reflective).
- The experience appears as unique *(not anything – Never – Ne'er – never)*.
- The personification of the city allows the poet to "share" its feelings.
- General impression of a moment suspended in time.

The individual results of our analysis can now be presented in essay form, as a continuous text. Remember that your statements must be verified in the text by means of direct quotations (in which the quoted bits receive quotation marks) or by referring to the relevant line or lines (e.g. cf. lines 6 – 8).

It is generally a good idea to start off with an introductory sentence in which you mention the poet's name and the title of his poem. You may also want to point out the genre (e.g. that the poem under discussion is a sonnet) and what the poem is about. Afterwards all the significant details of your analysis are presented one after the other and a final overall interpretation of the poem based on these points is given.

In William Wordsworth's sonnet "Composed upon Westminster Bridge" the poet describes an experience he had when he was crossing Westminster Bridge very early in the morning. → introductory sentence

The speaker of the poem, who appears to be the poet himself, is struck by the overwhelming beauty of what he sees around him at daybreak and feels that there is nothing more beautiful on earth than this sight of the City of London at this time of day – "Earth has not anything to show more fair" (line 1); the city is "touching in its majesty" (line 3). The poet obviously desires to relive this wonderful moment in his poem, and he does in fact make the moment come alive – not only for himself, but also for the sensitive reader. → the speaker

→ poet's intention

The whole poem is presented in a basically iambic rhythm, with some important variations here and there. These breaks in the rhythm not only help to avoid monotony; they also mark certain statements as being particularly important. The basically iambic rhythm gives the poem a serious tone so that the few trochees sound particularly assertive, especially at the outset: "Eárth has not ánything …" → iambic rhythm

→ trochees

unusual vocabulary ➜ *When the poet opens his text in such a startling way and then goes on to talk about something so "touching in its majesty" that only a very dull person would pass it without noticing, the reader certainly takes notice. One must bear in mind here that the speaker is talking about a subject he has yet to identify. Suspense is built up and the reader is indeed surprised when the subject is at last named in line 4 – the City of London.*

unusual simile ➜ *The surprise is deepened when an unusual simile is employed, namely the city wearing the morning's beauty "like a garment" (l. 4). This simile is strange and arresting for two reasons; we do not normally think of cities as "wearing" anything, and it is difficult to imagine how beauty might be a "garment". But it is precisely because the simile is so vivid that the reader is forced to pause for a moment, much as the poet himself was made to stop by what he saw. In other words, in this way the reader is made to feel what the poet felt. He is thus drawn into the poem and invited to share the experience of the beauty of London in the early morning with the poet, a sight we are told is "touching in its majesty" (l. 3).*

imperfect rhyme ➜ *The imperfect rhyme of "majesty" is put to good use here as, again, it forces the reader to pause for a moment and take in what is being stated. This word "majesty" certainly has connotations of the city being intended by God to represent his kingdom on earth. It is this quasi-religious tone that characterises the poem throughout.*

religious connotations ➜ *It is quite clear that the overwhelming experience he had strikes him with the force of a revelation and appears to have a religious significance for him. So it is certainly not by accident that a few vocabulary items from the field of religion are used in the poem (soul, temple, God) to build up connotations of the metaphysical quality of the poet's experience. The London he sees at that moment thus takes on features of the Heavenly Jerusalem, the eternal City of God, "bright and glittering" (l. 8) and steeped in "splendour" (ll. 9/10).*

syntax ➜ *He describes his impressions of the beauty of the city in the octave and then gives his reactions in the sestet. It is significant that he starts off both sections of his sonnet with negative phrases – the octave with "… not anything to show more fair," l. 1, and the sestet with "Never" (l. 9), a word he repeats twice (l. 11), so that the uniqueness of the experience stands out very sharply – Earth has nothing to show more fair and never has the sun steeped "in his first splendour" "valley, rock or hill" (l. 11) "more beautifully", and never has he seen or felt "a cálm so déep" (l. 11).*

An image of perfect calm is achieved, and the poet feels the need to cry out to God at that point ("Dear God!") because the fusion of the external calm of the city and the internal calm he feels within himself is so overwhelming. The poet's feelings are thus connected with the → personification *"feelings" of the city, which is personified throughout and regarded as a living organism. It can wear "the beauty of the morning" "like a garment" (ll. 5/4) and contains houses that "seem asleep" and is a "mighty heart" that "is lying still" (l. 14) at that precise moment.*

The ending can thus reinforce the impression of the life of the city being → final *suspended in time, underlining once more the stillness, silence and* interpretation *angelic perfection of London at the break of day. The entire poem, therefore, portrays something like a magnificent frozen moment in time.*

2 Drama

2.1 The nature of drama

2.1.1 Literature that walks and talks

A printed drama text has a number of distinctive features that make it easy to recognise it as such, as the sample text below can show. It is an extract from the fourth act of *Pygmalion* by George Bernard Shaw (1856 – 1950):

Eliza Doolittle, a common flower girl, has been taking speech lessons from Professor Higgins who claimed that he could pass her off as a duchess within a period of six months. He bet Colonel Pickering a lot of money that he would teach her to speak English so well that nobody who listened to her would suspect her humble origin. Eliza has just triumphantly won his bet at an Embassy party and they are now back home where realization begins to dawn on Eliza that she doesn't really know what's to become of her now.

A pause. Eliza hopeless and crushed. Higgins a little uneasy.

HIGGINS *(in his loftiest manner)*. Why have you begun going on like this? May I ask whether you complain of your treatment here?

ELIZA. No.

HIGGINS. Has anybody behaved badly to you? Colonel Pickering? Mrs Pearce? Any of the servants?

ELIZA. No.

HIGGINS. I presume you dont pretend that I have treated you badly.

ELIZA. No.

HIGGINS. I am glad to hear it. *(He moderates his tone.)* Perhaps youre tired after the strain of the day. Will you have a glass of champagne? *(He moves towards the door.)*

ELIZA. No. *(Recollecting her manners.)* Thank you.

HIGGINS *(good-humored again)*. This has been coming on you for some days. I suppose it was natural for you to be anxious about the garden party. But thats all over now. *(He pats her kindly on the shoulder. She writhes.)* Theres nothing more to worry about.

ELIZA. No. Nothing more for y o u to worry about. *(She suddenly rises and gets away from him by going to the piano bench, where she sits and hides her face.)* Oh God! I wish I was dead.

HIGGINS *(staring after her in sincere surprise)*. Why? In heaven's name, why? *(Reasonably, going to her)* Listen to me, Eliza. All this irritation is purely subjective.

ELIZA. I dont understand. I'm too ignorant.

HIGGINS. It's only imagination. Low spirits and nothing else. Nobody's hurting you. Nothing's wrong. You go to bed like a good girl and sleep it off. Have a little cry and say your prayers: that will make you comfortable.

ELIZA. I heard y o u r prayers. "Thank God it's all over!"

HIGGINS *(impatiently)*. Well, dont you thank God it's all over? Now you are free and can do what you like.

ELIZA *(pulling herself together in desperation)*. What am I fit for? What have you left me fit for? Where am I to go? What am I to do? Whats to become of me?

HIGGINS *(enlightened, but not at all impressed)*. Oh, t h a t s whats worrying you, is it? *(He thrusts his hands into his pockets, and walks about in his usual manner, rattling the contents of his pockets, as if condescending to a trivial subject out of pure kindness.)* I shouldnt bother about it if I were you. I should imagine you wont have much difficulty in settling yourself somewhere or other, though I hadn't quite realized that you were going away. *(She looks quickly at him: he does not look at her, but examines the dessert stand on the piano and decides that he will eat an apple.)* You might marry, you know. *(He bites a large piece out of the apple and munches it noisily.)* You see, Eliza, all men are not confirmed old bachelors like me and the Colonel. Most men are the marrying sort (poor devils!); and youre not bad-looking: it's quite a pleasure to look at you sometimes – not now, of course, because youre crying and looking as ugly as the very devil; but when youre all right and quite yourself, youre what I should call attractive. That is, to the people in the marrying line, you understand. You go to bed and have a good nice rest; and then get up and look at yourself in the glass; and you wont feel so cheap.

*Eliza again looks at him, speechless, and does not stir. The look is quite
lost on him: he eats his apple with a dreamy expression of happiness, as
it is quite a good one.*

HIGGINS *(a genial afterthought occurring to him).* I daresay my mother
could find some chap or other who would do very well.

ELIZA. We were above that at the corner of Tottenham Court Road.

HIGGINS *(waking up).* What do you mean?

ELIZA. I sold flowers. I didnt sell myself. Now youve made a lady of me
I'm not fit to sell anything else. I wish youd left me where you
found me.

HIGGINS *(slinging the core of the apple decisively into the grate).* Tosh,
Eliza. Dont you insult human relations by dragging all this cant
about buying and selling into it. You neednt marry the fellow if
you dont like him.

ELIZA. What else am I to do?

HIGGINS. Oh, lots of things. What about your old idea of a florist's
shop? Pickering could set you up in one: he has lots of money.
(Chuckling) He'll have to pay for all those togs you have been
wearing today; and that, with the hire of the jewellery, will make
a big hole in two hundred pounds. Why, six months ago you
would have thought it the millennium to have a flower shop of
your own. Come! youll be all right. I must clear off to bed: I'm
devilish sleepy. By the way, I came down for something: I forget
what it was.

ELIZA. Your slippers.

HIGGINS. Oh yes, of course. You shied them at me. *(He picks them up,
and is going out when she rises and speaks to him.)*

ELIZA. Before you go, sir –

HIGGINS *(dropping the slippers in his surprise at her calling him Sir).* Eh?

ELIZA. Do my clothes belong to me or to Colonel Pickering?

Notes
in his loftiest manner: in a most haughty and arrogant fashion – *dont:* here and
in the rest of the text of the printed play Shaw follows his own ideas on spelling
– *writhes:* twists as if in pain – *genial:* cheerful – *grate:* fireplace – *tosh* (infml)*:*
nonsense, rubbish – *togs* (infml)*:* clothes – *shied:* threw

A first observation to be made here is that this extract consists almost entirely of dialogue. The action is carried forward by what the characters say (the names of the speakers are shown in small capitals). We notice, secondly, that sometimes we also get told, as in a novel, what the characters do. Their actions, but sometimes also indications of their state of mind or of their feelings, are shown in the text by statements in italics, often, as here, put in brackets, e.g. *(staring at her in sincere surprise)*.

These hints about the characters' actions, their feelings and their state of mind are known as stage directions – they are intended to help the reader of a play to imagine the scene better, and they can help the director staging it with a troupe of actors to know how the dramatist imagined the scene. Here we learn for instance that Eliza pulls herself together "in desperation" and that Higgins "*thrusts his hands into his pockets, and walks about in his usual manner, rattling the contents of his pockets, as if condescending to a trivial subject out of pure kindness*", etc.

It is obvious to the people in the audience that they are witnessing a conflict. There is tension at the beginning of the scene between the two characters and this tension never lets up despite the fact that Higgins seems to be largely unaware of it. Conflict, a struggle between characters or between a character and his surroundings is in fact among the most important elements of drama. A drama without a conflict of some kind is difficult to imagine. The conflict here is between Eliza and Higgins, the two main characters. The action carried forward by the dialogue is not difficult to follow.

- At the beginning of the scene, Higgins speaks like a prosecutor cross-examining Eliza to find out what is the matter. When he has satisfied himself that nothing is wrong (in his view), he moderates his tone and becomes like a condescending and rather self-righteous father talking to a naughty child.

- He imagines himself to be in a teacher – pupil relationship in which the teacher is always right and knows what is best. So he appears self-centred, bossy and condescending.

- Eliza, by contrast, is merely on the defensive, showing by her uncommunicative attitude that she is upset and hurt and that she resents the role of a child that Higgins forces her to play.

The audience in a playhouse are not told about any stage directions, of course, because they are present at a live performance and have no need to be informed about what the characters do, what their feelings are and what their state of mind is – all this can come across through the character of the production and the actors' efforts. Perhaps most of the people in the auditorium will never even bother to read the text of the play and yet their enjoyment of the dramatist's text and of what the theatre artists make of it when they put it on the stage is far greater than that of people who merely read the play.

The fact is that drama has a *dual nature* – it exists both as text, which can be printed and sold in book format, and as an actual performance. It is both literary art and representational art.

There is an enormous difference between a play and any other form of literature. Even though in fact plays are often studied as text and read in silence, they are not really intended for reading but for stage production. Drama can thus be called three-dimensional art – it is literature that walks and talks before our very eyes.

2.1.2 The playwright's contribution

It could be argued that the dramatic text is similar in character to the texts of ballads and songs in oral poetry; they can only truly come to life in actual performance. A skilful rendering of such oral poetry in recitation or song breathes life into what before was only plain text. We could also point to the world of music where a musical score, the musical notation of a work, also needs people, in this case musicians and possibly a conductor, to make it come to life. In much the same way a dramatic text begins to live fully only when actors and actresses and their director (and his assistants and the theatre artists generally) produce it on a stage.

The situation is different in the case of closet-dramas, which are stories presented in dramatic form, i.e. they employ characters and dialogue, but are not intended for theatrical production. We can ignore them here, because the vast majority of plays are stage-dramas to be seen and experienced in the theatre. The world of the playhouse must therefore be seen as an integral part of the dramatic world.

This is not to say that the playwright's contribution is insignificant or that he is no more than a mere scriptwriter, providing a few lines for some actors to deliver. After all, the play originates with the dramatist and the efforts of all the theatre artists are dependent on his initial creation – without his contribution there could be no performance. It is the dramatist who conceives the plot of the play and the various characters that are to act out the conflict his play is concerned with. The characters' motivations for behaving as they do also originate with the playwright. He furnishes the dialogue and specifies the physical movements with which the characters express themselves as living people. His text is thus the life and soul of the play and it is the words of a play that keep ringing in our ears.

Theatre artists, and especially stage directors, tend to see things differently and often insist on the overwhelming significance of the theatrical production. In their view the text of a play is not a fully finished artistic creation; it simply provides the basis for theatrical production, no more and no less. They may be prepared to admit that the meaning of the text of a play may well create a more enduring impression than a performance of that play. Generally speaking, however, the play's inherent message is seen as a relatively minor element – it is what happens on the stage that counts.

The contribution of the author to the theatrical experience is not unimportant, in the case of a dramatic masterpiece it is perhaps the most significant element, but even dramatic masterpieces demand the creative cooperation of artists other than the playwright. The text of a play, like the musical score of an opera or the scenario of a ballet, is no more than the raw material from which the performance is created. Not the dramatist, but the stage director is thus the most important factor for the success of a theatrical production because it is he who interprets the action, determines the production style and then directs all the other theatre artists in such a way that an artistic unity is achieved.

It is this latter view of the dual nature of drama that is behind the often-experienced phenomenon that people come to witness the performance of a play they are very familiar with and then suddenly find themselves confronted with an interpretation that is far removed from the way they had been seeing the play until then. The particular director in charge of such a production obviously saw the dramatist's text as nothing more than raw material from which to fashion something entirely new.

Ideally, the dramatist can cooperate with the theatre artists in preparing the play he has created for production on the stage. This is not an unusual situation and has in fact been common practice since the rise of the modern stage in the sixteenth century. The works of deceased playwrights, however, and especially of playwrights whose work is no longer protected by copyright, have occasionally been subjected to far-reaching changes – some would speak of "mutilations" – at the hands of energetic and ambitious stage directors.

Synopsis

Drama

- has a dual nature.
- is both literary and representational art.
- is literature that walks and talks.
- is intended for theatrical production.
- can truly come to life only in performance.

The play action

- is based on conflict.
- is carried forward by what the characters say / by dialogue.

Stage directions

- indicate what the characters do and what motivates them.
- are intended for the readers of a play.

The playwright

- creates the play.
- conceives the plot of his play.
- invents various characters to act out the conflict the play is concerned with.
- makes the most important contribution to the play.

The theatre artists

- tend to see the dramatist's text only as the basis for the theatrical production.
- do not generally regard the play as a fully finished artistic creation.
- insist on the overwhelming significance of their contribution.
- are likely to view the dramatic text as no more than a script / as raw material from which to create the performance.
- have been known to fashion out of the dramatic text something entirely new.

2.2 Drama in the theatre

2.2.1 Theatrical conventions

Much greater demands on the reader's visual imagination are made in the novel and in other narrative literature than in a play, because the audience can at least see and hear the actors and skilful stage lighting will direct their attention to particularly important elements in the production.

Yet even in plays an undisguised appeal is often made to the audience's imagination. The audience must use their imagination for anything that cannot be represented on the stage especially when there is very little scenery or none at all, as was the case on the Elizabethan stage. Shakespeare, for instance, often had to trust to the power of his poetry to create the setting and scenery for his plays. In his *Henry V*, for example, he talks quite openly about what the playwright has to do in this respect:

> Let us […]
> On your imaginary forces work.
> Suppose within the girdle of these walls
> Are now confined two mighty monarchies,
> […]
> Piece out our imperfections with your thoughts;
> Into a thousand parts divide on man,
> And make imaginary puissance;
> Think when we talk of horses, that you see them
> Printing their proud hoofs i' the receiving earth;
> For 'tis your thoughts that now must deck our kings,
> Carry them here and there; jumping o'er times,
> Turning the accomplishment of many years
> Into an hour-glass […]

Notes

your imaginary forces: the powers of your imagination – *girdle:* (here) border – *two mighty monarchies:* i.e. England and France – *Piece out our imperfections with your thoughts:* improve our imperfect representation with the help of your imagination – *make imaginary puissance:* imagine whole armies fighting – *deck:* clothe with finery

The quoted passage is an extract from the Prologue in which the actor who speaks it appeals several times to the audience to collaborate with the dramatist in establishing the illusion of the play by using their imagination.

The audience are thus expected

- to accept the idea that the stage area represents parts of England or France, as the situation demands;

- to be able to conjure up battle scenes and indeed fully-fledged battles, including cannons, horses and thousands of soldiers;

- to be fully prepared to ignore the telescoping of time that is involved here – that a number of years can be condensed into a single hour (or into a length of time no longer than the duration of the performance).

The speaker could easily have mentioned more "conventions" that are essential for the acceptance of the stage action as representing real human action. In fact, without such tacit agreements between the theatre artists and their audience, a play could not take off. In a way, it is amazing to observe to what lengths people are prepared to go to "suspend disbelief", as the great poet Samuel T. Coleridge famously put it, in order to throw themselves into the spirit of the action of a play and to regard it as real. They are willing to enter into the dramatic illusion and to accept, for the duration of the performance, even puppets or animals as representing real people. As long as the "characters" involved in such shows are endowed with human characteristics and exhibit typically human feelings, the audience can identify with them and somehow accept them.

Conventions are a necessary and indeed inevitable element in theatre, and in art generally, because the artistic illusion – that the work of art represents reality – could not be established without them.

Some theatrical conventions are so universal and so much taken for granted that we need to remind ourselves of the fact that they are indeed conventions. Thus it is by convention

- that the stage itself, as a physical object, is accepted without question as representing the scenery and setting of the play action wherever the dramatist may have placed it.

- that the actresses and actors on the stage are taken to be the people they make pretend to be.

- that we expect these actors always to try to face at least partly towards the audience whenever they can, even in intimate conversation, so that their words can be better heard and understood and their facial expressions and their gestures better seen by the audience.

- that the people in a play are far more articulate and well-spoken than most people are in real life and that the actors conventionally raise their voices far above the level normally used in everyday conversation so that even whispered words are not lost to the audience. This is known as a *stage whisper*.

- that the device of the *aside is* tolerated by the audience even though it is anything but a realistic element. Elizabethan and Jacobean dramatists were quite fond of the aside, because it allowed them to reveal certain ideas to the audience, but not to other characters on the stage. The aside thus refers to a few words that are spoken to the audience by one of the characters, often a comment on somebody's behaviour, and these words are taken to be inaudible to the other characters on the stage, but not to the spectators.

- that on the English-speaking stage all the actors speak in English irrespective of the nationality of the characters in the play they are impersonating. All the actors in Shakespeare's *Julius Caesar* communicate in English, for instance, and not in the Latin of the historical Caesar's time.

- that the characters often speak in verse, usually in *blank verse,* a highly stylized form of communication nobody would dream of using in real life. And when characters break into song in the middle of a play, often to musical accompaniment, this sudden loss of realism is also fully accepted, as is in fact the presence of musicians on or off the stage who provide a kind of sound track to the action presented on stage.

Another universally accepted convention involves the idea that the audience can see into the interior of houses and be present when a scene is set in one of the rooms. The stage may show three walls, possibly even a ceiling, but the fourth wall enclosing the room is missing; it is where the dividing line between stage area and auditorium is (in many playhouses there is a curtain here, but it is drawn up, of course). This is known as the convention of *the fourth wall*.

Ever since actresses were allowed on stage, the convention of a disguise being thought impenetrable has caused some spectators some problems, but on the whole this convention is still readily accepted. It involves the assumption of male disguise by a female character, and then this woman is thought to be a man by everybody on the stage, but not by the audience, of course. A famous example occurs in

Shakespeare's *The Merchant of Venice,* when Portia, the heroine of that play, disguises herself as a male lawyer, and of course gets away with it. Not even her husband can recognize her, and audiences since Shakespeare's day have quietly accepted this device whenever and wherever *The Merchant of Venice* has been put on the stage.

We must bear in mind at this point that in Shakespeare's day there were no women on the stage and that all the roles, even the female ones, were acted out by male actors so that a man who played a woman who dressed up as a man was not so very strange after all. Experiments with producing Elizabethan plays with all-male casts have shown however that there are limits to what audiences will tolerate. People want to see real women playing the female roles – anything else is felt to be profoundly unnatural. It is only for the sake of the story, which wouldn't work otherwise, that Portia and other female characters who dress up as men are conventionally accepted for what they pretend to be.

In sum, many conventions are alive and still going strong in the theatre, and even in the much more realistic world of film a number of conventions cannot be done without, e.g. that the actors are in fact the people they pretend to be, or the idea of a soundtrack helping to provide atmosphere.

2.2.2 Preparing a production

Producing a play for performance in the theatre is a complex business. The dramatist's text does not of itself translate into a cohesive stage action, but must be set out in such a way that an artistically satisfactory whole is achieved.

The responsibility for bringing all the various elements of a theatrical production together lies with the director. It is his job to see to it that all the individual artists cooperate in such a manner that a convincing production of the play that is to be shown is accomplished, but a good or even brilliant result is by no means guaranteed, as a look at the following review of a recent production in London of one of Shakespeare's best-known plays can show:

> Macbeth has seized the Scottish throne and is bumping off nobles left, right and centre. Macduff, his countryman, is in England visiting the rightful king when he learns that his own family has been murdered. Deranged with grief, he cries out for his "pretty ones". Somewhere in the Barbican Pit audience, sniffing starts. A nose is blown. [...] There are some fine

performances in this production, not least from Jonathan Nibbs as the bereft and vengeful Macduff. Gyuri Sarossy is splendid as [...] Macbeth, sick and sour with his own corruption; Zoe Aldrich is doubly chilling as Lady M and one of the "weird sisters" [...]. There's even that rarest of theatrical animals – a genuinely comic drunk, in the form of Roland Oliver's Porter, gasbagging on about brewer's droop as Duncan lies slaughtered in his bed.

Yet it never entirely gels. Director Andrew Hilton and his Bristol-based company, Shakespeare at the Tobacco Factory, bring a real freshness to the more intimate scenes, but the moment bodies crowd the stage, the spell is broken. Too much rushing about, sword-clutching and generic alarum;

too little feeling or intelligence. If you weren't familiar with the text [...] you might find it impossible to follow the politicking or the military developments. There are even a couple of fluffed lines.

The sparse set makes much use of trap doors, flipped open in the stage to suggest the witches' cauldron or a larger body of water. Something's not quite right when you catch yourself worrying that one of the actors might fall in.

(Phil Daoust in the Guardian, 25 September 2004)

Notes
Seized: taken over – *bumping off* (slang): killing, murdering – *deranged:* quite beside himself – *Barbican Pit:* seats at the lowest level at the Barbican theatre where the play was showing – *bereft:* feeling a great loss – *vengeful:* bent on revenge – *gasbagging* (coll.): talking too much without really saying anything – *brewer's droop:* refers to temporary impotence caused by too much drink – *gels:* comes together, works out properly – *generic alarum:* typically too much noise – *fluffed lines:* wrong lines, not true to the original – *sparse set:* very little scenery is used on stage – *cauldron:* a very large pot

This review is an example of the technique of "damning with faint praise", i.e. a number of elements are given full credit, especially the actors' performances, but the overall impression of the production that comes across is that it is a failure. According to the critic, a number of things are wrong (the production "never entirely gels" and it shows "too little feeling or intelligence"), and there are "even a couple of fluffed lines."

Yet apart from these observations, the review contains several interesting aspects:

- It mentions audience participation, or at least audience reaction ("... sniffing starts. A nose is blown ..."). This is to say that during the performance the critic saw the people interacted with the performers and exhibited signs of an emotional reaction to what they were being shown – they were feeling Macduff's pain and sorrow and so they became tearful. (This interaction between actors and audience is an important feature in the theatrical success or otherwise of the production.)

- It underlines the fact that stage design ("the sparse set makes much use of trap doors") is a significant element in the production of a play (and so are the contributions made by other theatre artists).

- It rates the way the actors play their parts as first-class ("there are some fine performances in this production"), but it also suggests that it is the director who is to be praised for bringing "a real freshness to the more intimate scenes" by directing his company so well. And yet his success in this area is marred by his failure to produce a convincing artistic whole, at least as this critic sees it.

The conclusion to be drawn is that the production can only be as good as the overall quality of the director's artistic conception and the way he gets the various theatre artists to convert this conception into practical theatre work.

We shall look at all these elements in turn – at the role of the audience, at the importance of stage design and at the significance of the theatre artists generally.

2.2.3 The role of the audience

There is no theatre without an audience. Its very existence depends on the presence of a crowd of spectators. Since it is a performing art and as such has no permanent substance and leaves no tangible record, theatre lives only as long as an audience is actually watching its presentation.

Yet it is not enough for the spectators simply to be present; for a performance to go well, the crowd in the auditorium must respond to it, i.e. there must be interaction between performers and spectators. Theatre depends more than other art forms on audience response, and if the auditorium is half empty, the performance loses force and simply cannot go well.

This is to say that the role of the audience in the creation of theatre can hardly be overstated. It is the audience which to a large extent determines

- the choice of certain types of play a theatre company will offer the public;
- the production style – anything the audience dislikes will have to be dropped quickly,
- the cultural role of theatre in general.

Since the success of his plays depends largely on the willingness of audiences to become fully integrated in the creation of the art of theatre, a dramatist must try to achieve a universality of appeal. All theatre must in fact aim to be "popular" in appeal in order win over the audience for whatever a particular play is trying to achieve. If the dramatist and the theatre artists are not skilful enough in manipulating audience response in such a way as to guide it towards the desired effect, the audience will refuse to cooperate, destroy the performance and ultimately stay away from the theatre altogether, if they feel they are not getting what they want. And if audiences stay away, theatre cannot take place.

All audiences are somewhat disparate in nature, and so the dramatist will be more successful if he can include in his plays a number of elements which appeal to widely-different tastes and expectations and thus satisfy deep communal needs and also meet a whole range of individual interests.

People go to the theatre for various reasons. They may go

- in search of diversion and entertainment in the widest sense;
- for reasons of prestige, as when the opening night of a new production is seen as a society event and then used by socially prominent people to show themselves in the limelight;
- because they love fine acting or like seeing a particular actor or actress perform;
- because they have a particular interest in a certain play (because it is being read in class, for instance);
- in order to witness intellectually demanding performances of the great works of dramatic art.

Good drama can only start from where the audience starts, and the very best dramatists have always known how to capture its attention and holding it spellbound, as it were, by appealing to a wide range of interests. The great William Shakespeare inevitably comes to mind here. He managed to include even in his most serious tragedies popular elements of intrigue, disguise, clowning, madness, blood and horror, but knew at the same time how to turn each of these elements to the advantage of his theme.

The shape of the theatre in any given period is bound to reflect the dominant audience preferences and tastes. If, for instance, a large majority is willing to tolerate only entertainment of a very shallow sort, then theatre will offer precisely the type of play which provides this shallow entertainment.

At present there is a wide spectrum of stage activities. We have absolutely first-rate playhouses with first-rate companies staging artistically outstanding productions, but we also have cheap commercial theatre churning out extremely poor adaptations. There are many other types of theatre in between these two extremes – from the highest reaches of theatrical art to the lowest pandering to the tastes of the vulgar. What is true of the theatre proper is also true for the related arts of opera, musical, variety shows of all kinds, and cinema and television; there is an extremely wide range of all forms of stage activity The point is that this wide spectrum simply reflects the composition of our society – we do not have a unified society, and consequently we do not have a unified theatre.

Another point must be mentioned here. We have a far better theatre and generally a much better arts scene than could be expected if only audience tastes were taken into account. The fact is, however, that the state makes it its business to see to it that radio and television programmes, for instance, do not merely reflect commercial interests. Governing bodies have been set up to guarantee balanced programmes in the sense of giving cultural activities a fair chance and an ensured place in the programmes. The continued existence of first-class opera and theatre companies is also regarded as a concern of the state – the productions are heavily subsidized with the taxpayer's money, the singers and actors are often state employees, and the performances take place in buildings which have been erected with public money.

If it were not for these lavish subsidies and generally the notion that first-class cultural activities are a concern of the community at large, commercial interest would probably take over completely, with the inevitable result that the general artistic standards would drop, because intellectually demanding productions would not be likely to draw big enough audiences – audiences prepared to buy tickets at the price of the real cost of the production. The principle of the long run would have to be introduced, i.e. that a play production would run for as long as enough people wanted to see it. Repertory theatre, i.e. several new productions per season, would have no chance at all – it would simply be too expensive.

2.2.4 The importance of stage design

From the beginning of theatre as we know it (in the sense of public dramatic performances), the area reserved for the performers, the stage, and the area reserved for the spectators, the auditorium, have been kept separate. This served a double purpose:

- it enabled all the members of the audience to watch the activities of the performers *(functional purpose)*;

- it allowed those in charge of the performances to fit out the stage area with a number of properties with which to stimulate the spectators' imagination *(artistic purpose)*.

The basic plan for such a public theatre remained much the same for a long time, even though there was a gradual evolution towards more elaborate theatre structures as time went on.

Here is a diagram of a Greek theatre based on the one at Epidauros:

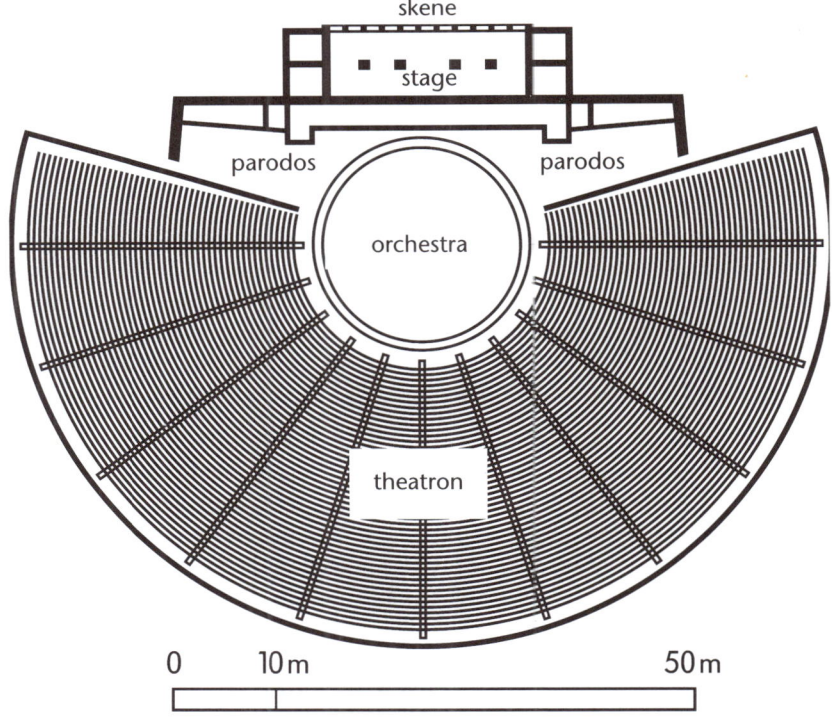

Greek plays were always performed in outdoor theatres where the audience could witness the performance, which usually centred on the exploits of a god or a hero. The chorus would dance and sing in a level circular area known as the *orchestra* (literally, *dancing space)* and would interact with the actors who were on the stage near the *skene* (literally, *tent)*. The *theatron* (literally, *viewing-place)* was where the audience sat or stood; it was often part of a hillside overlooking the orchestra, and surrounded a large portion of the orchestra (as in the diagram above). The *skene* was the building directly behind the stage, which was usually raised two or three feet above the level of the orchestra. It was directly at the back of the stage area and was usually decorated as a palace, temple, or some other building, depending on the needs of the play. It had at least one set of doors, and actors could make entrances and exits through them. There was also access to the roof of the skene from behind, so that actors playing gods could appear on the roof if necessary. The *parodoi* (literally, *passageways)* were the paths by which the chorus and some actors made their entrances and exits. The audience also used them to enter and leave the theatre before and after the performance.

Roman theatres were similar in structure, but had a much smaller orchestra, which was half a circle rather than a whole circle. This is partially due to the fact that Roman dramas did not use a chorus. The stage was also larger and there were three entrances in the back wall. An additional difference was that whereas Greek theatres were usually on the natural slope of a hill, taking advantage of the terrain and the acoustics, the Romans built theatres anywhere, even on flat plains, by raising the whole structure off the ground. This created more of an enclosed atmosphere, which was felt to be desirable.

This trend towards establishing an enclosed atmosphere is typical of later developments because a closer physical relationship between acting area and viewing area has an immense influence on play production, and thus also on playwriting. Three major stage designs have developed and they can all be found in the world of modern theatre – the *proscenium arch stage,* the *open stage,* and the *theatre-in-the-round.*

The proscenium [prə'si:niəm] arch stage is also known as the *picture-frame stage* because it is designed to be viewed only from the front, and because the opening (i.e. the proscenium arch) through which the spectators watch the progress of the action forms a frame for the actors and indeed the whole stage area. Often a curtain is used to shut off the stage area and it is drawn up at the beginning of the play action and comes down again at the end and possibly between acts, especially when changes in the scenery are to be made. It can be represented as a diagram like this:

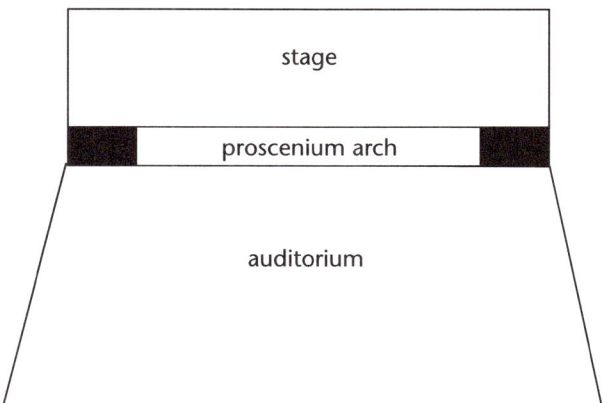

These are the physical properties of the proscenium arch stage:

- The stage is situated behind a frame-like opening in the front wall, the proscenium arch.

- The performance can be viewed only from the front; the audience watches the play action through the proscenium arch.

- A curtain is used to conceal or reveal the stage.

- Scenery may be placed at the three sides of the stage and a ceiling added. This is known as the *box set* (also known as the theatre of the fourth wall). When the curtain is raised, the imaginary, fourth wall between the stage and the auditorium is removed.

- The introduction of this box set in the nineteenth century has had a far-reaching effect on the theatre.

- It encouraged an increased visual realism, i.e. fidelity to external appearances.

- It led to a strong emphasis on theatrical illusion and indeed to the rise of a theatre of illusion by means of the introduction of more and more real objects on the stage:
  - elaborate costumes in keeping with the period in which the play is set;
  - cleverly designed (realistic) scenery, artificial stage lighting and sound effects to increase the effect of realism.

- It is responsible for the introduction of a new style of acting in which a psychological rendering of the portrayed character's behaviour was sought, with the actor trying to identify with the character he is portraying as completely as possible and totally ignoring the audience.

- And it finally led to an increased orientation of theatre towards domestic and private worlds and psychological analysis.

- It encourages a consumer attitude in the audience because there is little need for imaginative interaction with the actors and consequently little audience participation. In short, theatre basically becomes consumer art and is no longer participation art.

The advent of the new medium of film, which can achieve a virtually perfect surface realism, far more easily than the stage, has put a stop to the more extreme attempts at creating an illusion of reality in the theatre, but the influence of the theatre of illusion is still very strong and can be felt in many of today's productions.

On the other hand, attempts are being made to revive the theatre as a joint and communal experience between the actors and their audience and to get away from a view of theatre as *consumer art* and return to a view of theatre as *participation art*. One such attempt is the return to the open stage and its versatility and imaginative scope.

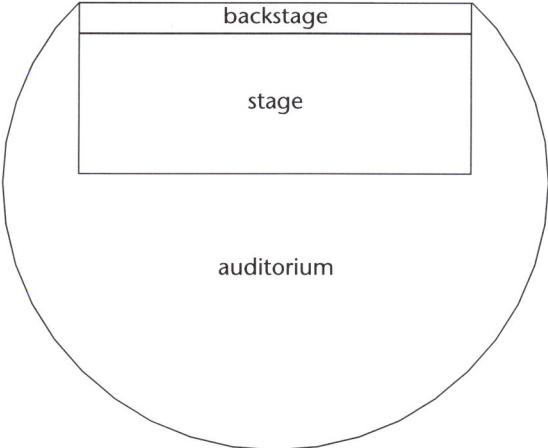

The physical properties of the open stage:

- The stage area is a raised platform projecting into the auditorium.

- The performance can be viewed from three sides.

- There is (usually) no curtain and little scenery.

The open stage, which is also known as *platform stage* or *thrust stage,* breaks down the distance between actors and audience. Seats are arranged around three sides of the stage so that the actors can play directly to the spectators, bringing actors and audience closer together. There is usually no curtain and little scenery; they would block the audience's view. An open stage has a limited capacity for realistic effects, but it encourages a theatre of range and versatility, with rapid changes of mood and great flexibility of tone, permitting high style in speech and behaviour. It makes undoubted demands on the audience's imagination and its willingness to accept the obvious make-believe but can then achieve an almost unlimited fluidity, permitting rapid changes of scene and action. What it loses in realism it gains in scope and variety.

The open stage was used to brilliant effect in Elizabethan times by Shakespeare and his contemporaries and has proved suitable for all presentational acting which is declamatory in character. Quite a few of the theatres built recently have opted for an open stage, hoping thus to create the external conditions for a theatre that allows lively interaction between players and spectators.

Theatre artists have largely been turning away from the picture frame stage and the tradition of the proscenium arch because

- they are no longer interested in theatrical realism at all costs;

- they are trying to achieve a more imaginative staging of plays and a greater fluidity in theatrical production;

- they are pressing for a revival of the theatre as a communal experience;

- they are dissatisfied with the view of theatre as consumer art and want it to be experienced again as participation art.

Theatre artists are often quite desperate to overcome the tradition of the proscenium-arch stage. The development of the theatre-in-the-round, also known as the *arena stage,* can be seen as a further attempt at getting rid of the limiting features of the proscenium-arch stage.

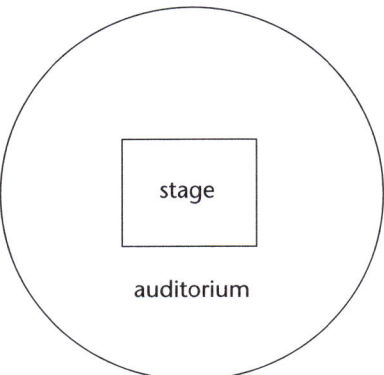

The physical properties of the theatre-in-the-round:

- there is no stage as such, but only a central acting area in the middle of the auditorium;

- the performance can be viewed from all four sides;

- there is no curtain and little scenery at most.

The theatre-in-the-round tries to go right back to one of the features of classical theatre, namely having a central acting area surrounded by a raised spectator area, and it tries to combine this principle with the idea of having the stage inside an enclosed theatre structure. But there is no stage as such – the actors perform in an open space at floor level in the middle of the auditorium. The audience sits around the central acting area and is thus very close to the action. As a result, the relationship between actors and audience is characterised by an even greater degree of intimacy and immediacy than is the case when an open stage is used. It is obvious that this intimacy and immediacy have a strong influence on the manner of production in theatres of this type.

- Scene changes must be carried out in full view of the audience, as there are no curtains, of course.

- Pieces of scenery, if scenery is used at all, must be brought to the acting area along the aisles of the auditorium and then shuffled around quite openly on the stage.

- The actors must effect their entrances and exits through the audience, and they have to turn frequently so that can be seen from the front as much as possible on all sides. They can then either ignore the audience completely or use a style of acting oriented towards audience involvement.

The theatre-in-the-round is particularly suitable for experimental and avant-garde plays, for revivals of medieval plays, and generally for experimentation with new forms of theatrical production. It is a development in stage design that is trying to move more firmly in the general direction of a more imaginative theatre and towards a greater fluidity in theatrical production.

A comparison of the three main forms of modern stage design can reveal their strengths and weaknesses.

The proscenium arch stage	
advantages	*drawbacks*
• can achieve a greater measure of realism • a psychologically convincing rendering of a character's behaviour is possible • domestic and private worlds can be portrayed well and psychological analysis can be carried a long way	• encourages a consumer attitude in the spectators • theatre as a communal experience between actors and audience is made virtually impossible • very little flexibility
The open stage	
advantages	*drawbacks*
• can break down the distance between actors and audience • great flexibility • encourages a drama of range and versatility	• a limited capacity for realistic effects • makes great demands on the audience's willingness to accept the obvious make-believe
The arena stage	
advantages	*drawbacks*
• a high degree of intimacy and immediacy, and great versatility and flexibility • lends itself particularly well to the staging of experimental and avant-garde plays, to revivals of old plays, and generally to experimentation with new forms of theatrical production	• realistic effects are virtually impossible • the actors have to turn frequently so that everybody in the audience can see them from the front as often as possible

2.2.5 The significance of the theatre staff

From the audience's point of view, the actor seems to be the central figure in theatrical production, because he is the focus of attention when he appears on the stage, and it is he who seems to dominate the performance completely and to carry the whole weight of the production.

Actors are among the few artists who cannot separate their means of expression from themselves. They create the characters they are meant to represent on stage with their own bodies and voices and their own psychological and mental qualities. They must use their bodies to represent a wide range of attitudes and reactions and they need to achieve great physical control and coordination. And they need to acquire similar flexibility, control and expressiveness in their voice.

Yet no matter how well trained actors are, they cannot use their skills effectively without some consistent working method. There are two basic systems of acting to choose from.

- The supporters of the first system believe that emotion may interfere with good acting and say the actor should merely try to create the external signs of emotions.

- The followers of the second system claim that only through feeling can performers project themselves into a character and situation. This second system is often called the Stanislavski method, after the great Russian director Konstantin Stanislavski who was convinced that an actor must be moved emotionally to act convincingly.

Whichever way of creating a role is chosen, the performers must solve several specific problems every time they play a new role. These problems include

- analysing the role, which starts with a study of the play as a whole, and leads to a deeper understanding of all aspects of characterisation and also to a realisation of how their role is related to the other characters and to the structure of the play.

- finding the appropriate movements and gestures to portray a character's walk, posture, and bodily attitudes. The performer works to understand the purpose or emotional reason behind each movement so he or she can perform every action 'in character.'

- achieving vocal characterisation by adjusting their voice to the demands of the role and of each different scene, some of which may be relaxed and others emotionally high keyed.

- pacing themselves so that the performance can grow in strength and interest instead of starting out at an emotional pitch that is too intense so that the rest of the performance will seem monotonous because they will not be able to build the intensity any further.

- achieving an artistic unity that results from the cooperative efforts of the entire cast (ensemble playing).

Yet the actors are by no means the only people involved in the production of a play. In the modern theatre there are a lot of others with supporting tasks.

Supporting personnel for the actors first became necessary with the emergence of changeable scenery and designed space, and ever since there has been an increasing specialisation in theatrical skills, so that each aspect of production became the responsibility of separate individuals. The designer's task, for instance, has by now come to be spilt up among scenic, costume, and lighting personnel and involves technicians, electricians, stage hands, builders, prop masters, wardrobe mistresses, and many others working together.

This increased specialisation of theatre work has made it necessary for one person to guide the entire presentation, because an artistic effort that involves the close cooperation of so many people simply cannot express the views of all the participants. It is the job of the director to see to it that all preparatory work is fully coordinated. It is he who is responsible for the various steps of preparing the play for public performance, gradually leading up to the opening night. In short, he is responsible for the entire production. He will usually follow a general schedule such as the following.

- The director first all makes himself thoroughly familiar with the play and interprets the dramatic text as it comes from the dramatist.

- He usually discusses his interpretation of the play with the scenic, costume, and lighting designers, but the final interpretation of the play is his. They study the structure of the play, noting its pattern of exposition, complication, crisis and resolution, and examine the devices the dramatist uses to present the action and to create suspense. They also analyse individual scenes and the behaviour and motivation of the characters and try to define the predominant mood of the play.

- He may very likely suggest changes and cuts to the dramatist's text with the intention of "pointing up" the play, i.e. making it more meaningful to the audience and generally putting the stamp of his interpretation on the entire production.

- He decides on suitable scenery, costume and lighting requirements after studying the sketches of the scenery and the costumes that the specialists have prepared and after considering their advice. And he also decides on what "props" are to be used in the play and what musical accompaniment, if any, is to be used.

- He finally discusses with the experts what the mood of the set is to be and what arrangements are necessary with regard to the flow of action and to its suitability as background for the play action. A compromise is usually worked out, from the experts' suggestions and the director's ideas and requests. They make sure that the proposed set will faithfully reflect the action, mood, theme, characters, and period of the play.

- He selects the most suitable actors and actresses for all the roles in the play, a process which is known as "casting." In doing this he will take particular care that the individual performers are not only suited to their roles but also combine with the others to form a balanced and varied cast.

- After the casting, the director (or one of his assistants, such as the *stage manager)* takes charge of the routine of *rehearsals*. The text of the play is broken down into scenes involving one or more actors. From then on the work proceeds according to a detailed schedule, sometimes in smaller, sometimes in larger groups, later by whole acts. This process is known as "blocking" the action.

- He or his assistants then arrange the patterns of the performers' movements and proceed to detailed work on problems of characterisation, line readings, complex pieces of stage business (a duelling scene, for instance), and changes in mood here and there. During this process, a *prompt-copy* of the script is prepared for the prompter. This prompt-copy contains in meticulous detail every movement and cue worked out in the course of rehearsing the play.

- The next step is the arrangement of a number of "run-throughs" – complete trial presentations of the play – before the final *dress rehearsal* in which the play is tried out for a last time before the first public performance.

- When the director is satisfied that all the individual elements of the production move together to carry the play to its climaxes, give it structure and shape and make it convincing, the production is ready for the *opening night* and for the one final spark that will make the performance come alive – the performers' direct contact with a live audience.

There is only one person in the world of theatre who is more powerful than the director – the producer. He is the man who is responsible for finding the money to finance the production and without a solid financial base theatre cannot proceed.

There may also be an artistic director, someone who is concerned with guiding the policy of the theatre and does not usually concern himself with details of administration or the preparation of any single production.

The hierarchy can naturally vary in different circumstances (size of the theatre, etc.), but in virtually all large theatres we find a producer, a director, and sometimes an artistic director. The situation is slightly different in the state-run theatres, in which there is obviously no need for a producer – the money that is needed for preparing the productions is mainly provided by the state authorities, i.e. it is tax-payers' money. In the case of a state-run theatre, the artistic director is usually responsible for deciding how the money available is best used, for instance on new productions, on improving the technical equipment of the theatre, on engaging new actors, etc.

The whole process of preparing a production can be shown in diagram form, like this:

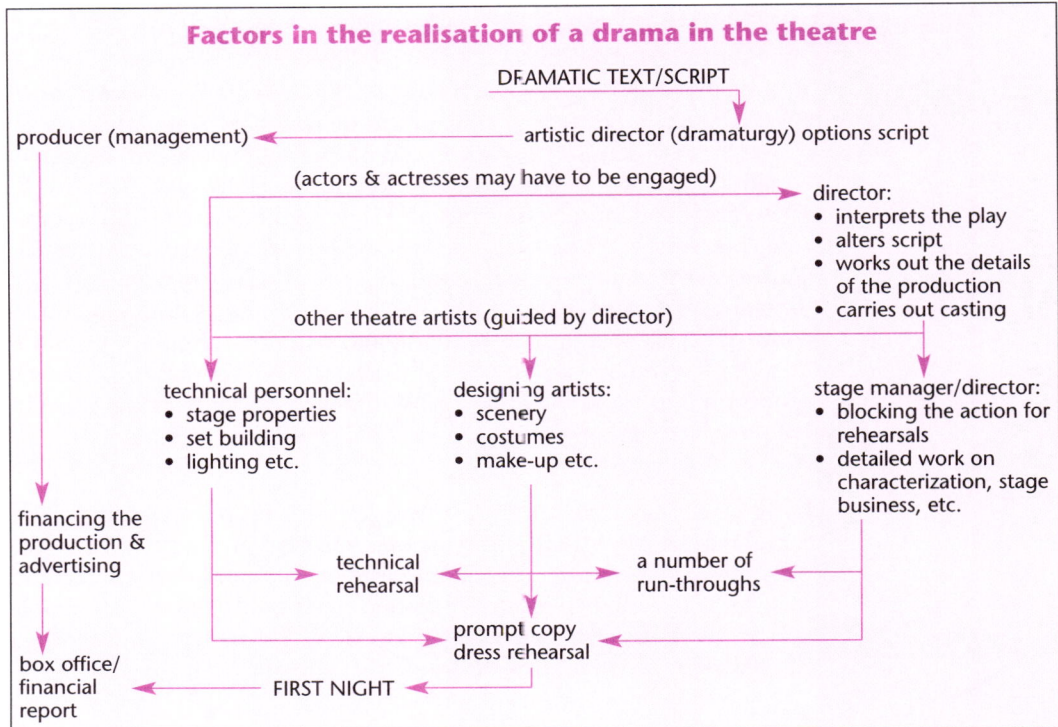

Factors in the realisation of a drama in the theatre

DRAMATIC TEXT/SCRIPT

producer (management) ← artistic director (dramaturgy) options script

(actors & actresses may have to be engaged)

director:
- interprets the play
- alters script
- works out the details of the production
- carries out casting

other theatre artists (guided by director)

technical personnel:
- stage properties
- set building
- lighting etc.

designing artists:
- scenery
- costumes
- make-up etc.

stage manager/director:
- blocking the action for rehearsals
- detailed work on characterization, stage business, etc.

financing the production & advertising

technical rehearsal ← a number of run-throughs

prompt copy dress rehearsal

box office/ financial report ← FIRST NIGHT ←

2.3 Types of play

2.3.1 A mixture of comedy and tragedy

In *A Midsummer Night's Dream* by William Shakespeare (1564 – 1616), there is a "play within the play" when the Athenian craftsmen produce a short scene, based on the story of Pyramus and Thisbe, for the Duke's wedding. This is how they introduce it:

> "A tedious brief scene of young Pyramus
> And his love Thisbe; very tragical mirth."
> Merry and tragical! Tedious and brief!
> That is, hot ice and wondrous strange snow. (Vi; i)

It is plain for everyone to see that almost the whole text consists of the most wonderful contradictions, e.g. *tedious* and *brief* or *tragical* and *merry*. All this promises to be good fun, and it is, of course. But it is also intended to parody and ridicule a marked tendency in the plays of many of Shakespeare's contemporary fellow dramatists to try and provide everything at once – laughter and tears, comic and tragic elements, all mixed together without any discretion.

As a playwright, Shakespeare himself did not hesitate to provide a lively mixture of various dramatic types in one and the same play, especially comedy and tragedy, but in his case all these diverse elements are made to contribute to the success of his theme. Though his *Romeo and Juliet,* for instance, is clearly a tragedy, it contains two superbly comic characters, namely Juliet's Nurse and Mercutio, and this arrangement – comic characters in a tragedy – works wonderfully well. Even in the most profound and agonising of his tragedies, *King Lear*, comic elements can be found, to the advantage of the play. Conversely, Shakespeare's comedies all contain serious elements in different measure. His *Merchant of Venice*, for example, is undoubtedly a comedy, a play with a happy ending and with lots of good fun, but it includes the figure of the Jew Shylock, whose fate takes on tragic proportions as the play progresses. Without Shylock's personal tragedy, however, something absolutely essential would be missing from the play.

In all this, Shakespeare, the playwright, is being true to our general experience of life – that it is a strange mixture of the comic and the tragic. And yet even if a certain measure of continual overlapping and even some tension between the different types of play seems acceptable if it serves a dramatic purpose, it is still useful to have some rough classification of what types of drama there are.

Shakespeare's first publishers must have been aware of this when they divided the collection of his plays they were bringing out into three basic categories, namely *Comedies*, *Histories*, and *Tragedies*.

The category of the History Play (or Chronicle Play, as it was also called) broadly refers to dramatic works based on historical materials, but we do not now speak as readily of the History as of the other two forms.

Plays dealing with historical events are usually serious plays. A relatively recent example is Arthur Miller's *The Crucible* (1953), which treats the Salem with trials of 1692, but has been interpreted by most critics as being an attack of the contemporary "witch hunts" of the McCarthy era in the early fifties; in this sense it could be classed as a "problem play" (for details see below).

Much more important is the traditional distinction between tragedy and comedy. A generally accepted definition is that tragedy is a play with a sad ending and a comedy one with a happy ending. In dramatic terms this usually means at least one death at the end of a tragedy and at least one wedding at the end of a comedy.

As in all the classifications of literature, however, the tone of the play and the emotional approach to the subject are more important than the nature of the ending. Tragedy treats life seriously and with a sense of its importance but also of its difficulties; it is concerned with conflict, dilemma and suffering. Comedy, by contrast, is presented in a light-hearted fashion and has often a better sense of proportion from the common-sense point of view, but does not show a similar emotional depth.

The diction of tragedy is generally more dignified, and dramatists writing tragedy are more likely to rely on poetic diction than dramatists writing comedy. The general attitude to life and especially to the problems of personal relationships exhibited in tragic plays is more austere and more responsible than in comedy, in which the stress falls clearly on providing fun and often quite shallow entertainment. Whereas in many of the best tragedies there is an almost continuous heightening of emotion from the beginning to the end of the play, we do not expect anything serious to happen in comedy. There is usually some tension at some point, but it is temporary and relatively easily overcome.

2.3.1 Tragedy

The term "tragedy" is broadly applied to serious plays which end in disaster for the main character, and possibly for others as well. Since this main character in a tragedy meets an unhappy end, usually death, the term came to be generally applied to any situation in life in which somebody suffers severe misfortune, often death. This is the sense of the word as Rita understands it in the following passage (from Act I, Scene 6) of Willy Russell's *Educating Rita* (1980). She has been to see a professional production of *Macbeth* and is deeply impressed. So she rushes over to Frank's office from her place of work at a hairdresser's to tell him about it, because she "couldn't get over […] how excitin' it was." The scene goes on like this:

RITA. […] Macbeth's a tragedy, isn't it? *(Frank nods.)*

RITA. Right. *(Rita smiles at Frank and he smiles back at her.)* Well I just – I just had to tell someone who'd understand,

FRANK. I'm honoured that you chose me.

RITA *(moving towards the door)*. Well, I better get back. I've left a customer with a perm lotion. If I don't get a move on there'll be another tragedy.

FRANK. No. There won't be a tragedy.

RITA. There will, y' know. I know this woman; she's dead fussy. If her perm doesn't come out right there'll be blood an' guts everywhere.

FRANK. Which might be quite tragic – *(He throws her the apple from his desk which she catches.)* – but it won't be a tragedy.

RITA. What?

FRANK. Well – erm – look; the tragedy of the drama has nothing to do with the sort of tragic event you're talking about. Macbeth is flawed by his ambition – yes?

RITA *(going and sitting in the chair by the desk)*. Yeh. Go on. *(She starts to eat the apple.)*

FRANK. Erm – it's that flaw which forces him to take the inevitable steps towards his own doom. You see? *(Rita offers him the can of soft drink. He takes it and looks at it.)*

FRANK *(putting the can down on the desk)*. No thanks. Whereas, Rita, a woman's hair being reduced to an inch of stubble, or – or the sort of thing you read in the paper that's reported as being tragic, "Man Killed By Falling Tree", is not a tragedy.

RITA. It is for the poor sod under the tree.

FRANK. Yes, it's tragic, absolutely tragic. But it's not a tragedy in the way that *Macbeth* is a tragedy. Tragedy in dramatic terms is inevitable, pre-ordained. Look, now, even without ever having heard the story of *Macbeth* you wanted to shout out, to warn him and prevent him going on, didn't you? But you wouldn't have been able to stop him would you?

RITA. No.

FRANK. Why?

RITA. They would have thrown me out the theatre.

FRANK. But what I mean is that your warning would have been ignored. He's warned in the play. But he can't go back. He still treads the path to doom. But the poor old fellow under the tree hasn't arrived there by following any inevitable steps has he?

RITA. No.

FRANK. There's no particular flaw in his character that has dictated his end. If he'd been warned of the consequences of standing beneath that particular tree he wouldn't have done it, would he? Understand?

RITA. So – so Macbeth brings it on himself? […]

Notes
get a move on: hurry – *dead fussy:* very hard to please – *blood an' guts:* dire consequences – *flawed:* less than perfect – *doom:* destruction – *stubble* (here): closely-cropped hair – *sod* (sl.): fellow – *pre-ordained:* somebody or something willed it beforehand – *brings it on himself:* is himself responsible for it, has only himself to blame for it

Several things emerge from this extract or seem to be implied, and many of these points are useful in a discussion of what makes a play a "tragedy".

- There is a *popular meaning* of "tragedy" (in the sense of somebody having a serious and possibly fatal accident).

- There is also a *technical meaning* of the term (in the sense of the main character of a serious play being ultimately defeated).

- He is defeated and destroyed by forces outside himself and beyond his control, but he is somehow himself responsible for his downfall.

- His ruin is his own fault because there is a "flaw" in his character.

- Watching this doomed character move through the play action to his destruction does not leave the spectators cold; they feel with him and pity him, and his death, when it comes, is not felt to be devastating, but seeing him meet his death eye to eye is somehow an uplifting experience for the viewers.

Generally speaking, a tragedy is first of all a serious play. It presents a character of admirable qualities and important position who is brought low by a fault in his character – in Macbeth's case, for instance, it is ambition, in Othello's it is credulity, etc. The protagonist's character must be richly developed so as to be believable; our sympathy cannot be enlisted for a pale, insignificant or shadowy figure. In short, he must be a round character, not a flat one. Whereas *flat* or *two-dimensional characters* tend to be constructed around a single idea or quality and are presented without much individualising detail, *round* or *three-dimensional characters* are many-faceted and complex and are presented with psychological subtlety.

The nature of the tragic hero and the nature of the conflict he is engaged in have changed as man's ideas about himself and his world have changed.

- The Greek tragic hero is a man of high estate, or royal or noble position (e.g. Agamemnon, Oedipus or Orestes). He or his ancestors have transgressed the moral law, embodied in the gods and the state, and the play shows him struggling to avoid the consequences of the transgression, showing a fatal pride in the process. His conflict, however, is with forces outside himself, and he is inevitably the loser in the struggle.

- The Elizabethan tragic hero is also an eminent man, but his conflict is an inner conflict. He is a person of generally admirable character, but there is this "tragic flaw," which is demonstrated in the play as leading to his downfall.

- The modern tragic hero is no longer a person of the highest social position; he is a member of the middle classes. His conflict, although it has broad moral implications, is usually of a domestic or social nature. Examples of such heroes include characters from the plays of Henrik Ibsen (1828 – 1906) or Willy Loman from Arthur Miller's *Death of a Salesman* (1949).

What all these tragic heroes have in common is that at some point their lack of understanding of what is happening to them gives way to a new insight. There is a moment of truth somewhere when the tragic hero realizes something important about his own situation or character that he did not see before. It is the process through which he becomes aware, for instance, of the part he himself has played in bringing about his ruin. There must not be many twists and turns of plot (one main reversal, or *peripety*, is common), for we need to concentrate on a character in a single situation.

The hero arrives at this recognition (the Greek word is *anagnorisis*) through pain and suffering and discovers to his horror that at some crucial point in the course of events he has done the wrong thing, made the wrong choice, for example, or becomes aware of this weakness in his character (Gk *hamartia*), the destructive passion inside himself that is ultimately responsible for his ruin.

There are various degrees of recognition, of course. It may be minimal, as when the protagonist becomes aware of what he has done but learns little or nothing about himself; or there may be almost total awareness on the hero's part. Yet even where the hero's recognition is considerable, it is never quite complete. A final element of puzzlement and wonder always remains. Why was he, and not somebody else, chosen for suffering the disaster which is about to crush him? He is baffled to the last over the how and why of his fate, but the enigma cannot be solved.

This element of discovery is central to the hero's tragic experience, and the manner in which he responds to it and faces up to his fate decides his essential worth as a tragic figure and also his ultimate tragic status.

Tragedy is said to arouse pity and fear – pity for the tragic hero and fear for ourselves, because the tragic hero's dilemma can be seen to be one of universal significance. He suffers vicariously for what may be in store for others as well. The hero's tragic fate has measured for us the value of human life – he goes down, it is true, but his downfall at the same time reaffirms the essential dignity of human life, a dignity that comes from within and expresses the tragic importance of human existence. So at the end of a tragedy we are left with a sense of the greatness of man as well as of the suffering involved in human life. These passionate characters who struggle with their destiny are strangely important; they symbolize for all of us what it is to be human – a creature endowed with an inalienable dignity. This is indeed an uplifting, even exalting idea so that the experience of theatre goers throughout the ages is borne out again and again – the experience of witnessing a tragedy on the stage has not left them shattered and devastated but curiously satisfied, an experience also known as *catharsis*.

143

There are two types of play which are in many ways similar to tragedy and yet must be strictly distinguished from pure tragedy; they are the *problem play* and *melodrama*.

The problem play is typically intended to make people aware of a problem and to think intelligently about it. The playwright is concerned with a particular social or moral problem and discusses it in his play. It is usually somewhat tragic in tone in that it naturally deals with painful human dilemmas; it is the type of play that, by implication, asks a definite question and either supplies an answer or leaves the audience to find one. Most of the plays of Henrik Ibsen and some of George Bernard Shaw (1856 – 1950) belong here, but the problem play is not principally a thing of the past. In fact, it is highly popular today and is likely to be popular in any period when ideas change and society develops rapidly, as at present. It is a type of play that naturally appeals to thoughtful minds and can thus hope to make a small contribution to human progress, yet many plays in this category tend to be short-lived and ephemeral in character as the problems they concern themselves with are superseded in society by others. They are apt to over-simplify things for the sake of dramatic effect and show a tendency to be over-melodramatic.

Melodrama has been called a poor relation of tragedy, and the description seems to be peculiarly apt. It can have dignity, stature, and importance and can frequently be exciting and satisfying drama. There are, however, several features of melodrama which sharply distinguish it from tragedy.

- Unlike tragedy, melodrama is not interested in bringing the hero to a point of self-discovery or recognition – there is not much for the hero of melodrama to learn about himself, because characterization tends to be generally more superficial in melodrama than in tragedy, and the characters are also less complex and their conduct less ambivalent.

- Melodrama characteristically uses stock or type characters who can definitely and clearly be divided into "the good guys" and "the bad guys." They are constructed around a single dominant trait in their nature; thus we find the miser, the clown, the lovesick young man, the hypochondriac, the clever servant, the schemer, and many more.

- The issues are clear-cut and direct, there is no moral ambiguity, and virtue will be rewarded and evil will be punished in the end. The conflict tends to be presented in black and white.

- Perhaps the decisive test by which we can distinguish melodrama from tragedy is in the kind of emotional reaction each of them produces in the spectator. Both types can produce thrills, but if thrills are the principal effect of a play it is melodrama. Tragedy, by contrast, does more than this, because it evokes in the more thoughtful spectator overtones of reflective emotion. Generally speaking, melodrama is content with arousing pity and fear, whereas it takes tragedy to create compassion and awe.

The fact that melodrama does not address such deep questions and problems does not invalidate it as a type of drama. There is certainly nothing wrong with plays which set out to provide thrills and entertainment and, by a skilful use of all the established theatrical devices for moving an audience, actually manage to do so. There is a great demand for this type of play, especially in the commercial theatre and even more so in the cinema. Most adventure and detective films, the westerns, and even the bulk of serious films are pure melodrama, with their insistence on spectacular scenes, sensational effects, often a sentimental love interest, and a happy ending.

The life of melodrama is thus action and thrills, which are generally more significant than motivation. Incident is piled on incident in rapid succession, so that what happens tends to be far more important than to whom it happens or why. And the plot of a fast-moving action will usually generate a thrill of suspense, which creates more and more suspense as the events are proceeding towards a thrilling climax, in which, perhaps, the hero arrives on the scene to rescue the heroine from a truly desperate situation at the last possible moment. The various steps in the villain's persecution of hero and heroine, the man-hunt for the villain, and many other exciting scenes are also very effective in producing thrills.

A further characteristic of melodrama is its constant attempt to satisfy the audience's desire for wish-fulfilment by presenting what is essentially a dream world; it embodies elements of the world as we know it but is basically a world as it ought to be, a world in which things come out right in the end. Melodrama thus provides an opportunity for escape. Uncritical spectators can lose themselves in the story and enjoy the vicarious satisfaction of seeing hero and heroine defeat the machinations [ˌmækɪ'neɪʃnz] of the villain.

2.3.3 Comedy

If the essential function of tragedy is to make people think and feel more deeply, the essential function of comedy is to amuse. It features an unheroic action that shows the follies of mankind in the light of recognizable standards of social conduct. It distributes penalties, punishing the bad, and rewards, rewarding the good, as we would wish life to do, and it affirms life as ultimately good.

The amusement brought about by comedy may range from a quiet smile to loud laughter. Comedy can be highly sophisticated and quite simple and it can be warm-hearted and human or brilliant but heartless. Since it can show so many different facets, it seems useful to divide it into several sub-categories.

- There is a type of comedy in which the plot consists of a series of mistakes of identity or fact, or misinterpretations of action or character, which results in much talk at cross-purposes and some general confusion before the situation can be cleared up. A great deal in such a comedy of errors depends on the convention of disguises being impenetrable, so that husbands and wives, parents and children, pairs of friends and of sweethearts, cannot recognize each other. The disguise may be as simple as a mask or boy's clothes on a girl and the other way round. On the stage most audiences have little difficulty accepting this. Shakespeare's *Twelfth Night* and *She Stoops to Conquer* (1773) by Oliver Goldsmith (1730? – 1774) may be considered masterpieces in the genre.

- The comedy of manners is a type of play in which the amusement arises chiefly from the portrayal of a number of current fads. This type of comedy relies heavily on presenting recognized social types such as the vulgar *nouveau-riche*, the social climber, the gossip, the snob and so on. The chief pleasure for the audience of this type of play derives from the wit and sparkle of the dialogue, and from the habits and foibles portrayed. Shakespeare's *Love's Labour's Lost* and *The School for Scandal* (1777) by Richard Brinsley Sheridan (1751 – 1816) are well-known examples. Some plays of this type not only make an attempt at satirizing current foibles but suggest better modes of behaviour.

- Sentimental comedy, as the name implies, is comedy which tries to play to some extent on our sympathies as well as making us laugh; it may even be out to draw easy tears. Historically speaking, sentimental comedy was a reaction to the brilliant but heartless Restoration Comedy with its scandals and its satirical stance. Yet the genre is far from extinct as a number of more recent productions can show, *Dear Octopus* (1943) by Dodie Smith (1896 – 1990) among them. The chief market for sentimental comedy is now however the world of film, both with regard to TV films and to full-length feature films. Hollywood has provided abundant examples. TV audiences will be familiar with TV films based on stories by Rosamunde Pilcher (1924 –).

- The Comedy of Humours can be mentioned here, though it is now mainly of historical interest. It was Ben Jonson (1572 – 1637) who specialized in the comedy of humours, which is a simplified *comedy of character* in which people are described by means of a single characteristic. Thus we have the ill-tempered person, the lazy person, the jealous man, and so on, much like some of the characters in the *Commedia dell' arte*, which is based on stock characters.

- Of much greater interest is the Drama of Ideas made popular by George Bernard Shaw. Shaw considerably widened the scope of comedy beyond the usual conflicts revolving around the "boy meets girl" theme. His plays show characters involved in social, political, and philosophical problems. Thus he takes up the subjects of war (*Arms and the Man*, 1894), patriotism (*The Devil's Disciple*, 1897), economics (*The Millionairess*, 1935), religion (*Major Barbara*, 1905), and many others, including his famous play on the importance of the right accent (*Pygmalion*, 1912). The type of comedy he created has provided constant delight for theatre audiences the world over, even though it must be said that many of the issues discussed in his plays are now obsolete (e.g. his attack on slum landlordism in *Widowers' Houses*, 1892).

The success of the "drama of ideas" rests firmly on Shaw's unrivalled ability to create characters that are just sufficiently lacking in balance, just sufficiently distorted to be truly comic. He knew very well that surprise is an essential element of comedy and did not hesitate to include surprises in most of his plays. The unexpected transformation of Eliza Doolittle's father from a dustman into a millionaire (in *Pygmalion*) is a case in point.

- The burlesque [bɜː'lesk] is a type of comedy that is presented entirely in the satirical mode. Its main characteristic is that it is written in imitation of another play, or type of play, and that it greatly exaggerates certain features of the original so as to produce a comic and satirical effect. It can appear in the form of parody, which ridicules the style of the original but departs from it in subject matter, and in the form of *travesty*, which keeps the original subject matter but treats it in a totally inappropriate style, thus making it appear as ridiculous. (The three terms burlesque, parody and travesty are often used interchangeably).

Famous examples in English literature are the Pyramus and Thisbe sequence in *A Midsummer Night's Dream* (c. 1595), in which Shakespeare was ridiculing the tradition of the "Interludes" of earlier generations, and Shaw's *Arms and the Man* (1894), which can be seen as a burlesque of the extravagance of "patriotic" plays – Shaw deflates them thoroughly.

- This leaves us with farce, which is to comedy roughly what melodrama is to tragedy. It aims at producing simple and hearty laughter and provoking mirth of the most basic kind. There is generally a rapid succession of amusing and often ludicrous situations of a rather crude type, and highly exaggerated type characters are employed. Clowning, buffoonery, slapstick and horseplay are usually involved, such as the throwing of custard pies and other messy things so that farce is also known as *custard-pie comedy*.

Farce is virtually without intellectual content and concentrates exclusively on elements of *low comedy*. Whereas *high comedy* characteristically produces "thoughtful laughter" and perhaps a smile at the spectacle of human folly, pretentiousness and the incongruity in human behaviour that is presented, low comedy arouses laughter by boisterous and clownish activity and by using slapstick humour and "gags."

If melodrama can be said to fulfil an important function by providing an opportunity for experiencing the intense and exciting moments of life in concentrated form, farce can do much the same thing for the widespread human urge to be amused by ludicrous situations and undignified and grotesque behaviour. This is why farces are still popular and always will be. A classic example is of course *Charley's Aunt* (1892) by Brandon Thomas, which still delights audiences. A widely known recent example of the type is Michael Frayn's uproarious farce *Noises Off* (1982), which has been one of the most frequently produced plays the world over in the last two decades.

2.3.4 Other types of play

Over the last century or so, playwrights have turned to new techniques to demonstrate their discontent with traditional ways of creating plays. Above everything else, this new drama tried to be anti-realistic, turning away from the dogma of stage illusion at all costs and from the representational style of play production.

A first such anti-realistic movement was symbolism. Its influence can still be felt whenever attempts are made to substitute suggestion for direct statement and wherever simplified settings and non-realistic styles of stage design are used.

A second anti-realistic movement was expressionism, which was intended to show that reality does not exist until the human mind has shaped it and that the surface appearance of things is important only as it reflects an inner vision.

A third counter-movement against realistic drama was the epic theatre developed by Bertolt Brecht (1898 – 1956). The ideal epic play has a clear pragmatic goal – to make people want to change their society, but the epic theatre has not on the whole achieved a real breakthrough on the English-language stage.

The greatest single force for change in the drama has undoubtedly been the Theatre of the Absurd, which offers a vision of humanity struggling vainly, and therefore absurdly, to control its fate in a world that is indifferent to it, if not actively hostile. Most absurdist drama has been concerned with the anxieties of individuals trying to survive in a world that seems bent on destruction.

The plays that have been grouped under the heading of the Theatre of the Absurd have a number of things in common:

- They have tended to emphasize the confusing and illogical elements in life rather than its positive points.

- They have questioned, if not flatly denied, the existence of any identifiable meaning whatsoever in life.

- They therefore regard life as essentially meaningless, or absurd.

- The general atmosphere of absurdist plays is one of futility and hopelessness.

All these movements have experimented with the traditional play structure and have developed play structures of their own.

The traditional play structure is typically based on clear division lines, like this for a five-act play:

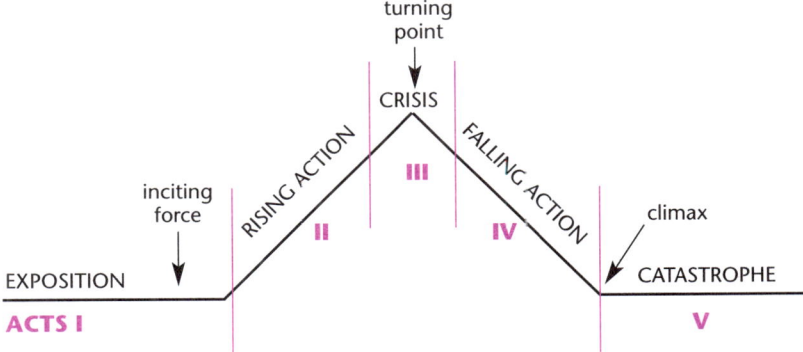

The diagram typically refers to the plot movement in a tragedy ending in the hero's death (catastrophe). But up to a point, this play structure can also be applied to comedy because the fortunes of the hero and the heroine must also undergo a certain development before the happy ending is achieved. (The Roman numerals roughly indicate the act divisions.)

The general division of a play into the categories of *exposition – development – resolution* can be regarded as standard and can be represented like this:

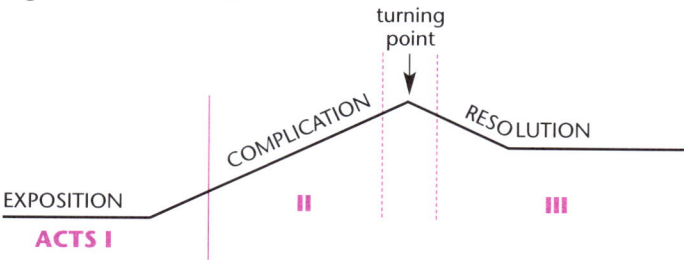

The situation is almost totally different for a play in the tradition of the Theatre of the Absurd. There is exposition, it is true, but there is little else that corresponds to the traditional play structure. The following diagram can show what is meant:

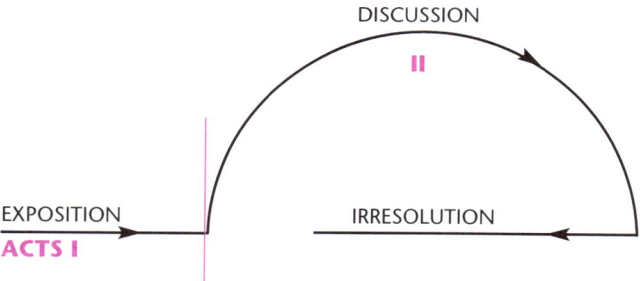

There is no rising action here which could lead to a turning point, no obstacles need to be overcome by the lovers before they can be united, and above all, there is no resolution at the end. We are almost back at where we started. There is a great deal of discussion, but it doesn't lead anywhere. It is as if the play is turning back on itself. And this is precisely what the dramatists writing in this tradition want to say – people fool themselves if they think that happy endings can be achieved. Life is essentially meaningless and therefore there can be no "direction" in which characters might be moving and none of their efforts has any value whatsoever. Consequently, those plays are based on something resembling a circular structure; at the end we are back at the beginning. The situation is just as hopeless as ever and human activities are absolutely futile.

Synopsis

Tragedy
- is a serious play which ends in disaster for the main character.
- is concerned with conflict, dilemma and suffering.
- presents a character of admirable qualities and important position who is brought low by a fault in his character.
- often relies on poetic diction for effect.

The tragic hero
- is a many-faceted and complex character.
- becomes aware at some point of the part he himself has played in bringing about his ruin.
- in his downfall reaffirms the essential dignity of human life.

The problem play
- is concerned with a particular social or moral problem.
- often deals with painful human dilemmas.
- tends to over-simplify things for the sake of dramatic effect.
- is highly popular today.

Melodrama
- is based on action and thrills.
- presents conflicts in black and white.
- presents a dream world, a world in which things come out right in the end.
- provides escape.

Comedy
- is a play with a happy ending.
- is intended to amuse and provide fun and entertainment.
- affirms life as ultimately good.
- is presented in a light-hearted fashion.
- does not show the same emotional depth as tragedy.
- can be subdivided into a number of different types.

The comedy of errors
- is based on a series of mistakes of identity or fact.
- often depends on the lavish use of disguise.

The comedy of manners
- portrays a number of current fads and foibles.
- is basically satirical in character.

Sentimental comedy
- tries to play on our sympathies.
- may be out to draw easy tears.
- is especially popular in film.

The Drama of Ideas
- is concerned with social, political, and philosophical problems.
- is basically comedy because its characters are truly comic.

The burlesque
- is written in imitation of another play.
- is presented entirely in the satirical mode.
- can appear as parody or as travesty.

Farce
- concentrates exclusively on elements of low comedy.
- is based on clowning, buffoonery, slapstick and horseplay.
- employs highly exaggerated type characters.

Symbolist drama
substitutes suggestion for direct statement.

Expressionist drama
intends to show that the surface appearance of things is important only as it reflects an inner vision.

Epic theatre
aims at making people want to change their world.

The Theatre of the Absurd
is concerned with the anxieties of individuals trying to survive in a world that is essentially meaningless.

2.4 Drama and film

2.4.1 The study of film

Most people have seen, continue to see and will in their lifetime see many more movies than they will watch theatre plays or even read books. Most people thus experience drama not primarily as theatre, but as film. Film – whether as cinema or as television – has become the dominant medium in the Western world. *Hollywood* is a household word and at various times in history, Mickey Mouse, Charlie Chaplin, Marilyn Monroe, John Wayne, Julia Roberts, Tom Hanks and a number of other film stars have been more widely known throughout the world than presidents, popes and top class athletes. The names above, thrown out with little effort, attest to the power and pervasiveness of film, especially American commercial cinema.

Since film is generally commercially oriented, however, many people feel that a study of film has nothing to commend it. They say that movies with their tendency to rely as heavily as they do on sex and violence are unworthy of study; and that Hollywood is nothing but a "dream factory." They point out that films

- routinely ignore a deeper realism

- freely use melodramatic plotting

- use sentimentalities and trite dialogue

- rely on stock characters and stock situations

- are often based on gross improbabilities.

This is however a serious misconception both of the cultural significance of film and of the value of screen education generally. The point is that visual language is too much with us to be ignored. Films are too powerfully popular with young people to be pushed aside and dismissed as worthless. People, especially young people, need to observe and interpret their world, and electronic media, least of all their form of expression, the film, cannot be excluded. Films are simply an overwhelming presence that won't go away in a hurry.

All too often what happens when one asks somebody about films they have seen and films they like, is that they talk about the narrative or action, with little sense of how the visual composition conveyed the story. In showing them how to 'read' film, we have to draw their attention to the various elements of film language.

The use and study of film has in fact become commonplace in many classrooms and with the advent of VCRs and DVDs, film has been made easily accessible. The general aim of studying film is to increase media literacy, but improving film literacy also affects the ability to interpret clues, to think critically and analytically as well as to engage in creative expression.

The key lies in a heightened awareness of screen studies as a discipline like any other, where students take popular culture seriously and learn that film criticism is both more complex and more rewarding than they had previously considered. Through this approach, similarities become apparent between screen and written texts; both provide recognition of how culture, whether popular or otherwise, intersects with the social, political and ethical dilemmas of everyday life. Rather than considering one approach academically superior, it becomes clear that each approach can be used to enhance the other.

Films are more than stories with pictures. Themes are important as is the message of the film, but what is vital and so often sadly missing in the study of film is an understanding of the way in which a story is told in film. It is vital to understand how a film director uses *camera*, *lighting* and *sound* to create a mood and to communicate his vision.

In the following diagram, an attempt is made to point out how the various aspects of literary study, dramatic analysis and the study of the cinematic approach to a work of fiction are all interrelated. So it makes sense to study the contribution of cinematic aspects, too, when dealing with a work of fictional art, especially if there is the story as text and a film version of that same story. Comparisons can then be very instructive.

Literary aspects	Dramatic aspects	Cinematic aspects
narrative	acting	camera shots
characters	costumes	camera angle
setting	scenery	camera movement
theme	location / props	sound and vision
point of view	make-up	colour / lighting
genre and mood	lighting	montage / editing

It is a well-established fact that nearly all viewers find that the study of films

- increases their enjoyment of them;

- heightens their appreciation of the effort and creativity involved in making a film;

- can also help them understand how different filmmakers have used the medium;

- shows up the medium's possibilities and limitations;

- teaches them about the various genres of fictional films, such as western and science fiction;

- helps them understand familiar films in new ways and appreciate the meaning of films in greater variety and depth.

The three aspects of study set out in the diagram above correspond to a number of questions that can be asked about a film. Here is a selection:

Literary aspects	Dramatic aspects	Cinematic aspects
Who are the characters and what is their relationship and their conflict?	Did the actors make me forget they were acting, and how did they do it?	What vivid visual images did I note, and what was my reaction to them?
Where is the story set?	Did costumes, make-up and set contribute in equal measure to the effect of the film?	What can I remember about the soundtrack? What did it make me feel in certain situations?
What is the main story line?	In what scene or scenes was an actor's voice particularly effective? How?	What scenes did not need any dialogue, and why not?
Who tells the story? Whose point of view is used?	What scene or scenes must have been particularly difficult to act? How did the actors manage? (movements and body language)	Which scenes were edited very effectively and unusually?
What is the theme of the film? What is it mainly concerned with?	In what scene was facial expression important? What feelings were expressed in this way?	Did the film use special effects, and did they add or detract from my enjoyment of the film?
What is the mood of the film?	How did the actors establish character – more through dialogue, movement or facial expression?	What unusual camera angles or camera movements did I notice? What did they signify?
What symbols did I notice?	Is this film like or unlike others by the same director? Does this director have a recognisable "style"?	How does the film use lighting? Are shadows important? Why?

From the moment people begin watching a film they start getting involved. The first few images of a film, i.e. the opening sequence, are very important as they give many clues as to what the film will be about.

- The opening shots of place and time help to put the film into some context.

- The actors provoke assumptions about their characters and roles in the film and their relationship to each other.

- The sound, which is often predominantly music at this stage (and not other noises), and the tone and beat of this again give further clues as to how the film will develop.

The viewers do all this automatically – at this stage they are extremely receptive and actively involved. Without realising it, they have entered into the world of the film and begun to read the signals that have been set up for them; they have begun to *decode the film language*.

In all language, words often have a deeper, hidden meaning behind the literal meaning of the word. They may embody a "signal" and symbolize something quite different. For instance, the sun is literally a yellowish ball in the sky, but the word "signals" to us meanings such as warmth, cheerfulness, life, etc. A teddy bear is a stuffed, brown plaything but it "signals" comfort and childhood innocence to us. These are known as the *denotative* (literal) meaning and the *connotative* (hidden signals and implications) meaning of a word.

Films use the same signals or coding systems. For instance if we see a picture of a wooden thing with branches on screen, our mind thinks "tree". If the tree is a gnarled, large, spiky and leafless image, shot in black and white, we read the signal of disaster, threat, maybe horror. If the tree is drawn in bright crayon colours and is rounded and "lollipop-like", it signals "children", "happy birds nesting", etc. to us.

The codes films make use of are not necessarily visual. The use of sudden loud music can signal that something dramatic is about to happen. An extreme close-up shot of a person's face signals that this character's reaction is very important, and so on. Most viewers have learnt to recognise many of these film codes.

Reading, i.e. decoding a film is similar to reading a book, except that instead of looking at a printed page we are looking at a cinema screen. When we watch a film we are interpreting the film language as we see it; we are considering why we think the filmmaker made certain choices and what the film means to us.

If a printed text produces a certain effect on the readers, for instance if it makes them scared, we can look closely at the way the text has been put together to see how the writer has used the tools at his disposal to create this fear. Reading a film works in exactly the same way except that the tools that are used to create meaning are different. The most important of them are the use of the *camera*, of *lighting* and of *sound*.

2.4.2 Uses of the camera

The filmmaker's camera has been likened to the writer's pen (or his typewriter or word processor); it is the main tool he has for "telling" his story. It is mainly through the lens of a camera that the viewers experience the film. The sounds mostly play a subordinate role.

The basic unit from which a film is put together is the shot, which is a single "run" of the camera. The duration of such a shot depends on its purpose and on the tempo of the sequence (i.e. a series of shots depicting one action) in which it occurs. We distinguish three basic camera shots:

- the long shot,

- the medium shot,

- and the close up shot.

In the long shot, also known as *wide shot* or *establishing shot*, the camera is placed at a certain distance from the subject being filmed so that the whole scene can be taken in. The long shot is often used to show the place in which action will occur, frequently at the beginning of a scene or sequence. It can thus set the stage for the action and the viewer gets something like an overview of the location of the action, especially if the long shot is combined with a *panning movement* of the camera (for details see below) to show an even wider area.

The medium shot is a middle distance shot in which the camera is placed nearer the subject and it focuses the viewer's attention on this subject. The camera is close enough to pick up detail, though still far enough away to allow the viewers to follow the actors' movements. The medium shot is very useful if the aim is to let the viewers have a closer look at a subject.

The close up shot moves the camera very close to the subject or scene and is thus great for showing detail, such as a person's facial expression. It is consequently often employed to show a character's emotions or his reactions to something he witnesses or is told about.

Of course, there are any number of gradations between these basic types of shot, which are also known as field sizes. These field sizes help determine what details will be noticeable, what objects will be included and excluded from the frame, and how large the subject will appear within the frame. By changing the field size (the camera distance) between shots or even during a shot, filmmakers can change perspective – the relative size and apparent depth of objects in the photographic image.

It is quite astonishing what different effects can be achieved with different field sizes, especially if they are combined with other uses of the camera, such as different camera movements, which are significant for creating meaning.

The panning shot already mentioned, i.e. a camera movement from side to side from a stationary position around the vertical axis, can lead smoothly from one image to the next or from one character to another. If the camera is moved up and down, for instance to show the height of a building, we speak of a tilt.

More commonly known is the zoom, which is often used for a close-up of a face to suggest emotion. Technically speaking, it does not really describe a camera movement because the camera as such is not moved at all. The zoom effect is produced by a system of lenses whose focal length is adjusted during the shot. When the camera *zooms in*, the viewers are shown more and more detail, when it *zooms out* (reverse zoom), the shot is moved further and further away.

Generally speaking, filmmakers and their cameramen use shots with movement sparingly. Rapid pans, tilts and repeated zooms might make the viewer woozy or at least disoriented.

Significant meaning can be created by a number of camera angles. The shot angle is the level from which the cameraman looks at the subject through his camera. We distinguish

- eye-level angle shots
- high angle shots
- low angle shots.

Eye-level angle is the perspective most familiar to all of us – we usually see things from our own eye-level. It is a neutral angle, not usually suggesting anything about the person filmed. It is frequently employed to convey the idea of realism, authenticity and objectivity.

This is different in the case of a low angle shot, in which people and objects are filmed from below. The fact that the camera looks up at the subject makes it seem important and powerful to the viewer, or perhaps larger than it really is.

In the high angle shot, the camera looks down on the subject, making it seem smaller and less important. In an extreme form, it becomes a *bird's eye view*.

The exact shot framed by the cinematographer can communicate a number of things to the viewer. It can suggest power or weakness, for instance. Or it can give the impression that someone is bigger and more important or weak or smaller and less significant, as the case may be.

The meaning or general significance of all these shots in cinematographic terms can be summarized like this:

Shot	Definition	General significance
long shot	shows setting and characters	suggests context, scope, public distance
medium shot	(most of the) body	shows relationships
close-up	shows face only	creates intimacy, shows emotions
panning shot	camera moves horizontally	gives overview, takes in everything
tilt	camera moves vertically	suggests height
zoom in	camera moves in	provides a focus, shows detail
eye-level angle	camera is at eye level	suggests authenticity and objectivity
low angle	camera looks up	conveys an impression of power and influence
high angle	camera looks down	conveys a sense of smallness, weakness

Special effects can be achieved with different camera lenses. Wide-angle, normal and telephoto lenses all have different properties and create different images.

Wide-angle lenses tend to suggest that something is not right, they emphasise distances between subjects or between subjects and setting. The *normal lens* causes minimum distortion of image and movement and is thus ideal for creating images that are close to what the human eye would see in the same circumstances. When a *telephoto lens* is used, however, only the objects close to the camera are in focus, whereas the sides of the image are not, especially when a shallow focus is used.

A slightly blurred shot makes the subject seem more attractive. If this is the intention, *diffusers* may be placed in from of the camera lens to soften facial lines – to glamorise or to lend a more spiritual or ethereal look. The possibilities seem endless.

A special effect can be achieved with a hand-held camera. If the director is interested in creating a sense of anxiety or confusion, he may want to exploit the unsteady movement of a hand held camera. A hand-held shot in which a character is approached from behind often suggests that someone is being followed and is about to be pounced upon.

A shot is normally ended with a cut, a simple switch from one image to the next. Other possibilities of linking shots are the fade-in, in which the screen is black at the beginning, but gradually gets brighter and brighter. Fade-out is the opposite movement, of course. When the filmmaker opts for a dissolve, the first image gradually disappears (fades out), while another appears (fades in) so that for a few moments the two are superimposed.

2.4.3 Other aspects of cinematic art

The use of lighting effects is a well-established way of creating mood and atmosphere in film. Light and shade are important codes of meaning and are major signifiers of genres. (By *genre* we mean the kind of narrative being presented, e.g. detective, sci-fi, western, feature film, etc.). Since film, like theatre, presents absorbing and interesting stories to which people can relate but tends to massively oversimplify reality by grouping people into "good guys" and "bad guys", the lighting generally follows suit. What we get in films is *hard lighting*, which is used to create unflattering images of people, and *soft lighting*, which tends to be flattering because it fills in imperfections in the surface of the subject and obliterates or lessens sharp lines and shadows.

Hard lighting, also known as *high-key lighting*, is achieved when the light comes directly from a source, whereas soft light, or *low-key lighting*, comes from an indirect source. High-key lighting leads to bright illumination of the person and often creates a harsh image of that person, but it can also create or enhance a cheerful mood, depending on the situation. Low-key lighting, by contrast, involves little illumination on the subject and can often reinforce a dramatic or mysterious effect or create a romantic atmosphere. The mood and meaning of an image can be changed by the direction from which light reaches the subject.

Like hard or soft light, shadows can be used expressively in a number of ways, for instance to create a mysterious and threatening environment.

Much the same goes for the use of colour. Colour associations vary from culture to culture, and the impact of a particular colour depends on the context – where and how the colour is used. In Western society

- warm colours, namely reds, oranges, and yellows, tend to be thought of as hot, dangerous, lively, and assertive;

- greens, blues, and violets are generally characterised as cool, but they are also associated with safety, reason, control and relaxation, and sometimes with sadness or melancholy.

Extra effects can be achieved if colour is saturated, i.e. intense and vivid, or if it is de-saturated, i.e. muted, dull and pale.

When shooting is finished the individual parts of the film must be joined together to create the film as the spectators will see it. The process by which this is achieved is known as editing. It involves decisions about which shots to include, the most effective take of each shot, the arrangement and duration of shots, and the transitions between them. We must bear in mind here that the individual shots are generally shot out of sequence, i.e. not in the order as we later see them. So they need to be edited after filming to make sense.

Underlying the process is a technique known as *pairing*, i.e. a story is built up by alternating one set of shots with another. Common instances of pairing include

- a conversation or confrontation between two characters. The shots alternate from one to the other; camera angles may be used to suggest inferiority (high level shot) or superiority (low level shot).

- shots of a character alternated with shots of what this character sees. The first shot of the character serves as the point of view, i.e. it establishes who is looking.

- *cross-cutting*, which is a sequence of shots alternating between two different locations. This technique is employed in many situations, for instance when a criminal is creeping into a house where an unsuspecting victim lies sleeping. The cross-cutting builds to a climax and of course ends with the two cuts coming together.

An important consideration in the process of editing is the *editing speed* (tempo). We can distinguish between *fast editing* and *slow editing*. The cuts are very short in fast editing, lasting only for a second or two. In this manner excitement and anticipation are built up, as for example in a chase sequence. Slow editing, by contrast, has much longer shots of about 3 to 10 seconds' duration so that the opposite effect is achieved – not exciting but calming and relaxing the viewer. Slow editing is typical of love scenes, for instance.

The placing of separate shots together to create a meaningful relationship between them, but not a continuous reality is known as montage [mɒn'taːʒ].

A montage is frequently used to compress time, i.e. a number of facts are established in one sequence, or film may begin with a montage which establishes a particular time and place. Using the technique of montage, a director can also show, for instance, what is going on in a character's mind. Various methods of montage can be employed.

- *Continuity edits*, especially *matched cuts*, where two shots seem naturally and smoothly to fit together, make the editing process almost unnoticeable; they create a realistic and seamless flow of the story where one event leads "naturally" to the next.

- *Jump edits*, by contrast, are dramatic edits emphasising the difference between subjects; using this method, the cutter, *the editing specialist, cuts from one person to the next without transition.*

- *Parallel editing*, also known as *cross-cutting*, allows the filmmaker to follow different actions at the same time, i.e. the shots of several scenes are intermingled. Parallel editing can be used to achieve various ends, including to give a sense of simultaneous events, contrast two actions or viewpoints or create suspense about whether one subject will achieve a goal before another subject does.

- *Flashbacks* and, to some extent, *flash-forwards* enable the director to insert scenes or sequences from the past into the narrative present tense of the film action or scenes that have a future reference, as the case may be.

- Particularly common is a sound edit known as a *sound-bridge*, in which the sound from one shot is carried on into the next to create a sham continuity.

Generally speaking, the addition of a sound track is a most important element in film production. There is first of all the sound that is part of the scene itself, wind noise, for instance, but filmmakers also love to use extra sound elements from off screen. The four major components of the sound track are

- dialogue

- music

- sound effects

- and silence.

The use of *dialogue* is essential in the theatre (or when a play is broadcast on the radio); it is invaluable for revealing character – a character's ideas, goals, fears, and dreams. Dialogue is certainly also very important in film, yet many films rely far more on visuals and use vocals (dialogue) to a lesser extent.

Music can be used in countless ways in films – at different volumes, in varying tempos, and by different instruments. It may be employed to highlight a film's central conflict, establish time and place, suggest what a character is like, direct the viewer's attention, and in many other ways. Soft violin music, for instance, tends to evoke a romantic atmosphere.

Sound effects are sounds other than the human voice or music. There are many possible uses for them. They can help to intensify a mood, enhance a situation, create a sense of location, and so on. Unusually loud footsteps in a thriller or a horror movie, for instance, are likely to increase the suspense and create a spooky atmosphere.

Even *silence* – the absence of sound – may be put to good use by filmmakers. It can, for instance, be employed during the showing of dreams, it can be used to suggest dying or death, and it can generally be employed when a break in the regular rhythm of the sounds of everyday life appears to be indicated.

2.4.4 The production of a film

Fictional films (i.e. non-documentary films) are based on a script, which may be an original story but more often is not. A film script is usually based on

- historical events
- a fictional work (most commonly a novel)
- a (theatre) play
- a TV show or series
- other films.

Much more so than in the theatre where the director and his staff expect a dramatist to provide them with a fully-fledged play, the scriptwriter working on a film script prepares a text that only gives a rough indication of the settings, the action and dialogue and some of the camera work. The finished film will more often than not be quite different from this script, which is hardly more than a first draft. In the end it is rarely clear who contributed exactly what, but shooting a film is much more of a communal effort than is the preparation of a play.

When a screenplay has been approved for production by a major studio, the director begins to work it through, trying to imagine how it might play out on screen. A good script is the foundation for a good film, but even the best one needs to be developed to work well in the cinema. Sometimes the producer will develop a script and then hand it over to the director. In other cases, the director may work with the writer early on to help develop a script from its infancy. Nowadays, the planning for a film is often underway before there is a script. A director or producer purchases the rights to a story and then hires a screenwriter. Whatever the route from script to screen, it is the director's vision that shapes the look and feel of a film. He is the creative force that holds a film together and he is ultimately responsible for turning the words of a script into images on the screen.

One of his first jobs is to assemble the cast and crew for the film. Both the actors and the crew who will make things work behind the scenes, are crucial to the film's success. The right people will understand and respect the director's vision, work well with one another, and bring their own unique talents to the filmmaking process.

- A production designer is responsible for the believability of a film's scenery and sets. In essence, the production designer is the architect of the film, working to make the director's vision a reality. The production designer also works closely with the art director and set decorator, making certain all the visual details are accurate and the style and period of the film reflect the director's wishes.

- The cinematographer [sɪnəməˈtɒɡrəfə], or director of photography, helps to translate the director's vision to film, scene by scene, planning shots and supervising camera operators. His job is to create and capture the images that best tell the story.

- In the end it is the actors who will bring the story to life. The film's producer normally hires the crew, but the director will usually be consulted over crucial hires such as the lead actors. Often a casting director or producer will help select the cast.

After months of development, delays, and rewrites, the final script is set and the film goes into pre-production. During this phase,

- budgets are detailed

- scenes are planned and designed

- a shooting schedule is drawn up

- storyboards – visual representations of every shot – are prepared.

This is to say that even before a single frame is shot, the film is planned from beginning to end on paper. The final stages of pre-production include periods of rehearsal, set construction, and finding the best locations.

Before shooting can begin, the set must be constructed by a group of specialists known as the "swing gang". Quite a number of people must contribute to get the scene done, each of whom has an important role in the making of the movie.

- The *cinematographer* is responsible for the lighting, choice of film, correct exposure, correct use of lenses, and supervision of the camera crew.

- The *mixer* is responsible for recording the sound.

- Other sounds are added during post-production by *foley artists*. They are the people who create and record many of the sound effects. Sound effects are rarely recorded at the same time as dialogue and action, since the sound mix is so difficult to balance; the foley artist listens to the dialogue track for the (usually quite faint) sounds of footsteps, for instance, a door slam, etc. and records them onto a new track in synch with the action on screen. The foley artist also adds sounds that may not exist at all on the original track: for instance, thumping watermelons or cracking bamboo to create the sounds of a fight.

- The *gaffer* is responsible for making sure all the lighting equipment is where it should be and operating correctly. The gaffer sets the lights so that the finished picture will have the desired effect.

- The *key grip* is responsible for the rigging (carpentry) and for moving and getting the sets and the camera ready.

- The *set dresser* decorates the set.

- The *property master* ensures the sets and actors have all the necessary dressing and props.

- The *wardrobe master* is responsible for all wardrobe needs.

- The *make-up person* is responsible for all make-up.

- The *assistant director* keeps order on the set and makes sure the production moves according to schedule. Sometimes this involves prodding the director to finish the shots planned for a particular day, or hunting down actors if they are not where they should be on the set.

The film industry has developed a special jargon for the individual actions that go into producing a shot.

When a scene has been rehearsed several times and the director is finally satisfied, he says, "Let's go for a take." The assistant director yells, "Quiet on the set!" The actors who appear in a particular scene move to their position. "Roll it," says the assistant director. Someone says, "Rolling." "Speed," says someone else. "Thirty-five, take one." An assistant holds a slate in front of the actor's face and snaps it shut. This "clacker" will later help the film editor in synchronizing the picture to the sound. "Action!" commands the director. Seconds later, the director calls out, "Cut. Do it again." The process is repeated until the director yells, "Cut. Print it."

The film shot that day is sent to a lab where it is processed and made into "dailies." Dailies are film clips that are viewed after each day's work in order to evaluate performances and spot any technical problems.

Once shooting is over, hundreds of thousands of feet of film need to be assembled into a coherent story. Days or weeks of shooting result in only a few minutes of screen time. On average, the director will be able to complete filming for about three script pages per day, or the equivalent of about three minutes of screen time. In the editing room, the film and sound editor will complete the detailed technical work required at this stage. The "director's cut" of the film (the one the director works with the editor to create) may not be the final one the audience sees. The producers may decide to cut certain scenes or use a different film clip for a certain effect.

Occasionally, a director dislikes the final cut and decides not to be listed in the credits. If this happens, the credits list Alan Smithee as the director. Alan Smithee is not a real person, but an alias used as a substitute when a director refuses to be linked to a film.

Factors in the production of a feature film

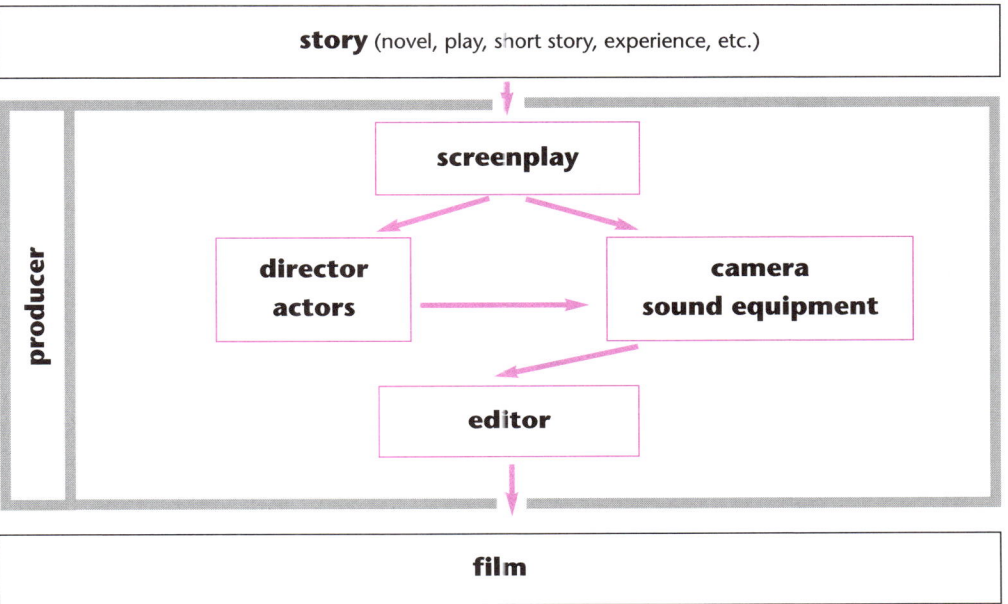

Synopsis

Film
- has become the dominant medium in the Western world.
- is powerfully popular.

The viewers
- must learn to "read" (decode) a film.
- ought to become familiar with film language.
- need to know about the codes used in film.

The camera
- is the filmmaker's main tool.
- is equivalent to / comparable to the writer's pen.

Field sizes
- The **long shot** (wide shot, establishing shot)
  - provides an overview of the location of the action.
  - can set the stage for the action.

- The **medium shot**
  - lets the viewers have a closer look at a subject.
  - focuses attention on the subject.

- The **close up shot**
  - is great for showing detail.
  - can show a character's emotions.

Camera movements
- The *panning shot* can lead smoothly from one image to the next.
- The *tilt* can provide a good impression of heights.
- The *zoom* can provide a close up or move the subject further and further away.

Camera angles
- The *eye level angle* conveys realism, authenticity and objectivity.
- The *low angle shot* makes subjects seem important and powerful.
- The *high angle shot* makes subjects seem smaller and less important.

Special effects can be achieved through the use of
- different camera lenses.
- a hand held camera.
- shadows.
- colour associations.

Lighting effects
- can be divided up into hard lighting and soft lighting.
- can create mood and atmosphere.

The sound track includes dialogue, music, sound effects and silence.

The script
- is no more than a first draft.
- needs to be developed to work well in the cinema.

The director
- is the creative force that holds a film together.
- is ultimately responsible for turning words into visual images.
- is supported in his work by the actors and the production team.

Editing
- involves decisions about
  - which shots to include.
  - the most effective take of each shot.
  - the arrangement and duration of shots.
  - the transitions between them.
- can be used
  - to promote continuity or disruptions.
  - to superimpose images.
  - to juxtapose shots to make a point, support a feeling or mood, intensify the viewer's reactions, or show parallel events.
  - to affect the viewer's sense of space, compress or expand time and convey an enormous amount of information in a brief time.

2.5 The interpretation of drama

It is customary to present for interpretation not a full-length drama but only a selected passage. There are usually several assignments attached to that passage so that various aspects of the dramatic text will have to be analysed. Typical assignments refer to aspects like

- the *structure* of the passage,

- the underlying *conflict*,

- the *characters* and the way they are presented,

- the contribution the passage can make to the general *theme*,

- the *genre* problem – what type of drama the play seems to belong to.

There may well be other assignments, of course, some of them going far beyond the text, asking for instance about the historical, social and generally the cultural background of the play, or demanding a comparison with another work, and so on.

If a film version of the scene is available, it will be useful to study how the filmmaker has used camera and sound track to guide the viewers and create the images he was interested in.

- Why has he filmed the scene the way he has?

- What can individual shots tell us about his intentions?

The following passage from the fourth act of *The Importance of Being Earnest* by Oscar Wilde (1854 – 1900) can be seen as fairly typical:

Jack Worthing wants to marry Gwendolen, Lady Bracknell's daughter, but she refuses to give her consent. Algernon Moncrieff, Lady Bracknell's nephew, wants to marry Cecily Cardew, Jack's ward, but Lady Bracknell again disapproves at first, on the grounds that Cecily is not from the right social class.

LADY BRACKNELL. ... May I ask, Mr. Worthing, who is that young person whose hand my nephew Algernon is now holding in what seems to me a peculiarly unnecessary manner?

JACK. ... That lady is Miss Cecily Cardew, my ward. *(Lady Bracknell bows coldly to Cecily.)*

ALGERNON. I am engaged to be married to Cecily, Aunt Augusta.

LADY BRACKNELL. I beg your pardon?

CECILY. Mr. Moncrieff and I are engaged to be married, Lady Bracknell.

LADY BRACKNELL *(with a shiver, crossing to the sofa and sitting down)*. I do not know whether there is anything peculiarly exciting in the air of this particular part of Hertfordshire, but the number of engagements that go on seems to me considerably above the proper average that statistics have laid down for our guidance. I think some preliminary inquiry on my part would not be out of place. Mr. Worthing, is Miss Cardew at all connected with any of the larger railway stations in London? I merely desire information. Until yesterday I had no idea that there were any families or persons whose origin was a Terminus.

(Jack looks perfectly furious, but restrains himself.)

JACK *(in a clear, cold voice)*. Miss Cardew is the granddaughter of the late Mr. Thomas Cardew of 149 Belgrave Square, S. W.; Gervase Park, Dorking, Surrey; and The Sporran, Fifeshire, N. B.

LADY BRACKNELL. That sounds not unsatisfactory. Three addresses always inspire confidence, even in tradesmen. But what proof have I of their authenticity?

JACK. I have carefully preserved the Court Guides of the period. They are open to your inspection, Lady Bracknell.

LADY BRACKNELL *(grimly)*. I have known strange errors in that publication.

JACK. Miss Cardew's family solicitors are Messrs. Markby, Markby, and Markby.

LADY BRACKNELL. Markby, Markby, and Markby? A firm of the very highest position in their profession. Indeed I am told that one of the Mr. Markby's is occasionally to be seen at dinner-parties. So far I am satisfied.

JACK *(very irritably)*. How extremely kind of you, Lady Bracknell! I have also in my possession, you will be pleased to hear, certificates of Miss Cardew's birth, baptism, whooping cough, registration, vaccination, confirmation, and the measles; both the German and the English variety.

LADY BRACKNELL. Ah, a life crowded with incident, I see; though perhaps somewhat too exciting for a young girl. I am not myself in favour of premature experiences. *(Rises, looks at her watch.)* Gwendolen! The time approaches for our departure. We have not a moment to lose. As a matter of form, Mr. Worthing, I had better ask you if Miss Cardew has any little fortune?

JACK. Oh! About a hundred and thirty thousand pounds in the Funds. That is all. Goodbye, Lady Bracknell. So pleased to have seen you.

LADY BRACKNELL *(sitting down again).* A moment, Mr. Worthing. A hundred and thirty thousand pounds! And in the Funds! Miss Cardew seems to me a most attractive young lady, now that I look at her. Few girls of the present day have any really solid qualities, any of the qualities that last, and improve with time. We live, I regret to say, in an age of surfaces. *(To Cecily.)* Come over here, dear. *(Cecily goes across.)* Pretty child! Your dress is sadly simple, and your hair seems almost as Nature might have left it. But we can soon alter all that. A thoroughly experienced French maid produces a really marvellous result in a very brief space of time. I remember recommending one to young Lady Lancing, and after three months her own husband did not know her.

JACK. And after six months nobody knew her.

LADY BRACKNELL *(glares at Jack for a few moments. Then bends, with a practised smile, to Cecily).* Kindly turn round, sweet child. *(Cecily turns completely round.)* No, the side view is what I want. *(Cecily presents her profile.)* Yes, quite as I expected. There are distinct social possibilities in your profile. The two weak points in our age are its want of principle and its want of profile. The chin a little higher, dear. Style largely depends on the way the chin is worn. They are worn very high, just at present. Algernon!

ALGERNON. Yes, Aunt Augusta?

LADY BRACKNELL. There are distinct social possibilities in Miss Cardew's profile.

ALGERNON. Cecily is the sweetest, dearest, prettiest girl in the whole world. And I don't care twopence about social possibilities.

LADY BRACKNELL. Never speak disrespectfully of Society, Algernon. Only people who can't get into it do that. *(To Cecily.)* Dear child, of course you know that Algernon has nothing but his debts to depend upon. But I do not approve of mercenary marriages. When I married Lord Bracknell I had no fortune of any kind. But I never dreamed for a moment of allowing that to stand in my way. Well, I suppose I must give my consent.

ALGERNON. Thank you, Aunt Augusta.

LADY BRACKNELL. Cecily, you may kiss me!

CECILY *(kisses her).* Thank you, Lady Bracknell.

LADY BRACKNELL. You may also address me as Aunt Augusta for the future.

CECILY. Thank you, Aunt Augusta.

LADY BRACKNELL. The marriage, I think, had better take place quite soon.

ALGERNON. Thank you, Aunt Augusta

CECILY. Thank you, Aunt Augusta.

LADY BRACKNELL. To speak frankly, I am not in favour of long engagements. They give people the opportunity of finding out each other's character before marriage, which I think is never advisable. [...]

Notes

Oscar Wilde (1854 – 1900): playwright, poet, story-writer, essayist – *ward:* G Mündel – *preliminary inquiry:* a few questions to start with – *persons whose origin was a Terminus:* as a baby Jack Worthing was found abandoned in a bag at Victoria Station – *whooping cough:* G Keuchhusten – *German measles:* G Röteln – *a life crowded with incident:* a life full of activity – *premature:* before the right time – *in the Funds:* G in festverzinslichen Wertpapieren – *I don't care twopence:* I don't care in the least, I couldn't care less – *mercenary marriage:* when somebody marries for money

Assignments

1. Analyse the *structure* (different parts and development of action) of this passage from Oscar Wilde's play.

2. What *conflict* is behind this passage?

3. How are the two women, Cecily and Lady Bracknell, portrayed in this passage? Take into consideration the direct and indirect *characterization*.

4. Compare Algernon's and Lady Bracknell's attitudes towards marriage (= *theme*) as revealed in this text.

5. What *type of play* does Wilde's drama seem to belong to?

Suggested answers

1. Analyse the *structure* (different parts and development of action) of this passage from Oscar Wilde's play.

● two different parts:
  – before the announcement of Cecily's fortune;
  – after this announcement.

● Development of action:
  – Lady B. strictly against the marriage of Algernon and Cecily;
  – turning point: Cecily has a fortune of £130,000 in the Funds;
  – reversal of the situation: Lady B. now all in favour of the marriage, which is to take place as quickly as possible.

Possible answer:
The passage is divided into two distinct parts – before and after the announcement of Cecily's fortune and the action develops accordingly.

When Cecily is first introduced to Lady Bracknell as Algernon's fiancée, she is treated with arrogant and sarcastic contempt. Lady Bracknell pretends not to have heard properly ("I beg your pardon?"), attributes the engagement to something "peculiarly exciting in the air of this particular part of Hertfordshire", and inquires whether Cecily has anything to do with London railway stations. Not even the information concerning Cecily's solid family connections can sway her, but a turning point comes when Jack tells her of Cecily's large fortune. A reversal of the situation takes place then, and Lady Bracknell is suddenly all in favour of a marriage between Algernon and Cecily, and as quickly as possible.

2. What *conflict* is behind this passage?

● conflict between the characters:
  – Jack, Algernon, Cecily: Algernon wants to marry Jack's ward Cecily
  – Lady Bracknell: refuses to give her consent

● conflict between different views of society and of life generally:
  – Jack, Algernon, Cecily: opposed to the snobbish attitude and behaviour of the "polite society"; interested in achieving personal happiness
  – Lady Bracknell: sees membership of society and belonging to the right class as the only goal in life; interested in "social possibilities"

Possible answer:

There is first of all a conflict between characters. Algernon would like to marry Cecily, Jack's ward, but Lady Bracknell refuses to give her consent. There is however a deeper conflict behind it. It concerns different attitudes towards life generally and towards society. Algernon declares quite openly that he doesn't "care twopence about social possibilities" and is interested in Cecily only because she "is the sweetest, dearest, prettiest girl in the whole world." He puts the achievement of personal happiness first.

Lady Bracknell on the other hand firmly puts money first and apparently believes that marrying into money and moving in the "right circles" will make a person happy. She despises people who she thinks are the wrong class and cares more for outward appearance and "social possibilities" than for a person's intrinsic qualities.

3. How are the two women, Cecily and Lady Bracknell, portrayed in this passage? Take into consideration the direct and indirect *characterization*.

Character in drama may be established through

-   the character's physical appearance, the clothes he / she wears and the objects he / she has surrounded himself / herself with
-   through the other characters' hints and comments
-   through the character's own dialogue and actions

Direct characterization is used when

-   other characters provide information
-   they comment on his or her past or present actions

Indirect characterization occurs when

-   a character reveals his / her nature and shows his / her opinions, attitudes and feelings, but also his / her social and educational level in the dialogue he / she has been given
-   a character establishes his nature by his actions, i.e. by what he / she does, or fails to do, or chooses not to do

Direct characterization of Cecily:
-   through various remarks by Jack concerning her social position and her financial situation
-   through Algernon's comments about her

Indirect characterization of Cecily:
- through her outward appearance ("your dress is sadly simple and your hair seems almost as Nature might have left it")
- through her modest and even humble behaviour:
    - she is rich, but does not parade her wealth
    - she obeys Lady Bracknell and turns around
    - she kisses her and calls her Aunt Augusta
    - she probably does not like her, but does not show it
- through her marrying Algernon even though he is poor

Direct characterization of Lady Bracknell – is not the case here

Indirect characterization of Lady Bracknell:
- through her language
- through her behaviour.

language:
- She refers to Cecily as "that young person"
- she uses stilted language (to underline her social superiority), e.g. "I think some preliminary inquiry on my part would not be out of place" or "That sounds not unsatisfactory"
- she begins using shorter and less complicated sentences as her excitement grows
- after hearing of Cecily's fortune she calls her "dear", "pretty child", "sweet child", "dear" and "dear child" again

behaviour:
- she "bows coldly to Cecily"
- shivers and crosses to the sofa to sit down as if she were really shocked
- pretends not to understand that Algernon is indeed engaged
- her excitement is growing, but she pretends to be in a great hurry ("Rises, looks at her watch")
- sits down again quickly after being told of Cecily's fortune
- "bends, with a practised smile, to Cecily"
- mentions "distinct social possibilities" for her
- gives her consent to the marriage
- asks Cecily to kiss her and to call her Aunt Augusta

Possible answer:

Cecily is directly characterized by the various remarks made by Jack Worthing concerning her social standing, which is good, and her financial situation, which is brilliant, and by the way Algernon speaks of her, namely that she is "the sweetest, dearest, prettiest girl in the whole world …".

But Cecily is also indirectly characterised both by her outward appearance and her behaviour. She is rich, but does not parade her wealth and generally behaves modestly and even humbly. Thus, for instance, she obeys Lady Bracknell's order to turn around; she even kisses her and calls her Aunt Augusta. Although she most probably does not like Lady Bracknell she does not show it. Also, she is willing to marry Algernon even though he is poor.

In short, she is a thoroughly pleasant character and the perfect counter-part to Lady Bracknell.

Lady Bracknell, by contrast, presents herself as a society snob and a schemer through her language and her behaviour.

At first, when she is still opposed to Algernon's marriage to Cecily, she refers to her as "that young person" and, to underline the social distance between them, uses stilted language when inquiring about her background. At this point her whole behaviour is still quite cold. She "bows coldly to Cecily", shivers and crosses to the sofa to sit down as if she were really shocked. Her unkind behaviour towards Cecily also shows when she pretends not to understand that Algernon is indeed engaged to Cecily and when she asks questions about the girl as if she were not present.

When she is informed of Cecily's social position, however, her excitement seems to grow, which becomes evident in her exclamation "Markby, Markby, and Markby?" and her statement "So far I am satisfied." She also begins to use shorter and less complicated sentences, which further demonstrates her excitement.

When she hears that Cecily is not only from a good family but has a vast fortune, her behaviour changes completely. She smiles at her, calls her "dear", "pretty child", "sweet child" and "dear child", says she can see "distinct social possibilities" for her, and gives her consent to the marriage. She allows Cecily to kiss her and to call her Aunt Augusta, accepting her as a member of the family.

In sum, Cecily appears to be a thoroughly pleasant character and is the positive counterpart to Lady Bracknell who characterises herself as a snob, a schemer and a highly superficial person who is interested in little else apart from "social possibilities."

4. Compare Algernon's and Lady Bracknell's attitudes towards marriage *(= theme)* as revealed in this text.

● Algernon:
    – wants to marry for love (cf. his statement "Cecily is the sweetest, dearest, prettiest girl in the whole world. And I don't give twopence about social possibilities."
    – He regards marriage as a way to happiness.

● Lady Bracknell:
    – sees marriage as a means of social promotion (for Cecily, because her nephew has aristocratic connections)
    – but also views marriage as a means of gaining material advantages (for Algernon, for he is penniless)

Possible answer:
Algernon's and Lady Bracknell's attitudes towards marriage as they are revealed in this text could not be more different. Algernon wants to marry for love and regards marriage as a way to happiness. Lady Bracknell, on the other hand, sees marriage exclusively from a socio-economic perspective. For her, marriage is a means of achieving social promotion (Cecily is going to marry into an aristocratic family) and of gaining material advantages (Algernon will profit from Cecily's fortune, as he himself is penniless).

5. What *type of play* does Wilde's drama seem to belong to?

Comic effects based on language:
● "… that young person whose hand … Algernon is now holding in what seems to be a peculiarly unnecessary manner?"
● "… the number of engagements that go on seems to me considerably above the proper average that statistics have laid down for our guidance."
● "Ah, a life crowded with incident, I see; though perhaps somewhat too exciting for a young girl."

In all these instances, the language used to describe a particular situation is not in keeping with that situation.

Comic effects based on contrast:
● "A firm of the very highest position in their profession. Indeed I am told that one of the Mr. Markby's is occasionally seen at dinner-parties." ["highest position in their profession" and being seen at dinner parties form a ludicrous contrast]

- "As a matter of form, Mr. Worthing, I had better ask you if Miss Cardew has any little fortune? … A hundred and thirty thousand pounds! And in the Funds! Miss Cardew seems to me a most attractive young lady, now that I look at her." [Lady Bracknell's turnaround comes very suddenly and unexpectedly, which creates a comic effect]
- "Few girls of the present age have any really solid qualities, …" ["solid" here seen ironically – not in the sense of solid character, but in the sense of financial position]
- We live, I regret to say, in an age of surfaces." [contrast between what she says and what she herself stands for]
- "I do not approve of mercenary marriages. When I married Lord Bracknell I had no fortune of any kind. But I never dreamed for a moment of allowing that to stand in my way." [a paradoxical statement]
- "To speak frankly, I am not in favour of long engagements. They give people the opportunity of finding out each other's character before marriage …" [contrast between general expectations and the reason Lady Bracknell gives].

Comic effects based on Lady Bracknell as a comic figure:
- the way she speaks produces a comic effect
- the way she behaves reinforces this comic effect
- her use of language and her behaviour are both distorted and incongruous – this makes her a figure of fun and not a serious character

Possible answer:
Various elements in the passage clearly mark the play out as belonging to the genre of comedy. They concern the use of language, which produces a comic effect, the introduction of a number of contrasts, which reinforce the comic tone of the play, and the character of Lady Bracknell, of course; she can be seen as a truly comic figure so that the general impression of the play is that it is quite clearly a comedy.

There are many instances of comic effects being produced by an unusual use of language in the passage. Right at the beginning of the passage Lady Bracknell's question, "May I ask, Mr. Worthing, who is that young person whose hand my nephew Algernon is now holding in what seems to me a peculiarly unnecessary manner?" is a case in point. It is difficult to imagine lovers holding hands in a "necessary" or "unnecessary" fashion – the whole question is ludicrous. And much the same is true of Lady Bracknell's statement that "the number of engagements that go on seems to [her] considerably above the average that statistics have laid down for our guidance." The statement is farcical and bears little resemblance to ordinary dialogue or to ordinary sentiments – as if lovers had ever been guided in their relationships by statistical evidence. In those two examples (and in many more instances throughout the text), the language used to describe a particular situation is not in keeping with that situation.

Many of the comic effects in the passage result from the competent use of contrast. One instance occurs when Lady Bracknell seems to be in a great hurry, but the moment she hears of Cecily's financial situation she suddenly has all the time in the world and sits down again. Here the comic effect derives from the contrast between her prejudices against Cecily and her unexpected fascination with her money. Her prejudices seem to disappear in a flash and she suddenly finds Cecily very attractive. Another comic effect originates from the contrast between Lady Bracknell's obvious attitude towards money and marriage and her statement that she does not approve of mercenary marriages, since it is only too evident that she wants Algernon to marry the girl only for her wealth. There are many more examples of contrasts in the passage.

Finally, Lady Bracknell presents herself as a figure of fun, as a truly comic figure. Her statements are often ironical and paradoxical, usually in an inappropriate register, and the reversal from cold disdain to warm-hearted and almost gushing acceptance of Cecily too sudden and unexpected for her to be believable as a serious character.

All these factors point to the play being a comedy.

Useful language material

▪ Structure
- The passage divides into … paragraphs.
- The text can be divided into … distinct parts.
- The text falls into two main parts.
- The action is developed in several steps.
- The turning point is reached when …
- There is a reversal of the situation when it is revealed that …
- A reversal of the situation takes place at this point.

▪ Conflict
- The characters are locked in a conflict.
- There is conflict between … and …
- The conflict concerns different attitudes towards …
- The conflict is based on different ideas on …
- The conflict seems insoluble at this point.
- The conflict involves a dilemma for the main character.
- There is a deeper conflict behind this situation.

▰ Character
- The hero is a complex, three-dimensional character.
- The main character is a round character.
- He / She is shown as a many-faceted individual.
- The personality and motivation of X are fully established.
- A is a subordinate / minor character.
- B is no more than a type / stock character.
- C appears to be two-dimensional or flat.
- D is constructed round a single idea or quality, namely …

▰ Characterisation
- may be attempted in a number of ways.
- can be achieved by various methods.
- is sometimes attempted in extensive stage directions.
- may be helped along by the character's physical appearance.
- is often made easier when other characters make comments about a particular character (direct characterisation).
- is most frequently based on what the character says and does (indirect characterisation).

▰ Theme
- The passage is about …
- The general theme of the passage is …
- The play addresses / deals with the problem of …
- The dramatist explores the theme of … in his play.
- The writer is concerned with / discusses … in this play.
- The playwright obviously follows a strong moral interest here.

▰ Type of play
- This play is a comedy / tragedy / tragicomedy.
- The play belongs to the genre of comedy.
- The writer has devised a play action that is full of high comedy.
- The dramatist introduces a comic effect when …
- The playwright has invented a number of comic characters for his play.
- The tone of the play marks it out as a comedy.

3 Fiction

3.1 The concept of fiction

"Fiction" is a complex term with many overlapping uses.

- Often it is taken to refer exclusively to novels, short stories and other works of prose writing,

- sometimes short narrative forms like anecdotes, fables and parables are also included under this heading.

- Frequently the term "fiction" is used synonymously with the term "novel."

- In an inclusive sense, "fiction" is any literary narrative (whether in prose or in verse) that is invented instead of being an account of events that really happened.

In this section, we shall exclusively be concerned with "fiction" in the sense of "imaginative literature", namely works of literary art in prose in which the authors present actions and events, people, places and situations, all of which they have invented, or at least modified to suit their own purposes, even if some of their materials have been adapted from real life, as in the case of historical novels. In other words, fiction is here taken to mean fictional narratives that refer to a world created by an author, to a fictitious reality. Such works of fiction are always presented to the listener or reader through a narrator (chosen by the writer) whose point of view governs what is being told.

3.1.1 Escape fiction and great fiction

People love fiction mainly for two reasons. Stories can comfort and entertain readers with fantasy, and they can satisfy people's curiosity and their desire for an insight into reality.

It is not only children who play fantasy games; adults do it, too. Many are usually quite shy about their fantasies, perhaps even ashamed of them. Some of these fantasies are downright ridiculous, often ignoble, always selfish. Fantasy is not useless, however. It is an easily accessible pleasure and an emotional safety-valve. It may even teach people about their real wishes, weaknesses and intentions. Fantasies can become harmful only when people confuse them with reality. Then they may lead them to expect too much of others, deceive themselves about their own motives, expect problems to solve themselves, or feel grievances against the imperfections of others and against the difficulties of life in general. Many novels have touched upon the dangers of self-deceiving fantasy, but have usually included some elements of how people are educated by life out of fantasy towards a better grasp of reality.

Yet even from light reading, readers may pick up a good many scraps of useful general knowledge and notions of epochs, backgrounds and occupations different from their own. They will usually also find some sensible insights into character, motive and morality. In detective tales, in police fiction, and even in the more callous thrillers, readers may find nuggets of good sense, even of compassion, and reminders that people's actions do affect other people.

Even someone whose reading never rises above the level of escapist fiction is likely to be better informed, more tolerant and at least a little wiser than someone who never reads anything but a scrappy newspaper. A trivial novel will also often be helpful in taking someone's mind off illness, injury, the loneliness of old age or the difficulties of growing up. Entertainment helps keep people sane and provides an escape from reality that gives people the strength to face it once more. We can say that the novelist creates fantasies for a large audience and thus provides comfort and escape.

At its best, fiction can do more, however; it can strengthen people's imaginative sympathies and insights by providing an essentially true and illuminating picture of life. It can thus move beyond mere escapism and enlarge the readers' awareness of human realities. Generally speaking, there are a number of features that distinguish great fiction from mere escape fiction.

Escape fiction (at its worst)	Good fiction (at its best)
stock characters and stereotypes that are either "good" or "bad"	complex and psychologically convincing characters showing a mixture of good and evil in the same person, as in real life
a world of black and white, of hero and villain, in which the moral issues are simple – right or wrong	highly complex situations involving moral ambiguities – right and wrong cannot always be distinguished with absolute certainty
a reduction of the complexity and range of human emotions	an awareness of all the implications of the conflict, of the complexity of the issues involved, and of the multiplicity of options in conduct or attitude

Escape fiction (at its worst)	Good fiction (at its best)
the psychological motivation of the characters remains largely in the dark	a psychologically accurate picture based on deep moral and psychological insights
plays up to the readers' expectations and flatters their moral sense – the bad are punished and the good are rewarded	concerned with presenting a sincere, well observed and enlightening picture of an aspect of human life
is concerned with truth only on a superficial level	reaches a profound level of truth
credibility both of character and plot is sacrificed for the sake of sensation and emotional manipulation	all the elements that make up a work of fiction are interrelated and each in its own individual fashion highlights the general character of the whole
violence, sensationalism and a heightening of feeling for its own sake, not as an integral element of structure	a balance between external action and character
almost exclusive stress on the presentation of a fast-moving narrative	an organic unity among the elements that make up the story
no interest in originality, but in producing stories according to a bestselling formula	familiar human situations are shown in a new and fascinating light
is interesting only as a means of escape but not in itself	possesses a rich aesthetic value, i.e. is interesting on many levels

The differences are not always quite as stark as in this table – there is a lot of literary trash on the market, it is true, but there is also much escape fiction that is reasonably good literature. And not all novels intended as serious fiction come up to the highest standards.

3.1.2 The pressures of the market

As a work of literary art, fiction is a literary product, but the writer's finished manuscript is usually also a marketable commodity; it can make money for him if he can get it published.

Fiction is not produced in a vacuum. Most writers do not only write for themselves, without a thought of ever publishing what they have written, but are keenly aware of the law of supply and demand on the literary market. They have thus to bear a number of points in mind when, and even before, they put pen to paper.

In the case of famous bestseller writers, the publishers will forward a contract as soon as writer and publisher have agreed on a new book, and the publisher may even pay the author a certain advance whilst he is writing his book. The situation is different for first-time authors or writers who have not yet established a certain reputation. They will have to think particularly hard about what they want to do. The following diagram can help to explain what pressures there are on the modern writer and how the finished product, the writer's new novel, for instance, finally gets to the reader.

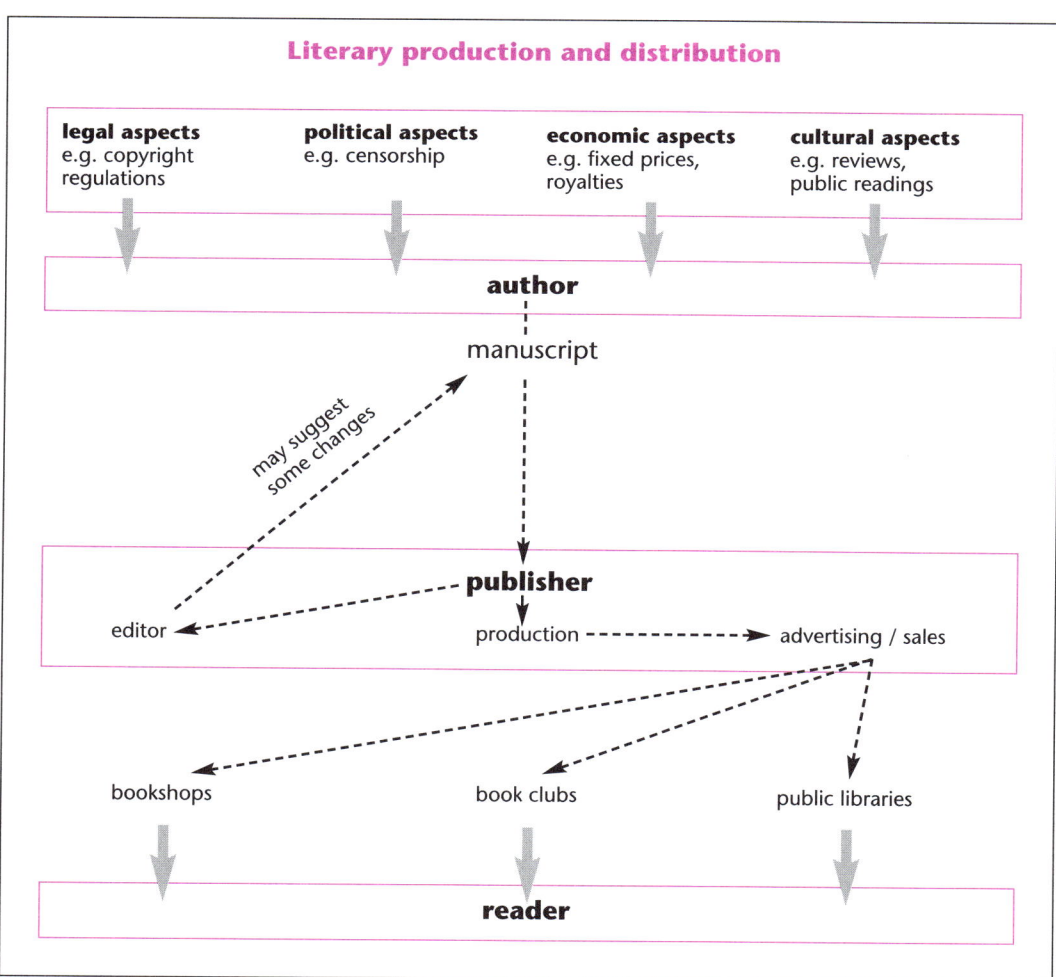

Our author must of course first of all decide if he wants to write to a formula and be successful in this way, or if he wants to produce good literature that may win him prizes and praise from the critics, perhaps even a place in literary history. His first choice is thus whether he wants to write entertainment and escape fiction or serious literature. His decision at this point will vastly influence his selection of themes and various other aspects of the writer's craft (for details see below under 3.2). Many a good writer has certainly been lured away from trying his hand at serious fiction by the promise of quick money in the huge market that exists for escape fiction, and many have undoubtedly squandered their talents by writing for a mass market.

3.1.3 Modes of fiction

The distinction between serious fiction and escape fiction is only one possible grouping of the countless works of fiction that have been produced. We can also start from a different angle and say that not all works of fiction focus on the same area of interest and then group them into three main "modes of fiction:"

- fiction in the social mode,
- fiction in the psychological mode,
- and fiction in the symbolic mode.

Fiction in the social mode generally presents a group of characters in a clear social context. It may depict whole societies with many characters whose actions are followed over time, or a representative cross-section of a class. Social fiction gives readers a vicarious experience of the particular situation, drawing them into the world being described.

- The main characters tend to define their problems and seek to solve them through interacting with other people, usually in a series of encounters.

- Most of what happens is not internal, within the character, but is acted out between individuals. Social fiction emphasises the outward manifestations of behaviour, not the internal sources of motive.

- There is also concern with the tensions within the society, mainly with ethical questions. These questions are answered in the crises undergone by the individual characters, showing how individual behaviour is affected by the social order.

In short, readers are invited to discover insights about the social interaction in human societies, and thus about their own lives.

The organisation and structure of fiction in the psychological mode depends on the inner experience of one or more characters.

- The focus is on individual development – personal, interior conflicts and developments and the presentation of a particular character's mind and sensibility are at the centre.

- Time is dominated not by objective chronology, but only by those moments that are psychologically significant and intensely meaningful for a particular individual. The use of repeated flashbacks is typical; any impulse or sensory perception felt by the character may trigger memories and start new trains of thought.

- The reader is invited to share these experiences, to see the world through this character's eyes, in his unique individual way. The aim is to project the reader into another person's consciousness, and by doing this, to enlarge the readers' own sensibilities.

To sum up, fiction in the psychological mode is preoccupied with individual experience rather than social and historical events.

Fiction in the symbolic mode is intended to dramatise a theme or philosophical concern, which is given sharp dramatic focus.

- The world exists chiefly in the protagonist's mind; what happens in the story is a reflection of his emotional state or a projection of the way he sees himself and everything around him.

- The action described must not be taken too literally; in fiction of this mode, action is often symbolic – no more than a projection of the hero's emotional state. It is intended as a dramatisation of an idea, state of mind, or mood.

- Characters appear to have no complex emotions and are two-dimensional only – in the grip of a single emotion or a powerful overwhelming obsession.

- The reader is projected into the dramatic context, mainly through a natural fascination with the protagonist's actions and a compelling interest in the events described.

In sum, symbolic fiction presents a fictional world in which an aspect of society or human behaviour is singled out – an idea, emotion, state of mind, or a cluster of notions and feelings. It can thus reach deep emotional intensity, sharp focus and a high degree of artistic integrity.

3.1.4 Universal story types

There is a third way in which fiction can be grouped, namely according to story type. Three basic story types can be distinguished:

- adventure,
- romance,
- and mystery.

Stories involving heroic action are usually very different from stories where a girl meets a boy and love follows. These differ again from stories of the unravelling of a mystery, or imaginary adventures in a fantasy world. These three types – adventure, romance, and mystery – can be found chiefly in popular fiction, but all literature uses them occasionally.

In an adventure story, an individual or a group of people, has to overcome obstacles and dangers to accomplish some sort of mission. Sometimes the problems are caused by the machinations of a villain, who will be overthrown in the end. The hero normally receives, as a kind of side benefit, the love of a young lady. This last element is however not really important; the true focus is the hero and the obstacles to be overcome.

This is the simplest and the oldest story type. It belongs with the myths, legends, and epics of pre-history, cultivated in some form by every society. The surface appeal is obvious – a character with whom the reader identifies passes through perils to triumph.

Most stories of adventure have a male protagonist, in stories of romance the central character is usually female. The development of a love relationship dominates a romance story, everything else is of secondary importance. An element of adventure, and perhaps mystery, is found in many romances, but the dangers and mysteries function merely to challenge and perhaps strengthen the love relationship. Happy marriage is the usual outcome, after social or psychological barriers have been overcome.

Sophisticated romances may end in the lovers' death, but in a way this always suggests that the love has been lasting and permanent; it is the intensity of the love that seems to bring about the tragedy. The passion of the lovers for one another is so overwhelming that it simply cannot continue – it inevitably results in the death of one or both of the lovers (*Liebestod*-motif).

Until the arrival of the "classical detective story," mystery was only a subsidiary issue in adventures and romances. This is because the investigation and discovery of hidden secrets, which is basic to the structure of action in a mystery story, is mainly an intellectual activity. The search for mastery of the secret (in a detective story finding the criminal) involves making deductions from clues and putting them in a scheme of cause and effect. The emphasis is on man's reasoning powers, thought, deduction and inference, leading to rational solutions. The pure mystery story has its limitations because of the intellectual demands it makes on readers; people prefer mystery to be used to intensify and complicate heroic and romantic action, increasing suspense and uncertainty, and not to be followed for its own sake, as it were.

A variant of the mystery story is the *encounter with the supernatural*, ghosts and demons, for instance. In stories featuring such encounters, the mystery concerns something outside normal experience, something inexplicable that is never cleared up but only dealt with in some way. The mystery ultimately remains unsolved.

Synopsis

The term "fiction"
- has several meanings.
- sometimes refers to all fictional narratives in prose and verse.
- is often taken to be synonymous with the term "novel."
- generally refers to imaginative literature in prose.

Escape fiction
- can comfort readers with fantasy.
- is generally not much more than entertainment.
- can be helpful in taking people's minds off everyday problems.
- provides escape from reality and from a humdrum existence.

Great fiction
- can satisfy people's desire for insight into reality.
- gives an essentially true and illuminating picture of life.
- enlarges the readers' awareness of human realities.
- is psychologically convincing.
- reaches a profound level of truth.
- possesses rich aesthetic value.

The writer of fiction
- wants his manuscript to be published.
- intends to make money from his writing.
- decides if he wants to write escape fiction or produce serious literature.

Universal story types

- Adventure stories focus on a hero who has to overcome obstacles and dangers to accomplish some sort of mission.
- Stories of romance are dominated by the development of a love relationship.
- Mystery stories deal with the investigation and discovery of hidden secrets and emphasise rational deduction.

3.2 The writer's craft

3.2.1 Verisimilitude – truth in fiction

When the storytellers of the past recounted the exploits of the heroes of the past, they drew on known and well-established facts, but they also embroidered the facts a little. Their stories were thus a blend of fact and fancy. But at some point people began to distinguish between two kinds of narrative, calling one *history* and the other *fiction*.

The particulars of fiction, unlike those of history, are "made up," or invented; they are *fictitious*. It seems perhaps natural, therefore, to think of history as true, and of fiction as basically false, as a mere fabrication, but that would be misleading. In saying that history is true we only suggest that history deals with what actually happened, insofar as this can be determined, whereas fiction does not. But in another sense fiction can be quite true, because the range of truth is not confined to being faithful to externals. Fiction can even make use of materials that are demonstrably "untrue" in the sense of not being part of life as we know it, or of our range of experience. This is the case, for instance, when elements of magic are introduced (as in fantasy literature) or an alternative world is shown (as in a great deal of science fiction). And yet what is shown to the reader in those stories is often true to our understanding of the psychology of the characters, or of moral truth. In other words, the characters in such stories must be "true to life;" they must show human emotions (even if they are animals, as in fables) and their behaviour must correspond to what we know of human behaviour.

A work of fiction is "true" when it gives a sincere and enlightening picture of a portion of life; when it is based on verisimilitude, on a likeness to life as it really is. But what is "likeness to truth," and how can the writer achieve an effect of verisimilitude?

- Many writers have tried to do it by paying *close attention to detail*, hoping to convince the reader that if so much detail turns out to be true to life, his story must be, too. Details of the external world will be presented as accurately and convincingly as possible, and genuine research and close observation can no doubt be important for gaining credibility for the story.

- Such a surface realism is certainly helpful, but doesn't go as far as the deeper realism shown in great fiction. In great literature another level of truth is reached, beyond the concrete and practical. The characters may show emotional complexities and moral developments but also elements of self-deception and a slow and painful evolution of awareness of themselves and others. This kind of verisimilitude will be nearer this deeper level of truth that lies in portraying something of the tangled, inexhaustible complexity of people's emotional, social and moral selves and of their relationship with others. The works of fiction that force us to look into ourselves are harder to read than the stories that provide escape and let us forget our surroundings for an hour or two, but there is much more of verisimilitude in them – a closer adherence to life as it really is.

- The deepest level of verisimilitude found in the greatest works of fiction lies however in their insights into the complexities of the human heart. Society and its demands, people in relation to family, friends and others – all these points and others besides are taken up by the skilful writer. He concentrates on showing us moral truth, even though we are not all agreed about many questions of morality. If we always knew what was right, there would be no dilemmas. In great fiction we do often recognize certain fundamental moral probabilities, for instance that an important factor in achieving a worthwhile life is learning to shoulder the right responsibilities and turning away from the wrong ones. It may perhaps be said that a large part of the moral truth of many works of fiction is the awareness of moral ambiguities.

No work of fiction can give "total truth," but good novels leave us with some sense of fragmentary truthfulness; and a great novel gives us a very complex impression of a portion of life and its problems, communicating many diverse insights, some explicitly, some by implication. The great novelist must genuinely want to tell the truth and he must enable the reader to believe that the fictional world he has created is true to life. In short, he has both to be sincere and to reach verisimilitude.

Typical assignments

- Does this work of fiction give a picture of life as it really is?

- How has the writer tried to achieve verisimilitude?

3.2.2 Composition and structure

Before he puts pen to paper, the writer has to make up his mind about a number of structural elements of his text:

- He has first of all to select what will be his central purpose, the central ideas his story will embody – his theme.

- When he has developed such an overall plan he needs to make decisions about action, characters, conflict and resolution. Short stories have a single controlling idea or theme. Novels have a *dominant theme*, and usually a number of other less important themes. The author's central purpose provides a focus for the story, giving it unity and infusing it with meaning.

- Then the writer has to decide on an action to illustrate or dramatise the theme. Whatever he wishes to communicate has to be made concrete by action of some kind. It may be physical action *(external action)* or action involving thoughts and emotions *(internal action)*. The writer's main interest may be in character and motive, a moral problem, or the condition of society, or some social injustice or evil, he may wish to make us laugh, or merely entertain us. Whichever it is, he cannot express his intentions without action of some kind. Character, for instance, is revealed in action. Action makes the problem explicit.

- The action always involves one or two main characters, a hero and / or a heroine. This central character is known as the protagonist; his opponent is the antagonist. Between the two there is always some kind of conflict, which may be external (when the conflict is with others) or internal (when the conflict is within the character himself). Behind these surface conflicts is a deep-seated central conflict – essentially the forces of good are in conflict with the forces of evil. This central conflict is closely bound up with the theme.

- The interplay between characters – what they do, say, or think, and what happens – is the plot. It is the backbone of a story.
  - In an *episodic plot* a number of "adventures" of one person are strung together into a single narrative.
  - In an *integrated plot* the component parts are all directed towards a central effect; none of them is superfluous. The writer establishes a clear sequence from introduction, to complication, conflict, climax, and finally resolution.
  - A plot with a definite resolution of conflict is called a *closed plot* but it has now largely been abandoned in serious fiction. In most modern fiction the open plot is preferred in which

nothing is finally decided and a carefully finished but false interpretation of our complicated world is avoided.

- A *subplot* is a secondary story, possibly interesting in its own right, introduced into the narrative so as to broaden the reader's perspective on the *main plot* and to underline its meaning by similarity or contrast.

- *The movement of the plot* raises questions and appeals to the reader's curiosity – he wants to know what happens next. This uncertainty about the future course of events is known as *suspense*. Suspense is based on verisimilitude, on a close correlation between real life and the narrative, and also on causality. Of course, there may occasionally be unexpected developments, especially if we have been led to expect something else. This is the element of *surprise*. The interplay of suspense and surprise is a prime source of power and vitality in an on-going plot.

- Finally, to give his fictional creations coherence, the writer must impose order on his material. He must link cause and effect much more clearly than in real life. Important things are brought to the fore, irrelevant matters are pushed into the background so that a coherent whole is achieved.

Typical assignments

- What is the writer's theme / his central purpose?

- How is the theme developed?

- Describe the structure of the action in the story.

- Outline the (central) conflict in the story.

- Explain the character of the conflict and show where the climax is.

- What kind of action takes place? Is it mainly external or internal?

- How are the external action and internal action interrelated?

- Describe the chain of causes and effects making up the plot.

- Draw a diagram illustrating the plot structure of the narrative.

- Comment on the handling of turning-point and resolution.

- Analyse the mutual interdependence of main plot and subplot.

- How has the writer aroused the reader's curiosity?

- Show how the author has created suspense.

- Why is the outcome so surprising?
- Would you change the ending of the story? Give reasons.

3.2.3 The narrative process

There are many ways of telling a story, and the author has to decide which of them best suits his purpose.

- He has first of all to choose a suitable *narrator* from whose *point of view* the story will be told.

- He has to decide what *mode of presentation* to employ. He may want to tell us directly about the events and their significance, or alternatively to show the words and actions of his characters in a dramatic scene.

Many stories are explicitly presented as passing through the consciousness of a narrator. The story is told by this narrator and not by the author himself, as the device of having a narrator establishes some authority outside the author himself and thus considerably strengthens the illusion of reality the writer wants to achieve. By choosing this or that narrator whose point of view then governs everything, the author can provide the exact measure of authorial guidance he thinks is needed for the story to have its intended effect, for each story requires the establishment of a particular kind of illusion to sustain it.

- The difference between the author and the narrator of a work of fiction is obvious when we have an explicit or *dramatized narrator* who is a character in the story and is involved in the action. In this case his point of view – and not the author's, of course – completely dominates the tale he is presenting.

- The situation is not so obvious where there is an *undramatized narrator*, i.e. a narrator who is not a character in the story he is relating. But even in this case author and narrator are not identical, because a story is never told by the author as he is in real life, but by a „second self," the *implied author*. The picture of the author's "second self" that emerges from a narrative will not be identical with the one created before the reader's eye in another story by the same author. The implied author in Hemingway's famous short story "The Killers", for instance, is different from the picture of the author the reader gets from reading *The Old Man and the Sea*.

The writer can choose between quite a number of perspectives through which the reader is to perceive the events of a story.

Point-of-view:

- **Omniscience.** In many stories the narrator is in a godlike position behind the scenes, managing the characters like puppets on strings, knowing the thought-processes and feelings of each of them. Such a narrator is known as *omniscient*.
  - In what is called *editorial omniscience* the author will not only report what happens and what is in the minds of the characters, but will also criticize them and their plans, commenting on the follies of mankind.
  - The situation is slightly different if the author opts for *neutral omniscience*, staying away from interpolating ideas or comments.

- **Third-person narration.** When the narrator is outside the story, he refers to the characters by name, or calling them "he", "she", or "they".
  - This *third-person point of view* is often combined with omniscience, but the author may prefer to employ *impersonal narration*. Giving up access to inner feelings and motives, he describes or reports the action in dramatic scenes, making no comments.
  - Alternatively the author may use a *limited point of view* and tell the story in the third person, but confine himself to the point of view of a few or only one of the characters. His narration is thus limited to what is experienced, thought and felt by the character who occupies the centre of attention at a given time in the action, thus providing a "focus", "mirror", or "centre of consciousness".

- **First-person narration.** The story illusion becomes stronger when one of the characters adopts *first-person narration*, apparently telling the story, or their part of it, as "I".
  - This "I" may be a minor character, a disinterested observer or a witness, with no more than ordinary access to the thoughts and feelings of others who therefore can tell the reader only what any observer may reasonably be expected to know and discover from what he sees and hears.
  - In some stories the "I" of first-person narration is the central character. His role in the story limits the *protagonist-narrator* much more than the *witness-narrator*, who can have access to facts, places, people, etc., out of reach of the protagonist, who tends to become a fixed centre, compared with what has been called the "wandering periphery" of the observer-narrator.

- **Impersonal narration.** In their attempts to achieve complete objectivity some writers have dispensed with the narrator altogether – the story is made to tell itself.

- This is usually done by scenic presentation: only what the characters do and say is presented; what they think and how they feel is not given but may possibly be inferred from action and dialogue.
- Yet another method is the transmission of all the materials – the action and words, appearance and the setting – through the minds of the characters; the story is told as it is reflected in the mind of one or more of the characters.

● **Self-conscious narration.** On rare occasions the narrator seems to be aware of himself as a writer. Such a *self-conscious narrator* often discusses, either seriously or for comic purposes, the problems involved in writing the book.

● **Unreliable narration.** Sometimes a narrator's words cannot be taken at their face value, because he seems excessively naïve or innocent, may be blind to the moral problems involved in certain situations, and so on. He can thus give only a distorted view of the events, so that his narration is full of irony.

It is almost impossible for an author to hit on a perfect point of view. It is difficult to decide just how much guidance the reader needs so that the story can progress with proper effect. Each new story may require the establishment of a particular kind of illusion and thus a particular narrator. The following table lists some of the problems.

Point of view		
	advantages	disadvantages
omniscient point of view	affords the writer great freedom: he may follow any number of characters for any length of time, relate what he thinks is most interesting and comment if he wishes	the writer always stands between the reader and the story, so that the story illusion may suffer
limited point of view	great vitality can be achieved, and the story can be told very convincingly	the author is restricted to the experiences of one person only
impersonal narration	by presenting the action in dramatic scenes a vivid and fast-moving narrative can be achieved, so that the reader is quickly drawn into the story	the whole area of the characters' inner life is simply blocked out, with some inevitable loss of characterization in depth

What the author wants the reader to hear, feel and see can be conveyed as *telling* (also known as *summary*), or as *showing* (also known as *scene*), or – commonly – as a combination of the two. "Telling" and "showing" are modes of presentation, i.e. distinct ways of conveying a story.

- In *telling*, the narrator summarizes the events in his own words, e.g. "Many years passed."

- When *showing* is employed, the characters' words and actions are shown in dramatic scenes (dialogue and detailed action).

- When the narrator presents what goes on in the characters' minds, we speak of *stream-of-consciousness*. This dramatization in language of the workings of a character's consciousness tries to reflect the interior processes of perception, thought and speech of this character.

Variations of it are the technique of *interior monologue* (also known as *reported thought*), in which a character's stream-of-consciousness is "translated" into ordinary language and presented as first-person narration, and *internal analysis*, in which the narrator does not quote directly from a character's consciousness, but summarizes this character's thoughts and feelings in his own, the narrator's, words.

These narrative methods that have enabled writers of fiction to move inside the minds of their characters have provided literature with new conventions for the presentation of the processes of the mind and with new avenues to pursue in analysing and understanding the behaviour of characters. They have been widely used in recent fiction.

Telling (Summary)	Showing (Scene) dialogue	Stream-of-consciousness
• gives a general account or report of a series of events covering extended periods and a variety of settings • informs the reader about certain elements of the world of the narrative which are necessary to the tale but are not worth narrating in detail → provides a comprehensive and extensive view	• achieves an effect of immediacy by letting the characters present and interpret themselves in their own words and actions • shows an important action taking place • conveys an intense moment vividly → offers an intensive view	• introduces the reader directly into a character's interior life • gives the reader access to the easy and effortless intermingling of past and present events as they come into the character's mind by random association → explores the minds of the characters

Typical assignments

- From what position does the narrator tell the story?

- Explain the point of view from which this story is told.

- At what point in the story does a shift in the point of view take place? What is its function?

- Is the narrator reliable? Try to find some evidence in the text for your answer.

- Analyse the mode of presentation in this narrative.

- What effect is achieved when the narrator
  - shifts the focus from panorama to scene at this point in the story?
  - effaces himself completely and gives a direct quotation of the workings of this character's mind?

3.2.4 Characters and characterisation

It is remarkable how a writer, by putting words on paper, can create characters that seem real to us. When the writer knows his business, we feel that the characters are vivid and believable, that they "come to life." Even a relatively superficial reading of a story enables readers to feel the vital force of a character.

Characters in fiction closely resemble real-life people, and yet they are different. This is because they are *fictional characters*, specially created for a purpose. Their authors have selected certain aspects of ordinary people and developed some of them whilst playing down others, and finally put them together as they have seen fit. The result is not an ordinary person but a fictional character who exists only in a particular work of fiction.

There are some characters who seem to be fully alive, independent and original. They act, think and speak in a distinctive way, and they have many facets.

- They have a rich inner life,

- they are capable of growing and changing,

- the reader can follow them through a wide variety of experiences.

Readers feel that they know these characters well because their authors have opted to give them range, depth and richness. Such characters are also known as *three-dimensional characters* or as *round characters*.

There are other characters who are known both from the outside and the inside but who, nevertheless, are not as rich, varied or original as the ones outlined above. They are characters who have a much more limited life.

- Their authors have given them few characteristics,

- they do not develop or change very much,

- they rarely surprise the reader.

They are lightly sketched in with a few broad lines, but there is little light or shade to them. This is not to say that they have very little purpose in the fictional works in which they appear. Quite often their presence is very important, but in many cases the reader gains the impression that the author has put them there not because he or she is interested in them but because they serve a purpose in the total design of the work.

There is a third group of characters who have only one telling characteristic. This has the following consequences:

- they never develop,

- they rarely have any inner life,

- they never surprise the reader,

- they often repeat phrases.

The reader is never puzzled about them, because there is nothing about them to cause puzzlement. They can, however, be delightfully funny, and many of them, in consequence, are memorable. Such characters have been called *two-dimensional* or *flat characters*.

In short, writers create a very wide range of characters in terms of their fullness. There are not just the three types outlined above – *central characters, intermediate characters*, and *background characters* – but a scale running from deep and rich characters to very simple ones. The point is that all of these characters have a place in the overall design of a particular work of fiction, and their authors have created them with this purpose in mind. If some characters are fuller than others, it is therefore not necessarily a fault in the work; it is usually in accordance with the author's overall plan. The difference, therefore, between central characters, intermediate characters and background characters is based on their different functions for the narrative.

- The *central characters* are the protagonists of the story who are at the centre of attention and whose motivation and history are most fully established.

- The *background characters* may be almost anonymous, voices rather than individualized characters.

- Between the central characters and the background characters we find a wide variety of *intermediate characters* who exist mainly to serve some particular purpose.

The difference between flat and round characters lies in the extent to which they are individualized.

- A *flat character* is constructed round a single idea or quality and consequently presented only in outline and without much individualizing detail.

- A *round character*, on the other hand, is characterized by a mixture of good and bad features, of strengths and weaknesses, and is therefore a many-faceted and very complex character, with regard to both temperament and motivation.

Most fiction can do without three-dimensional characters. The vast majority of detective novels, for example, employ protagonists that are only two-dimensional. Agatha Christie's famous sleuths Miss Marple and Hercule Poirot or Arthur Conan Doyle's Sherlock Holmes are well-known cases in point. Their creators, it is true, have tried to give them some individualizing traits:

- well-versed in village gossip and expert at needlework and gardening (Miss Marple);

- immoderately vain and extremely proud of his enormous moustache (Hercule Poirot);

- fond of his pipe and his violin, but also addicted to opium (Sherlock Holmes).

The fact remains, however, that they are basically flat characters and have been characterized only insofar as is necessary for their function in the plot. What really counts, of course, is not their individuality as characters, but their superior powers of analysis and logical deduction, and in this sense they are certainly sufficiently equipped for the purposes of the stories in which they figure. In fact, any additional individualizing details would make them too complex, and this would detract from the central problem – the solving of the mystery – rather than enhance the reader's interest in it. It is not an accident, perhaps, that none of the three characters mentioned has a family and they are thus entirely free for their function – it is the mystery that is at the heart of the detective novel and not the character of the detective as a complex human being. There are notable exceptions, of course, e.g. Dashiell Hammett's Sam Spade (cf. *The Maltese Falcon*), who is much more complex as a person than other private eyes who are the heroes of detective thrillers.

Generally speaking, all fiction mainly intended for entertainment and escape tends to employ only two-dimensional characters, even for the protagonists. For the literary roles they play, they do not require the roundness of a Paul Morel (the hero of *Sons and Lovers* by D. H. Lawrence) or of a Leopold Bloom (a central character in *Ulysses* by James Joyce).

Character can be revealed in basically two ways – by direct characterisation and by indirect characterisation.

- When the author, through his narrator or through the remarks of another character in the story, mentions a character trait directly (e.g. "X is a mean old skinflint"), we are dealing with an instance of *direct characterisation*.

- The method preferred by most recent writers is however *indirect characterisation* – the readers have to infer what a character is like from what goes on in the narrative itself.

  Evidence may thus be deduced from other participants in a story; they may be foils to another character, by their difference from him or the ways in which they resemble him. They may embody and personify certain traits in his character, thus throwing light on his true nature. His servants, friends or acquaintances may discuss him, his person, past life and appearance, or comment on his behaviour, providing additional clues.

  The most important evidence usually comes from the character himself. He may make direct statements about himself or show the significant traits of his character through what he says and does; or, if the author prefers to employ the stream-of-consciousness methods we will know from his thoughts what sort of person he is. Modern writers usually use several of these methods in combination to achieve particular effects.

Typical assignments

- How are the characters presented in this story?

- Try to explain the devices the author has used
  - to characterise A;
  - to make the personality of B emerge;
  - to bring out the contrast between C and D.

- Trace the different stages in the development of X.

- Show that X and Y are two different types.

- Summarise the information the reader is given about X.

- What is the position of character X within the structure of the story? Is he a major or a minor character? Give reasons for your opinions.

3.2.5 Time, setting and atmosphere

Whereas the action of the medieval romances takes place in a timeless world and in an essentially static cosmos, there is a clock ticking away in every work of modern fiction, as E.M. Forster (novelist and critic) famously put it. This is to say that the present-day writer of fiction is keenly aware of reality as being essentially dynamic, i.e. constantly moving and changing. Modern fiction is therefore concerned with a presentation of events as they happen in time – with the inevitable consequence that the temporal setting of an individual narrative recedes further and further into the past as the years go by. If his work is to have a timeless appeal, the writer must therefore somehow bridge the ever-widening gap between the date of composition and the time of reading by successive generations. He can achieve this by creating an illusion of immediacy and directness in the reader's mind of the events, even though they are described in the past tense. The illusion can sometimes be so vivid that an impression of actual personal participation is conveyed. The reader becomes so engrossed that he yields to the illusion of actually participating in the action or situation, or witnessing it, though he knows it is only a fictional account devised by an author who may well have been dead for a hundred years or more. When the chronological past of the story's action is thus translated into the fictive present felt by the reader, the story illusion is complete – the reader forgets the present and thinks himself into the fictive present of the story. All the elements of a work of fiction have to contribute towards this effect, but the handling of the time scheme of the story plays a vital part in it.

A writer has three basic alternatives when selecting the time scheme of a narrative:

- He can opt for a close correspondence of acting time and reading time; the events described are transacted in approximately the same time as it takes to read about them.

- He may choose concentration and compression; the events described may span a period of many years, but this period is summarized by the narrator, so that it takes only a few moments to read about them.

- He may select expansion of chronological time; the events described last only for a few moments, but they are narrated in such great detail – because they are felt to be supremely important – that they take a long time to read.

Flexibility of tempo is so important in the creation of the story illusion, because the reader can lose himself in the events of the story much more easily if the writer indicates, by his handling of pace, the relative value of each occurrence within the plot.

Few works of fiction adopt only one of these three basic approaches. Writers of mainstream fiction usually vary the proportion of time allocated to particular incidents and thus achieve flexibility of tempo, which greatly helps the creation of the illusion of immediacy. Flexibility of tempo also helps to control distance. We can lose ourselves in the events of a story much more easily when the writer, handling pace with a deft and professional touch, indicates the relative value of each occurrence within the plot: an important event may be described at greater length than it took to happen, and long periods of time may be dealt with in a short paragraph.

The time scheme of a work of fiction is determined not only by the length of reading-time allocated to the events it describes but also by the order in which they are told. Even the simplest narrative is likely to blend perception, memory and speculation. An effective storyteller will appear to be everywhere at the same time, aware of the past, conscious of the present, and able to comprehend the possibilities of the future.

There are many ways in which a writer can handle the difficult problem of choosing a time scheme to suit his purpose in a particular story – what will be the best point in time to start the action in motion, how much of what happened before the action begins can be filled in later, when this should be done, and so on.

- The easiest way is to present action *in chronological order*, retelling events as they happen, in succession. This is the method mainly used in action-centred stories.

- Where the aim is to interest the reader in thought rather than action, as in psychological narratives, writers often delineate the character first, then work from period to period over the past. In this method, known as *reverted narration*, some parts of the story are told in the "normal" time-sequence, others in *flashbacks* filling in what happened before the point at which the work opened.

- Special effects may be created by the technique of *foreshadowing* or *anticipation*, where the narrator cleverly hints at what is to come, increasing suspense.

Some modern authors prefer an interwoven exposition and action with alternating or intermingled flashbacks and anticipatory glimpses. In this method the *focus* shifts continually; the relative past and present are continually dissolved; tenses are mingled or fused: the past is not distinct and separate from the present but part of it, absorbing it. Each moment is a condensation of earlier moments; the past is never completed, it is an ever-developing and unfolding changing present. For these writers there is only an eternal present in which the past is fused – there is no such thing as the past, only an unrolling present. This treatment of time as no more than an aspect of the ever-present is found mainly among impressionist writers using the stream-of-consciousness technique.

Everything that happens, happens somewhere at some time. That element of fiction which reveals to us the where and when of events is known as the setting. The elements of which setting is composed may be listed under four headings:

- the actual geographical location, including topography, scenery, even the details of a room's interior;

- the occupations and modes of day-to-day existence of the characters;

- the time in which the action takes place, e.g. historical period, season of the year, etc.;

- the religious, moral, intellectual, social, and emotional environment of the characters, e.g. the social group or groups in which the protagonists move.

Setting does not have equal importance in all fiction, or with all authors, some of whom assess the value of setting differently.

- The setting may simply be one of the elements of the structure of a work, a kind of "stage backcloth" in front of which events are acted out (neutral setting). Much popular fiction has a vaguely contemporary setting, either urban or rural. In such a case, it is obvious that the writer has no real interest in his setting and does not encourage such interest on the reader's part.

- The setting may be a negative example of what existing or possible trends might lead to; this is often so in utopian novels, such as Aldous Huxley's *Brave New World* and George Orwell's *1984*.

- It may be integral to the plot, as in works where an exotic setting helps to underline the strangeness of the events, or where an alien or strange background puts the participants into sharper relief. In fiction dealing with problems of human adjustment a change in the setting may serve to illuminate the problems more clearly.

- Details of the setting generally add to the sense of reality and three-dimensionality, but they may also function as symbols, as in Herman Melville's *Moby Dick*, where the isolation of the ship suggests Captain Ahab's spiritual isolation.

- Sometimes we find the setting directly influencing the characters, as in Edgar Allan Poe's famous tale *The Fall of the House of Usher*, where the landscape seems to take charge of the characters, and the story of a family's degeneration is apparently determined by the visual setting. The family is shaped, distorted and overshadowed by the overpowering surroundings. All moral qualities or choices are taken from them. As a result of the horrifying environment they seem to define within themselves the inevitability of their decadence and eventual decay.

When a setting evokes such a definite emotional mood, we speak of atmosphere. It may set up in the reader expectations about what will occur, especially if we are given the impression that the action will inevitably unfold towards a tragic conclusion. Atmosphere is thus a kind of mood or emotional aura suggested primarily by the setting. A suggestion of mystery and foreboding may be established, for instance, by a description of shapes dimly seen in the darkness. A stormy night carries with it one emotional aura, a sunny morning another.

Typical assignments

- In what sequence is the action presented in this story? Explain its time structure.

- What is the relation between acting time and reading time?

- Where has the writer used compression, where expansion? Explain the effects he has tried to achieve.

- Describe the setting in which the events occur and explain its function.

- Has the setting any symbolic significance?

- What kind of atmosphere is evoked in the story?

Synopsis

Truth in fiction
- is based on verisimilitude.
- closely sticks to life as we know it.
- lies in its insights into the complexities of the human heart.

Composition
- is the transposition of the writer's central purpose into an overall structural plan.
- involves decisions about the relationship between external and internal action.
- revolves around the central characters and the conflict they are involved in.
- relies heavily on good plotting.
- produces order and coherence.

The narrative process
- involves the choice of a suitable narrator and a corresponding point of view.
- relies on the interplay of certain modes of presentation.

The narrator
- may be a character in the story (dramatised n.) who employs a first-person point of view.
- may be an anonymous person outside the action of the story (undramatised n.) who uses a third-person point of view.
- can be omniscient.
- may prefer to employ impersonal narration.
- may have only a limited point of view.
- may be self-conscious or unreliable.
- often summarizes the events in his own words (telling).
- sometimes presents the characters' words and actions in dramatic scenes (showing).
- occasionally presents a character's stream-of-consciousness.

Characters
- are fictional individuals, created for a purpose.
- may seem fully alive, independent and original.
- can be three-dimensional, round characters.
- may be intermediate characters with some distinguishing features but without any real depth.
- may be two-dimensional, flat characters built around a single characteristic.

Characterisation
- may be direct or indirect.
- sometimes relies on direct statements, but is more often based on evidence derived from what a character says and does.

The time scheme of a narrative
- may show a close correspondence between acting time and reading time.
- may rely on concentration and compression as achieved in the narrator's summarising of the events.
- may employ an expansion of chronological time at moments of high emotional intensity.
- is often characterised by a flexibility of tempo.
- may be strictly chronological or make use of the "time-shift technique".

The setting
- may be no more than a kind of vague background before which the action unfolds.
- may be integral to the plot and thus make the conflict stand out more clearly.
- may add to the sense of reality and three-dimensionality.
- may occasionally directly influence the characters.
- may create a definite mood, a particular atmosphere and emotional aura.

3.3 The short story

3.3.1 Characteristics of the short story

If we attempt a definition of the short story, we can define it as a brief fictional prose narrative that deals with only a few characters and is shorter than a novel. The form encourages economy of setting and concise narrative and is usually concerned with a single effect conveyed in only one or a few significant scenes. Character is disclosed in action and dramatic encounter but is seldom fully developed.

Since the short story is a brief work of prose fiction it shares a number of elements with other types of fiction, especially with the novel.

- It organises the action, thought and dialogue of its characters into an artistic pattern.

- The plot form may be comic, tragic, romantic, or satiric.

- It presents the story from one of many available points of view.

- And it may be written in the mode of realism, impressionism, or fantasy.

The short story differs from the novel first of all in terms of length. The most important and most obvious characteristic of the short story is that it is *short*. But how short is "short?" Nobody knows for sure, because the very briefest of short stories are under 200 words and there are some others with 30,000 words or more. Generally speaking, the term "short story" is applied to works of fiction ranging in length from 1,000 to 15,000 words, Novels are thought of as containing about 45,000 words or more. Works of prose fiction from about 15,000 to about 45,000 words are commonly called *novellas*.

Edgar Allan Poe (1809 – 1849) settled the matter of a short story's proper length once and for all by stating that it should be short enough to be read at one sitting. He also said that it should be long enough to produce the desired effect on the reader. What could be clearer than that?

The short story also differs from longer fiction in the sense that the tightness of the short story form always imposes the need for economy of management.

In longer narratives, especially in the novel, the writer may devote a whole chapter or more to the *exposition,* explaining the situation, mentioning important antecedent matters, introducing the theme, the main characters, the environment and so on. The *complication*, sometimes called the *rising action,* begins when conflict develops. A *climax* comes when the conflict is at its most intense. From this climax point the *resolution* becomes inevitable. The movement or direction of the resolution may be made obvious in a passage indicating a *turning-point* or *crisis*; from then on, there is *falling action*, with the fortune of one of the two opposed forces declining and the other correspondingly gaining control of events. In the resolution or *denouement* (Fr. denouement, literally "un-knotting", pronounced [deɪˈnuːmãːŋ]) the outcome is decided; the action ends in success or failure for the protagonist.

All of this is not possible for the short story writer. He must get to the point very quickly and simply cannot afford the space for a detailed development of the plot as outlined above. He minimizes both prior exposition and the details of the setting, keeps the complications to a minimum, and clears up the conflict quickly – sometimes in a few sentences. The central incident is often selected to manifest as much as possible of the protagonist's life and character, and the details are devised to carry maximum import for the development of the plot.

The short story very often begins the story close to the climax, for the writer has no words to spare, no scope for deep and elaborate expository and introductory matter. All the writer's points – place, period, character, point of view, etc. – have to be developed in a paragraph or even less. This opening from *Interesting Things* by Kingsley Amis (1922 – 1995) is typical:

> Gloria Davies crossed the road towards the Odeon on legs that weaved a little, as if she was tipsy or rickety. She wasn't either really; it was just the high-heeled shoes, worn for the first time specially for today.

From this short opening extract we learn that the heroine is young, she is going to the cinema (the Odeon), she wants to look good but is uncomfortable, wearing new shoes that she doesn't know how to walk in ...

We are already right in the middle of the action and can expect it to develop quickly and decisively because the short story typically cuts out all circumstantial detail and quickly gets on with the action, which is commonly based on a single incident. Characters seldom develop in the short story, however. Rather, they are revealed to the reader, and in a relatively short period of time. The short story seems particularly suited to such effects of intensity and to uses of the elements of fiction that tend to such effects.

To summarize, we associate with the short story a quintessential brevity and also such qualities as compression, concentration, and intensity.

3.3.2 Different types of short story

Before the 19th century the short story was not generally regarded as a distinct literary form. People had been enjoying various types of brief narratives – jokes and anecdotes, short romances and moralizing tales, short myths and shortened historical legends. Yet none of these forms constituted a "short story" in the sense in which the last 200 years or so have defined the term.

The "modern" short story evolved from two separate strains of short fiction.

- There was on the one hand the realistic story in which the stress fell heavily on the attempt to deal objectively with what looked like real places and events involving real people. Many regionalist stories (e.g. by Bret Harte, 1836 – 1902) are of this type. The writers try hard to present a lifelike picture of the setting, stressing realistic details and concentrating on depicting objective elements.

- And there were also tales shaped by strongly impressionistic elements. The effect that resulted from such stories was achieved by letting the individual consciousness of the central character or the narrator's subjective psychological attitude dominate the presentation of the events. Of this sort are many of Edgar Allan Poe's impressionist short stories in which the hallucinations of a central character or the narrator provide the details and the "facts" of the story. The events become so distorted in this way that the reader cannot hope to look objectively at the scene he is being shown; instead, he only gets the narrator's subjective impressions of that scene.

These two strains became fused in the work of a number of writers, and many have experimented with the form, but the point is that the two tendencies in writing short fiction live on and have yielded a great many different types of short story.

In the beginning, when things were still in a state of flux with regard to the shape of the short story, it was Edgar Allan Poe who laid down some guidelines for the structure of the form. He gave it as his opinion that the definitive character of the short story was its unity of effect, and he was mostly concerned about craftsmanship and artistic integrity. His remarks do not prescribe subject matter or dictate techniques and that has left the door wide open for experimentation and growth.

His own contribution as a writer to the development of the short story is considerable. He especially excelled in

- the detective story (e.g. *The Murders in the Rue Morgue*),
- the Gothic spine-chiller (e.g. *The Pit and the Pendulum*),
- and a kind of early science fiction (e.g. *The Gold Bug*).
- He was also instrumental in bringing about the impressionist short story.

Poe's notion of a *unity of effect* has fascinated short story writers ever since and they have tried their best to achieve in their texts an artistic unity or unity of impression of the type Poe envisaged. Many have attempted to do this by

- concentrating on one action, in one place, on one day;
- dealing with a single character, a single event, a single emotion or a series of emotions brought about by a single situation;
- achieving an effect of totality.

Aiding them in such efforts has been the idea of a concentration of the movement of the plot, of a *tightly-knit plot* with

- an *immediate beginning*,
- a *turning point* somewhere in the story,
- a *surprise ending*.

Many distinguished short stories are of this type. They are generally described as plot stories. For this type of story, skilful plotting is an essential requirement. The stories tend to be action-centred and fast-paced, and they move quickly to a sharp climax that often leads to a surprise ending. Other stories depart from this model in various ways.

This is because when this formula is repeated too often, the plot story is in danger of becoming purely conventional in structure and mechanical in effect. Because of this, many sincere artists have sought inspiration from the other strain of story writing that Poe helped to pioneer – the impressionist story.

This type of story focuses on the impressions registered by the events in the characters' minds (and especially the narrator's), rather than the objective reality of the events themselves.

All impressionist stories distort ostensible reality in a way that reflects on the characters who are speaking. Poe's often-quoted story *The Tell-Tale Heart* (1843) is of this type, and so is Ambrose Bierce's famous *An Occurrence at Owl Creek Bridge* (1891) – in both these stories the reader sees a mind at work – distorting, fabricating, and fantasising – rather than an objective picture of actuality.

A number of writers went a step further and tried to abandon all notion that stories had to be built around a plot. Their aim was to achieve form, not plot, although form was more elusive and difficult. Narratives like *A Clean, Well-Lighted Place* by Ernest Hemingway (1898–1961) appear to some readers to have no structure at all, because hardly any action develops. "Nothing happens in these stories," they complain, but what they fail to see is that stories of this type are structured around a psychological rather than a physical conflict. In these psychological stories, physical action and events are unimportant except insofar as the actions reveal the psychological background of the story. The psychological approach

- shuns consistent plotting,

- tends towards inaction and formlessness,

- merely suggests character and does not reveal it openly,

- is primarily concerned with evoking mood and capturing the more elusive moments of life,

- focuses on showing inner life and especially the influence of the subconscious,

- often presents experience through the minds of the characters.

Others have experimented with selecting some especially telling moments of life and registering the impressions these moments make upon them, especially if these impressions constitute for them an "epiphany" of some kind. This epiphany idea goes back to the work of James Joyce (1882–1941), who believed that there are "moments of revelation" in life in which the veil is drawn away, as it were, from complex reality. The character who has such an eye-opening experience (an epiphany) will find some new insight and reach a deeper understanding of some mysterious and enigmatic aspect of life.

At present there are too many trends in short story writing – anything from an attempt at rendering inner action, including aspects of the subconscious, to symbolic writing – for anybody to be able to say with confidence which way the short story as a genre is moving. Many conventional stories continue to be written, it is true. Old forms like the animal fable (see for instance James Thurber's famous *Fables for Our Time*) and modern parables have been tried, and there is generally a great deal of experimentation still going on.

The short story is certainly very much alive today and appears to be seen by many writers as an ideal vehicle for presenting their vision of reality, especially if this vision is an expressionistic or a surrealistic one. Or they try to test out the possibilities of the genre by presenting stories that are basically collages of bits and pieces of graphic material, TV commercials, dialogue from Hollywood films, literary allusions and original prose (see for instance the work of Donald Barthelme, 1931 – 1989). Experimentation with the form of the short story is by no means over yet.

Synopsis

The short story
- is a brief fictional prose narrative.
- deals with only a few characters.
- reveals character but does not develop it.
- encourages economy of setting and concise narrative.
- aims at a unity of effect.
- tends to encourage experimentation.

The plot story
- is based on skilful plotting.
- tends to be action-centred.
- often moves quickly to a climax and to a surprise ending.

The impressionist story
- focuses on the impressions registered by the events in the characters' minds.
- distorts ostensible reality.
- is mainly interested in revealing the character who is speaking.

The psychological story
- develops hardly any action.
- at first sight appears to have no structure.
- focuses on showing inner life.
- often presents experience through the minds of the characters.

3.4 The novel

3.4.1 The novel as a "mirror of life"

When the first modern novels came to be written in the 18th century, the direction in which the novel would be moving was anything but clear. There had been something of a novel tradition in English before, but the prose stories that were called "novels" were not novels as we know them today. They either dealt with an imaginary world of romance, ideal love and chivalry among ladies and gentlemen pretending to be shepherds and shepherdesses, or they depicted the adventures of a rogue that involved a great deal of fighting, risky love affairs, practical jokes, etc.

What was missing from these narratives was that they were not interested in the light thrown by the stories they present on man's life and situation in the world, the nature of society, and the interplay between well-established characters – all elements that we now expect from novels. It was only when formal realism was introduced as an essential element in novel-writing and the concept of human character as the centre of the novel came to be firmly established that the novel was on its way to becoming the literary form that we know today. We expect to find in the novel

- fully-rounded individuals experiencing life and making moral decisions as we do,

- a minimum of an analysis of motives and emotions,

- an emphasis either on inner conflict or on outward action, or a combination of the two.

If we attempt a definition of the novel, we can define it as a fictional prose narrative of considerable length and a certain complexity that deals imaginatively with realistic human experience, usually through a connected sequence of events involving a number of characters in a specific setting.

Within this broad framework, the genre of the novel can encompass many styles:

- romanticism, realism, naturalism, impressionism, expressionism, and avant-gardism,

and an almost incredibly extensive range of types, for example:

- historical, picaresque, sentimental, gothic, apprenticeship, anti-novel, detective, mystery, thriller, best-seller, utopianism, science-fiction, fantasy, and so forth.

Incredibly long though this list may seem, especially with regard to novel type, it is by no means exhaustive. Many more categories could easily be mentioned; those listed above simply constitute the most common fictional forms. Theoretically there is no limit to the number of types available, since changing social patterns will provide fresh subject matter and new beliefs and new psychological theories will certainly lead to new fictional approaches to both content and technique.

Other novel types that could be mentioned include the *erotic novel* (which may be or may not be pornographic), *the satirical novel, the novel for children, the theological novel, the allegorical novel,* and so forth. Certain types have fallen out of favour, e.g. the *pastoral novel* about shepherds and shepherdesses frolicking in an Arcadian landscape, a situation which is felt to be no longer in keeping with the spirit of the times (but see below). Other novel types are no longer practised because their real-life referents have largely ceased to exist. A case in point is for instance the *colonial novel* (a famous example is E.M. Forster's *A Passage to India*, 1924), because the colonial structures that form the backbone of the setting have long been abolished and so the novel now makes sense only as a piece of historical fiction.

As new real-life referents become available, the novel stands waiting in the wings, as it were, to enable writers to provide a literary representation and discussion of the experience. Recent examples include the *Vietnam novel* (usually with an anti-war slant), the *novel of negritude* (allowing Afro-Americans to voice their concerns in a still predominantly WASP-oriented society), the *novel of drug hallucination*, and so on.

Though it is the youngest form of story-telling, the novel has been the most successful literary genre of the last two hundred and fifty years.

There are two main reasons for this development – one is social change, the other lies in the form of the novel itself.

- Social and political changes and a number of other factors such as increased literacy created the conditions for the growth of the novel. Focusing on individuals and their social behaviour at different levels, the novel has been ideal for showing how people are affected by socio-political circumstances in their attitudes and actions, and the implications of living in an increasingly complex social order.

- The novel functioned from its very beginning as a forum for discussing social and moral issues, and it has continued to express every topical concern in every age. It has been a testing ground for new ideas, and its continuing success is due to its unfailing adaptability and flexibility.
    - A novel can depict a social group without losing sight of the nuances of gesture, feeling, experiences, and attitudes of individuals within the group, describing all their elusive inner states and experiences.
    - It can portray social and historical affairs of great magnitude by means of intimate private thoughts and actions.
    - A well-written novel is highly convincing and the ideal medium for expressing the problems of the age.
    - No other art – neither drama, nor epic poetry, nor even the cinema – can match the ability of the novel to take you from place to place, present to past, pre-history to future, to see inwardly, to observe in a wide sweep or in meticulous detail, to rejoice in success, sigh at failure, weep at tragedy, laugh at comedy, and to bring immediate, passionate life to the ideas of sociologists, historians and psychologists.
    - There are few things the novel cannot do. There is an endless supply of subject matter. Novels are read by all sorts of people, not limited to being available and understood by specialists with esoteric knowledge or clinical interest.

But the enormous appeal and diversity which is the strength of the novel is also its greatest weakness; it is so easily adapted to triviality. The modern novel has no heroes in the classical or medieval sense; the protagonists are often imperfect, even absurd. Novels can be extremely profound and serious, but some types are very shallow: detective thrillers and sentimental melodramas, for instance. It can be vulgar, commercial, pornographic, or propagandist.

This is to say that the novel does not invariably achieve the highest reaches of literary art. The opposite is too often true. The novel can and does frequently descend to shameful commercial depths of sentimentality or pornography (easy tears and sex are part and parcel of a best-selling formula, after all). There is no doubt that the novel today is an all-purpose medium catering for all levels of literacy, from the lowest to the highest.

To summarize, the novel has become the mirror of society, reflecting an infinite variety of artistic images of the patterns of life in a number of societies. As long as human cultures continue to exist, the novel will exist alongside them, mirroring human life in all its diversity and complexity. In this sense, the novel has been the most successful artistic medium of recent times, even more successful, perhaps, than film, which, after all, is all too frequently based on fiction. Its popularity never seems to wane. More and more novels are published every year, and though the days of the hard-back are numbered, the huge sales of paper-back novels of all kinds bring reading within the grasp of almost everyone.

3.4.2 Styles of the novel

As the "mirror of society," the novel has faithfully reflected cultural trends.

Romanticism. The Romantic spirit which transformed intellectual life in Europe after the French Revolution and continued to be a potent force till far into the 19th century also found expression in fiction.

In keeping with this romantic spirit, which emphasised idealism, chivalry and strong emotional impulse, the aim of romantic fiction was less to present a true picture of life than to work a magical charm on the reader. The romantic novelist wants to arouse the reader's emotions by a depiction of strong passions and to fire his imagination with exotic, wonderful, or terrifying scenes and events.

This romantic impulse is still strong in fiction. Wherever we find strong erotic feelings, exotic settings, and generally emotional intensity, a sort of neo-romantic spirit is at work, but this fiction has a marked tendency to degenerate into the depiction of easy dreams and wish-fulfilment. Neo-romanticism all too easily shows life not as it really is but as we would like it to be.

Realism and naturalism. Realism came as a reaction to the idealism of romanticism, an attitude which the realists see as fundamentally wrong-headed. They do not want to present an idealized picture of human life as the romantics have done but seek to expose the hopelessness and shallowness of life and its social demands and appearances. It is typical of fiction in the realist style that there is no benevolence in life, only a pessimistic determinism which sees the world as hostile, tragic, devoid of meaning.

Out of realism came *naturalism*. The difference between those two moods is essentially one of degree. Naturalism differs from realism in concentrating on the physical and biological aspects – man is a product of social and natural forces, and genetic influences. The naturalist writers believe that fiction has to show the physical essence of man and his environment. So exponents of naturalism are utterly frank about the basic processes of life. Their outspokenness brought them into conflict with censorship – timid publishers, public outcries, confiscation and charges of obscenity, etc. The most significant fictional work in this style is James Joyce's *Ulysses* (1922), which is revolutionary in claiming absolute candour as an artistic aim. Joyce tries to follow this idea through by recording with absolute objectivity every aspect of one day, June 16, 1904, in Dublin, mirrored in the consciousness of three characters.

Since the publication of *Ulysses*, naturalism has been widely accepted and has in fact become commonplace as writers are still struggling to describe the raw realities of life.

Impressionism. The realist/naturalist desire to present life frankly and objectively, led novelists not only to present aspects of life previously avoided and looked upon as "unclean", but also to question conventional narrative techniques. The device of the omniscient narrator was felt to be particularly unacceptable. How could a godlike knowledge of everything be right? It seemed more reasonable to make the narrator a character in the story who can only recount what he actually sees and hears. This would be nearer the truth as we experience it.

Breaking up narration into what the participant observer-narrator sees and what he assumes he sees, achieves an effect somewhat like the works of the French impressionist painters in which the visible world is broken down into innumerable specks or splashes of colour to achieve brilliance and the appearance of light. The novelist achieves a comparable impressionist effect by "implication" – the reader has to fill in the omitted details. He is told what characters say or do, but there are no author's comments to help him to interpret action and speech. The reader's cooperation is essential when this style is used. Speech is presented as it is actually spoken, with all the halting utterances of real life. Most characters in previous fiction had been impossibly articulate but this has no place in a truthful picture of reality. This real-life speech technique is often combined with "stream-of-consciousness", which is typically impressionistic, enabling the writer to show thoughts, emotions and impressions without following the normal rational order, thereby achieving powerful immediacy. In impressionism chronological time is abandoned. Instead there are fragmentary impressions through which the total picture is perceived.

The impressionist style has had an immense influence. Techniques such as the interior monologue, unedited dialogue giving the words actually spoken, and the fragmented time-continuum are now generally accepted and widely used.

Expressionism. The outstanding feature of expressionism is the radical revolt against realism; instead of imitating reality, the writer depicts the world as it appears inside his mind, or in the mind – usually in a troubled or abnormal mental condition – of one or more of his characters. This can lead to a nightmarish atmosphere that can express man's alienation in this world. The characters in expressionist fiction are intended to represent anxiety-ridden mankind in an industrial and technological age that is moving towards final disintegration and chaos.

The central conviction of expressionists – that presentation of the theme is more important than imitation of reality – has exerted considerable influence on fiction, especially on works with propagandist or didactic aims. Though expressionism is still occasionally used by novelists, it is not a dominant force in fiction and has not become part of the mainstream of contemporary style. In one form or another, expressionism crops up in much twentieth century fiction, but it has a tributary effect and is not a decisive factor.

Avant-gardism. Innovation and change have dominated much of twentieth century fiction. This innovation has often taken the form of rebellion against traditional conventions – against the notion of realism, against the idea of mimesis (art imitating life), against conventional ways of viewing man and society, and even against traditional definitions of what reality is. Attempts at creating realistic pictures of life, the experimenters say, can capture only the surface, the illusion.

Their protest has taken many forms but they belong in essence to the tradition of either impressionism or expressionism. Realistic settings, logical reasoning and consistent plotting are often rejected in an attempt to reveal the senseless irrationality and absurdity of life, showing man as a lonely and deprived creature resentful of a God he cannot believe in.

There have also been experiments with the presentation of fiction – e.g. as a poem with a critical apparatus put together by a madman, or as "false-directional" novels in which the traditional order of the chapters has been abandoned; they can be read in any order. Sometimes there are compositions disclaiming all interest in the world of feeling, thought and sense. Not all of these experiments get published, and if they do not all of them are saleable.

3.4.3 Types of novel

Many types of novel that have developed over the last 250 years have now largely only academic interest. Novels of this type include the *psychological novel*, the *novel of manners*, the *epistolary novel*, and the *pastoral novel*. And yet some of their typical features can still be found in a great deal of contemporary fiction.

When it is claimed here that the psychological novel and the novel of manners are no longer active categories of fiction, the idea is not that novelists are no longer interested in psychological insight or that they ignore in their novels all elements of the manners of the society in which their stories are set. It is only that the analysis of the characters' inner states has by now become such a commonplace and indeed inevitable element in all fiction that we can no longer meaningfully speak of the "psychological novel" as a separate type of novel. And much the same is true of the novel of manners.

The situation is slightly different with regard to epistolary and pastoral novels. Both have ceased to exist as types of novel, but letters of course continue to form a possible element in a writer's presentation of his story, and aspects of the pastoral novel can also still be found in some fiction. They have to do with the age-old idea that sees in nature only goodness and innocence. The image of a rural Eden, a rural idyll away from the pressures of urban life, is a persistent one in Western culture.

The historical novel. Historical themes have always fascinated people and inspired novelists. But what exactly is meant by the term "historical?" Given that all fiction must be set in some period, even if it is fantasy literature (see below), is not then all fiction somehow "historical," and are some novels "more historical" than others?

To be deemed "historical", most people are agreed, a novel must have been written at least fifty years after the events described, or have been written by someone who was not alive at the time of those events (who therefore approaches them only by research). In this sense, historical fiction is "fiction set in the past," but this seemingly simple definition needs perhaps a little clarification.

Is it not frequently the case that the novelist uses the trappings of history but fails to really assimilate the past into the imagination? "Historical" novels of this type show modern-day characters dressed up and paraded around in period dress with a few old-time expressions thrown in for good measure, but the result is pure costume drama. Novelists who follow that course present a distortion of history rather than a portrayal of historical truth.

Authors, however, who write genuine "historical" novels centre their stories not on the historical setting but on the plot, which may help readers to better understand the differences (or parallels) between then and now, and on characters who manage to transcend time and speak to us from their own perspective in a way that we, today, can understand. So in such cases we may be dealing with fiction which is set in the past but which emphasises themes that have a bearing on the present.

Historical themes have always fascinated people and inspired novelists. The literary historical novel is extremely useful because the writers' fictional imagination can interpret remote events in human terms and can thus transform documentary material into immediate emotional experience.

Within this field we can also consider the following styles of novel to be historical fiction (often shot through with fantasy):

- *alternate histories*, which present stories in a historical setting that is all wrong in the sense that it presumes a different course of events e.g. that the invasion of England by the Spanish Armada (1588) was successful.

- *pseudo-histories*, in which historical developments are concentrated in an action that sums up in the experiences of a single protagonist what in reality happened over a lengthy period of time.

- *time-slip novels*, also known as time-warp fantasy, time-travel or past-time fantasy, which take the reader through the time-barrier to a period that is quite distinct from current time, usually a less complex one than the present time. The journey across time is generally spurred by some unhappiness experienced by the protagonist. There are a variety of ways in which authors have engineered their protagonists' entry into a different period of time. The reader's need to continue the adventure must allow for the dismissal of a known fact: that travel through time, as far as we know, is not possible. Usually entry is achieved through the use of a talisman of some kind, or through a door opening in the mind of the protagonist. The entry constitutes a shift in reality or a shift in the perception of reality. Because the method of entry is the only fantasy element in the story, it is essential that it is plausible and does not distract the reader from an otherwise realistic story. The method of entry must, in fact, make the story even more compelling.

- *historical fantasies*, in which the novelists give a purely imaginative account of happenings around a well-known historical or pseudo-historical figure, e.g. King Arthur and his knights of the round table.

- and *multiple-time novels*, in which the action is set in diverse periods.

The picaresque novel. The picaresque novel first developed in Spain but eventually found its way into many other cultures. In novels of this type, a *pícaro* (Spanish for a rogue, hence the term picaresque) has a number of adventures, usually in foreign parts, that involve a lot of fighting, love affairs, intrigues, practical jokes, and so forth. These adventurous episodes are almost complete in themselves but are loosely linked (through the person of the hero) to form a novel. Perhaps inevitably, with such a structure or lack of it, the attraction for the reader in novels of this type must come from an (unconscious) rejection of a settled bourgeois life, a desire for the open road and a half-formed wish for adventures in bedrooms and with people on the fringe of society.

Again and again one can detect elements of the old picaresque tradition not only in contemporary novels (usually in escape fiction) but also in the world of film. Road movies spring to mind, as do a number of James Bond adventures. The picaresque tradition is by no means dead yet, and it is possibly here to stay because it offers people vicarious adventure and some wish-fulfilment.

The sentimental novel has roots not only in the recognition of the importance of human emotion, but also in the works of eighteenth-century philosophers who established a close relationship between emotion and moral virtue. The popularity of the novels of Jean-Jacques Rousseau, with their emphasis on altruism, refined sensibilities and benevolent feelings, further aided the development of an appetite for the literature of sensibility. It is important to note, however, is that this was not in the beginning a literature of emotion for the sake of emotion, for self-indulgent expression, but a literature insistently moral and inescapably didactic.

The first novels of this type presented love as a passionate attachment between the sexes that transcends the merely physical. Later novels however are characterised by a sloppy emotionalism and a deliberate tear-jerking appeal. Writers of serious fiction have mostly avoided sentimental appeal, much contemporary escape fiction is however based firmly on it, and a sizeable sector of the book market is doing very well out of unashamed sentimentalism, or at least a considerable dash of it (known as "love interest").

The gothic novel. Scenes of horror, and wonder and delight in the mysterious and the irrational characterise novels of this type. They can be seen as a reworking of the fabulous and marvellous in a new guise. Their pseudo-medieval flavour seems to express the apparently inexhaustible human desire for the depiction of non-reality, and so the spirit of the gothic world with its dark, tempestuous, ghostly settings has been deliberately cultivated by a number of writers.

It is noteworthy that gothic fiction has always been approached in a spirit that suspends the ordinary canons of taste. Gothic fiction needs to be considered as ingenious entertainment; the pity and terror it generates are not aspects of a cathartic process (as in tragedy) but transient emotions to be, somewhat perversely, enjoyed for their own sake.

The novel of apprenticeship (G Bildungsroman). This type of novel about upbringing and education has always held a great attraction for writers. Many first novels are autobiographical in character and try to generalise the author's own adolescent experiences into something of a universal symbol of the process of growing up and emerging as an unmistakeable personality.

Portrait of the Artist as a Young Man (1916) by James Joyce, which depicts the struggle of the hero's nascent artistic temperament to overcome the repressions of family, state, and church, is generally considered the unsurpassable model of the form. Another famous instance, from American literature, is J.D. Salinger's *Catcher in the Rye* (1951), which deals with the attempts of an adolescent American to come to terms with the adult world in a series of brief encounters, ending however not in success but in his failure and his ensuing mental illness.

The anti-novel. This is a movement away from the traditional novel form. The aim is to devise a work of fictional imagination that ignores conventional elements such as plot, dialogue, and even human interest, concentrating on a minute description of non-human details of the setting, etc. Practitioners of the anti-novel try to dissolve individual character and consciousness into sheer "perception." Time is regarded as reversible, since perceptions have nothing to do with chronology, and memories can be lived backwards. Even the conventional format of the novel as a book ought to be changed – it must be possible to enter a novel at any point, like an encyclopaedia.

This new approach to the materials of the conventional novel can perhaps best show their value in their influence on traditional novelists who may as a result become extra-wary of the seduction of fast-paced action, contrived relationships, and neat resolutions.

Detective fiction, mystery, thriller. These three terms are frequently used interchangeably. The detective novel thrills the reader with the presentation of a mysterious crime (usually of a violent nature, mostly murder) and creates suspense by presenting a number of clues but also red herrings (false clues), pointing to the identity of the criminal. The clues are not often seen as such by the reading public and it needs the efforts of a superior mind – a fearless and intelligent amateur detective, a private investigator, or a police officer – to solve the mystery by a triumph of superior logical reasoning.

The detective story and the mystery are virtually the same thing, but the thriller can add an extra element of excitement and adventure. Fiction of this type has been highly popular with readers everywhere. The subcategories of the *novel of espionage* and the *novel of intrigue* have also found large followings. The types of novel grouped together here generally aim at entertainment, but quite a few of them are very well written; they show a skilful handling of suspense, a general economy of means, and often very artful plotting.

The best-seller. Some books sell much better than others. Those books that, for a time, lead all others of its kind in sales (numbers of copies sold), are commonly called best-sellers. From the beginning there has been a tendency among both critics and the general public to suppose that because a book is a best-seller it is bound to be trash and cannot have literary merit. This is not necessarily true, even though the success of a work of fiction is often due to ephemeral qualities such as the choice of a topical subject and lavish promotion by publishers and not so much to literary merit. It is a fact that novels of genuine aesthetic vitality often sell more copies than the most-hyped best-seller, but the sales are likely to be spread over many decades and even centuries rather than merely a few weeks or months.

Factors that are known to boost sales are

- an over-simplification of the subject-matter, an undertaking that an unsophisticated readership will not mind in the least;

- factual thoroughness (which gives readers the good feeling that they are being educated as well as entertained);

- a large dollop of sex, a measure of violence, quarrels and fights, and some adulterous relationships.

It is not exactly a secret that many potential best-sellers are carefully planned along these lines.

Utopian novels, fantasy literature and science fiction (SF) have much in common – they are all interested in showing life in an alternative world, but they go about it in different ways.

Utopian fiction is most often based on the idea that there is a place where all is well. A remote island is frequently used as the venue for the story and action *(desert island fiction)*. It holds a particular attraction because it can be placed right alongside the "real" world and is often an image of the ideal and the unspoilt. A further attraction can be found in the appeal to the reader's sense of adventure and his exploratory instinct, and the story can be used to criticise contemporary society and to propose better alternatives. The apparent impossibility of utopia has also produced its converse – *dystopia* or *anti-utopia*, in which the alternative world is not an earthly paradise but a nightmare. Fiction of this type is concerned with forecasting the doom awaiting mankind if it will not turn away from following avenues of destruction.

In some instances utopian worlds are almost indistinguishable from those in SF, but there is a decisive difference. SF deals principally with the impact of actual or imagined science and technology on society and individuals – there always is a scientific factor as an essential orienting component. SF is most commonly concerned with predictions of future societies on earth, with analyses of the consequences of interstellar travel and imaginative explorations of forms of intelligent life and their societies in other worlds, and some have used the form to criticise human nature and institutions.

Fantasy, by contrast, is not usually used for critical and satirical purposes. The fantasy author is content to show the reader strange characters moving in strange settings in other worlds and other times. Whereas SF is usually set in the future, fantasy actions take place in the distant past, and where SF is concerned with some aspect of science or technology, fantasy often relies for effect on the use of some form of magic and old ritual.

3.4.4 The novel – an all-purpose medium

There seem to be hardly any limits to what a good writer can do with the novel. The novel is a ready vehicle for the expression of many ideas, intentions and meanings. It can often transcend story telling and delineation of character and provide an interpretation of life, embody a view of the world, and comment on the meaning of life. It can offer convenient pleasure, informative entertainment and escape. Sometimes it has been used for propaganda purposes or for heightening the effect of factual reports. Finally, great novels express not only the spirit of their age but also timeless and everlasting truths.

An interpretation of life. Even though novels are not usually openly didactic, many express a distinct philosophy of life.

- In bourgeois fiction life is seen as being essentially reasonable and decent, with a well-ordered universe behind it.

- Writers in the tradition of realism cannot find any sense of justice at all so that evil and stupidity must prevail. Nothing happens for the best, and the universe is seen as being actively malevolent.

- Writers in the Catholic tradition tend to see life as mysterious and full of evil and injustice, but also full of hope because there is an inscrutable but somehow benevolent God behind it.

- Existentialist writers generally assume that man is imperfect and see life as absurd.

- Others again express in their fiction a philosophy of optimistic liberalism or a belief in the strength of "natural man," and so forth.

Entertainment and escape. Most novels on the market today have been written with the express intention of providing entertainment and diversion for the reader. However, novelists who merely try to whisk the reader away from a dull or oppressive daily existence are not usually highly regarded. Many critics apparently feel that every novel ought to be addressing a social wrong or be devoted to the propagation of progressive ideologies. Nevertheless, there are some counter-arguments:

- Adventure stories and spy novels have a healthy enough realism about them – not even impressionable youngsters will confuse those stories with real-life action and throw up their jobs to become secret agents.

- Novels of entertainment and escape are not all trash; many of them set themselves higher literary standards than some fiction with a profound social or philosophical purpose.

- Diverting stories can still hold on to the realities of human character.

- All good fiction is essentially entertainment, and if it also instructs the reader, it does so best through enchanting him.

- Providing entertainment and escape is a legitimate use of the novel, as the provision of laughter (for instance in comedy) and dreams has always been considered one of the legitimate occupations of literature.

- The use of the novel as a form of diversion is fully justified as long as a writer does not falsify life through over-simplification or through suggesting to the reader that reality is as he presents it. In other words, the use of the novel as entertainment is illegitimate or dangerous only if it functions as a mere narcotic.

Propaganda. The use of the novel for purely propagandist purposes does not work very well. Its weakness lies in the fact that it loses its value as soon as the wrongs it wants to expose are righted or are superseded by others. Only if the propagandist writer can give his attacks on social injustices a timeless human validity, for instance by presenting his material in the form of an intense dramatic conflict, can he hope to be read also in the future. Otherwise his novel will date very quickly. It will also be dull and unreal because all too often novels of propaganda regard man almost exclusively in terms of political or social phenomena and may perhaps even provoke readers to violent action.

If on the other hand the propagandist intention is combined with an aesthetic purpose, i.e. if the novelist manages to present his material in the form of an interesting action, then such a fusion of propagandist intention with aesthetic purpose may be regarded as one of the most valuable uses of the novel. The work of Charles Dickens (1812–1870) is a case in point. The genius of Dickens lay in his ability to transcend merely topical issues through the vitality with which he presented them so that his novels are still highly readable today; we read them for their human drama however and not for their propagandist purpose.

Documentary fiction. As Truman Capote's *In Cold Blood* (1965) and Norman Mailer's *The Armies of the Night* (1965) have convincingly shown, the documentary report can gain enormous strength from being presented in fictional form. Both writers managed to merge the art of fiction and the craft of reportage. Capote took the facts of a multiple murder in the Midwest of the United States and presented them with the force, reality, tone, and intense writing that distinguish his genuine fiction, and Norman Mailer recorded, in personal detail but in third-person narration, his part in a citizens' protest march on Washington, D.C.

It is certainly possible for a writer to use documents and other material taken from real life and incorporate them in a work of fiction (see also the historical novel). The literary quality of this work as *fiction* or with regard to its *concern with truth* cannot be decided on the question of how much factual material and how many actual events he has made use of, but according to the extent to which he has succeeded in blending such items into the whole and achieving an organic unity. Each work will have to be considered on its own merits, of course, as there is no generally valid answer.

The spirit of the age. The nature of a historical period (G Zeitgeist) can usually be understood only in long retrospect, and it is then that the novelist comes into his own, as it were. He can do better than others in summing up its essence. A novel can be said to be an expression of the spirit of its age when it manages to articulate the inchoate thoughts and feelings of a society and thus to give expression to the existing climate of sensibility.

- The spirit of the period following the First World War, for instance, has been caught in a number of novels by British and American writers, e.g. in Ernest Hemingway's *The Sun Also Rises* (1926) or in F. Scott Fitzgerald's *The Great Gatsby* (1925).

- Similarly, the unrest and bewilderment of the young in the period after World War II comes across most powerfully in novels of the time, e.g. in Kingsley Amis' *Lucky Jim* (1954).

It is however usually not the spirit of an entire society that is expressed in fiction but the segmented spirit of an age group, social or racial group. It is likely, on the other hand, that the *zeitgeist* has always found expression in a minority, the majority being generally silent. The reasons for the fact that there are so many expressions of the "spirit of the age" in the second half of the twentieth century may be found in the fragmented nature of life in the postwar world and the lack of a shared reaction to man's situation in the world based on a shared experience. There is no longer any consensus within society with reference to the attitude towards man, society and the world.

3.4.5 The future of the novel

As a result of the steadily increasing influence of visual and electronic communications, TV and the Internet, the popularity of literature in general has no doubt dropped considerably. Western societies have to a large extent moved from a book culture to a media culture. Within literature, though, the novel maintains its pre-eminence. It certainly remains more popular than poetry or drama, or even the short story.

In the second half of the twentieth century there has been a steady increase in the number of novels published every year. It is anybody's guess how many unpublished novels are lying around waiting to see the light of day, i.e. find a publisher, and it may well happen. Never in the history of literature have so many amateur writers put pen to paper or hammered away at their word processors to produce the novel of their dreams, hopefully a best-seller. It is significant that they are not interested in writing poetry and do not consider trying their hand at autobiography, the essay or the drama; they invariably choose the novel. The production of fiction requires no special training and those first novels can be quite readable, entertaining and absorbing, even if they violate the most basic rules of style.

The fact is that the novel tolerates a literary incompetence absolutely unthinkable in the poem or the drama. If professional writers stopped writing, there would be no shortage of fiction. It has been said that every person has at least one novel in him, and many try very hard to let it come out. The near-total literacy in the Western world has brought literature within the reach of many and has produced dreams of authorship in circles which a few generations ago one would not have associated with a love of literature let alone the drive to produce literature themselves.

At the beginning of the 21st century, the novel, one of the most flexible of literary forms, remains a powerful way for authors to represent the human experience both on the individual level and on the level of society. In countries all over the world, writers turn to the novel to give insight into people's actions, ideas, and aspirations. Novelists keep the form fresh by continuing to explore subject matter of vital interest to readers and by constantly innovating in form and technique. For more than 250 years the novel has been one of the most important ways for writers to comment on the human condition, and it shows no signs of weakening.

Synopsis

The novel
- shows individuals experiencing life and making moral decisions as we do.
- analyses the characters' motives and emotions.
- emphasises either inner conflict or outward action, or both.
- is a forum for discussing social and moral issues and a testing ground for new ideas.
- shows great diversity.
- is easily adapted to triviality.
- can achieve the highest reaches of literary art but also descend to shameful commercial depths.
- is an all-purpose medium catering for all levels of literacy.
- is a "mirror of society."

The novel can encompass many styles.
- Romantic fiction tries to arouse the reader's emotions and to fire his imagination.
- Realist fiction implies the hopelessness and shallowness of life and its social demands and appearances.

- Naturalist fiction is intended to show the physical essence of man and to describe the raw realities of life.
- Impressionist fiction is intended to give a truthful picture of reality by presenting real-life dialogue and the characters' stream-of-consciousness.
- Expressionist fiction depicts the world as it appears inside a troubled character's mind.
- Avant-garde fiction makes use of impressionist and expressionist techniques to reveal the irrationality of life or to experiment with the presentation of fictional material.

The novel can embody many types.
- The historical novel tries to interpret remote events in human terms.
- The picaresque novel shows a protagonist's amusing adventures in a number of difficult situations in an episodic plot.
- The sentimental novel today is usually characterised by sloppy emotionalism and a deliberate tear-jerking appeal.
- The gothic novel presents scenes of wonder and horror in dark, tempestuous, ghostly settings.
- The novel of apprenticeship traces a person's painful process of growing up and finding their way in the world.
- The anti-novel ignores all the conventional elements of fiction in an attempt to find a new approach to the materials of fiction.
- The detective novel (the mystery) shows a mysterious crime and a detective's search for its perpetrator among a number of suspects.
- The thriller adds an extra element of excitement and adventure.
- The best-seller is often based on the presentation of a well-researched but simplified topical subject garnished with sex and violence.
- Utopian novels show life in an alternative world, either as an ideal or as a nightmare.
- Science fiction deals principally with the impact of actual or imagined science and technology on individuals and society.
- Fantasy fiction shows strange characters moving in strange settings in other worlds and other times.

The novel as an all-purpose medium
- can function as an interpretation of life, expressing a distinct philosophy of life.
- may provide entertainment and escape.
- can be used for propagandist purposes in the sense of attacking social injustices.
- can transform documentary material into thrilling fictional narrative.
- can express the spirit of the age by articulating the inchoate thoughts and feelings of a society and by representing the existing climate of sensibility.

The future of the novel
- As the most flexible of literary forms, the novel is a powerful tool for presenting the human experience on the individual and social level.
- The novel can tolerate much literary incompetence.
- The novel remains more popular than other forms of literary art and shows no signs of weakening.

3.5 The interpretation of fiction

It is customary to present for interpretation not a full-length novel but only a selected passage. There are usually several assignments attached to that passage so that various aspects of the text will have to be analysed. Typical assignments refer to aspects like

- the context of the passage,

- the characters and the way they are presented,

- the contribution the passage can make to the general theme or to the underlying conflict,

- the setting and its importance,

- the genre problem – what type of fiction the novel the passage is taken from or seems to belong to.

There may well be other assignments, of course, some of them going beyond the text, asking for instance about the historical, social and cultural background of the novel, or demanding a comparison with another work, and so on.

If a film version of the novel and thus of the selected passage is available, it will be useful to study how the filmmaker has used camera and sound track to guide the viewers and create the images he was interested in.

- How has the filmmaker used the camera in this scene, and why has he filmed it the way he has?

- What can individual shots, camera movements and the use of the sound track tell us about his intentions?

- How is the film version different from the text version, and how can the differences be explained? Where exactly is the focus in film and text?

The following passage from *Pride and Prejudice* (first published in 1813) by Jane Austen (1775 – 1817), can be seen as fairly typical. It is the from the opening chapter:

> It is a truth universally acknowledged, that a single man in possession of a good fortune, must be in want of a wife.
> However little known the feelings or views of such a man may be on his first entering a neighbourhood, this truth is so well fixed in the minds of the surrounding families, that he is considered as the rightful property of some one or other of their daughters.

'My dear Mr Bennet,' said his lady to him one day, have you heard that Netherfield Park is let at last?'

Mr Bennet replied that he had not.

'But it is,' returned she; 'for Mrs Long has just been here, and she told me all about it.'

Mr Bennet made no answer.

'Do not you want to know who has taken it?' cried his wife impatiently.

'You want to tell me, and I have no objection to hearing it.'

This was invitation enough.

'Why, my dear, you must know, Mrs Long says that Netherfield is taken by a young man of large fortune from the north of England; that he came down on Monday in a chaise and four to see the place, and was so much delighted with it that he agreed with Mr Morris immediately; that he is to take possession before Michaelmas; and some of his servants are to be in the house by the end of next week.'

'What is his name?'

'Bingley.'

'Is he married or single?'

Oh! single, my dear, to be sure! A single man of large fortune; four or five thousand a year. What a fine thing for our girls!'

'How so? how can it affect them?'

'My dear Mr Bennet,' replied his wife, 'how can you be so tiresome! You must know that I am thinking of his marrying one of them.'

'Is that his design in settling here?'

'Design! nonsense, how can you talk so! But it is very likely that he may fall in love with one of them, and therefore you must visit him as soon as he comes.'

'I see no occasion for that. You and the girls may go, or you may send them by themselves, which perhaps will be still better, for as you are as handsome as any of them, Mr Bingley might like you the best of the party.'

'My dear, you flatter me. I certainly have had my share of beauty, but I do not pretend to be any thing extraordinary now. When a woman has five grown up daughters, she ought to give over thinking of her own beauty.'

'In such cases, a woman has not often much beauty to think of.'

'But, my dear, you must indeed go and see Mr Bingley when he comes into the neighbourhood.'

'It is more than I engage for, I assure you.'

'But consider your daughters. Only think what an establishment it would be for one of them. Sir William and Lady Lucas are determined to go, merely on that account, for in general you know they visit no new comers. Indeed you must go, for it will be impossible for us to visit him, if you do not.'

'You are over scrupulous surely. I dare say Mr Bingley will be very glad to see you; and I will send a few lines by you to assure him of my hearty consent to his marrying which ever he chuses of the girls; though I must throw in a good word for my little Lizzy.'

'I desire you will do no such thing. Lizzy is not a bit better than the others; and I am sure she is not half so handsome as Jane, nor half so good humoured as Lydia. But you are always giving her the preference.'

'They have none of them much to recommend them,' replied he; 'they are all silly and ignorant like other girls; but Lizzy has something more of quickness than her sisters.'

'Mr Bennet, how can you abuse your own children in such a way? You take delight in vexing me. You have no compassion on my poor nerves.'

'You mistake me, my dear. I have a high respect for your nerves. They are my old friends. I have heard you mention them with consideration these twenty years at least.'

'Ah! you do not know what I suffer.'

'But I hope you will get over it, and live to see many young men of four thousand a year come into the neighbourhood.'

'It will be no use to us, if twenty such should come since you will not visit them.'

'Depend upon it, my dear, that when there are twenty, I will visit them all.'

Mr Bennet was so odd a mixture of quick parts, sarcastic humour, reserve, and caprice, that the experience of three and twenty years had been insufficient to make his wife understand his character. Her mind was less difficult to develope.

She was a woman of mean understanding, little information, and uncertain temper. When she was discontented she fancied herself nervous. The business of her life was to get her daughters married; its solace was visiting and news.

From: Jane Austen, *Pride and Prejudice,* 1813

Notes

General note: The language of the text, esp. punctuation, spelling and syntax, has not been modernised.

chaise and four: a carriage drawn by four horses – *Michaelmas:* feast of St. Michael the Archangel, celebrated on 29 September – *four or five thousand [pounds] a year:* the equivalent of several hundred thousand pounds today – *engage for (archaic):* promise – *establishment:* a financially desirable marriage – *chuses (archaic):* chooses – *quick parts (archaic):* keen intellect – *develope (archaic):* understand – *mean (here):* inferior

Assignments

1. What news has Mrs Long brought and why is it important for the Bennet family?

2. What impression of the Bennets is conveyed to the reader? How is this achieved? Consider narrative perspective and mode of presentation.

3. What concept of marriage seems to be prevalent in this social group?

4. Describe the social background, including social conventions, of the characters presented in this chapter.

5. The novel was first published in 1813, at a time when the Romantic movement was gaining strength. Is it an instance of romantic fiction?

Suggested answers

1. **What news has Mrs Long brought and why is it important for the Bennet family?**
(a context question in two parts, testing general understanding)

Information in the text:

● news: Netherfield Park is let at last, taken by a young man of large fortune from the North of England. He is single.

● importance for the Bennet family: the Bennets have five grown-up daughters, and Mrs Bennet hopes that the rich young man will fall in love with one of them and marry her ("only think of what an establishment it would be for one of them.")

Possible answer:
Mrs Long has brought information about Netherfield Park – it is let at last. A young man from the North of England has taken it. He is unmarried and very rich.

This is important for the Bennet family – they have five grown-up daughters and Mrs Bennet is thinking of his falling in love with one of the Bennet girls and marrying her. It would be a very desirable match.

2. **What impression of the Bennets is conveyed to the reader? How is this achieved? Consider narrative perspective and mode of presentation.**
    (a question on character and characterisation, testing understanding of the writer's craft)

Information in the text:

Mr Bennet	*Mrs Bennet*
• not informed on the latest news and not interested in gossip.	• very keen on news and gossip
• pretends not to understand what his wife is getting at and refuses to pay a call on his new neighbour, Mr Bingley.	• regards the taking of Netherfield Park by a young man who is rich and unmarried as a golden opportunity for their daughters.
• regards his daughters as silly and ignorant girls, except Lizzy.	• wants Bingley to fall in love with one of her daughters and marry her.
• an odd mixture of quick intelligence, sarcastic humour, reserve and caprice.	• a woman of mean understanding, little information, and uncertain temperament.

• in short – an unusual couple, forming a contrast to one another

Narrative perspective / mode of presentation:
• omniscient narrator:

• knows everything about general feelings (first two paragraphs) and about the characters (final two paragraphs) – "telling"

• prefers to stay very largely outside the action, presenting the dialogue as a dramatic scene (middle section) – "showing"

Possible answer:
The impression conveyed of the Bennets is that of an unusual couple forming a contrast to one another.

Mr Bennet is not interested in news and gossip and likes teasing his wife about her love of these things, and while he regards his daughters as silly and ignorant girls (with the exception of Lizzy), his wife intends to make it her business to marry one of them to the new neighbour. Her lack of understanding and her uncertain temper form a sharp contrast to his quick intelligence and his sarcastic humour.

The scene is presented by an omniscient narrator who knows everything about general feelings and the characters. At the beginning of the scene and at the end of it the mode of presentation used is telling – the narrator sums up the relevant information. In the middle part he steps back, as it were, presenting the Bennets' dialogue in a dramatic scene, so that the reader can form his own picture of Mr and Mrs Bennet.

3. **What concept of marriage seems to be prevalent in this social group?**
   (a question on thematic content, testing background understanding)

Information in the text:

- a universally accepted truth: a rich unmarried man needs a wife

- such a man is considered the rightful property of some or other of the surrounding families' daughters

- this man might fall in love with such a girl and get married to her

- marriage to such a person would be highly desirable (higher social status, security)

- by favouring Lizzy, Mr Bennet appears to see marriage possibly in the modern sense of a partnership of equals – does not want Lizzy to be "married off" simply because a potential partner is rich

- conclusion: marriage seen as an institution in which a man can find love and women can find a higher social status and financial security, but Mr Bennet does not quite see it that way

Possible answer:
The concept of marriage prevalent in the social circles we are shown in the text seems to be based first of all on the idea that a rich man ought to take a wife. A second notion is that a woman's place in life is as the wife of a desirable man. Such a man is desirable because he is wealthy. He might marry for love, but a woman from the middle class marries to achieve a higher social status and above all financial security.

Mr Bennet, however, seems to favour the idea that a woman ought not simply to be "married off," but should follow her own ideas and make her own choice. This conflict appears to be unresolved at this point.

4.   Describe the social background, including social conventions, of the characters presented in this chapter.
     (tests understanding of the setting in its importance for the characters)

Information in the text:
- social background: middle class (families with servants, acquaintance with local squire, middle class ideas)

- social conventions: exchange of news and social calls are important; need for a male escort – ladies can't go out on their own

Possible answer:
The characters in this passage appear to belong to the middle class. We hear of families with servants and of the Bennets' acquaintance with the local squire, Sir William, and his family. People seem to have time on their hands for paying social calls, which also points to a middle class background. And Mrs Bennet at least (and presumably most of her daughters) hold typically middle class ideas with reference to marriage. Social conventions are felt to be important. The exchange of news and the custom of making social calls appear to be firmly established. The head of the household is expected to accompany his wife and daughters on such social calls as ladies can't make initial visits on their own and require a male escort.

5.   The novel was first published in 1813, at a time when the Romantic movement was gaining strength. Is it an instance of romantic fiction? Give reasons.
     (requires a knowledge of genres and styles of writing)

Background information:
- typically romantic:
  - idealism, chivalry and strong emotional impulse
  - a depiction of strong passions and to fire the imagination with exotic, wonderful, or terrifying scenes and events.

- nothing of this to be found in the passage

- instead: focus on individuals and realistic presentation of their problems, but tone of passage not in the style of realism (no pessimistic determinism, only a tone of satire and irony, esp. Mr. Bennet)

- Jane Austen found a style of her own

Possible answer:

Nothing that is typically romantic can be found in the passage. There is no idealism and no chivalry. Nor do we find a depiction of strong passions or exotic, wonderful, or terrifying scenes and events. The text focuses instead on individuals and a realistic presentation of their problems in society. It is not a novel in the style of realism either, which seeks to expose the hopelessness and shallowness of life; the tone is far too optimistic for that and we do not find anything of the pessimistic determinism that is typical of realist fiction.

Jane Austen apparently found her own individual style for this novel.

Useful language material

Character

– X appears to be an attractive / a friendly / benevolent character.
– Y seems to be an unattractive / evil-minded / a spiteful / dull / unpleasant character.
– X stands in contrast to Y / forms a contrast to Y.
– X appears in a new light when ...
– He / She shows a quick intellligence when ...
– X is characterised by his dry humour / sober-minded atttitude / one besetting emotion, namely ...
– A reversal of the situation takes place at this point.

Point of view

– The passage is presented from an omniscient / a limited point of view.
– The story is told as witnessed by the main character / a minor participant in the action.
– X is the viewpoint character.
– The events are portrayed from the point of view of a single character.
– The narrator tells the story from a remote standpoint / knows the meaning of the events / gives a distorted view of the events.
– The author / writer uses X as a focus / as a centre of consciousness.

▪ Mode of presentation

- The narrator uses the mode of telling / showing at this point / employs the dramatic method here.
- He skilfully blends telling and showing / presents this passage as a combination of telling and showing.
- He makes use of several narrative methods.
- He shifts the focus from telling to showing when …
- The writer employs telling to establish a comprehensive view.
- He uses showing for intense moments.

▪ Theme

- This extract deals with / is concerned with …
- The novel this passage is taken from is a study of …
- The problem of … forms the central theme / is the dominant topic.
- The writer is principally concerned with / interested in the presentation of …
- The conflict seems insoluble at this point.

▪ Genre

- The novel is an example of romantic literature / realist fiction / avant-garde writing / …
- The text is written in the style of …
- This piece of fiction belongs to / is an instance of historical fiction / fantasy literature / …
- The text unmistakably belongs to escape fiction / is a piece of serious writing.
- The author is mainly out to create suspense / provide thrills / …
- The writer's main aim is entertainment and diversion.

Index